FILM 71/72

An Anthology by the
National Society
of Film Critics

edited by
DAVID DENBY

Simon and Schuster   New York

FIRST PRINTING

SBN 671–21358–X CASEBOUND EDITION
SBN 671–21359–8 TOUCHSTONE PAPERBACK EDITION
LIBRARY OF CONGRESS CATALOG CARD NUMBER: 68–19946
MANUFACTURED IN THE UNITED STATES OF AMERICA

The reviews and articles in this book originally appeared, for the most part, in the publications for which the contributors regularly write. Thanks are hereby given by the contributors as follows:

Hollis Alpert, reviews of *Claire's Knee*, *The Last Movie*, and *Happy Birthday, Wanda June*, reprinted by permission of *Saturday Review*, copyright © 1971, 1972 by Saturday Review, Inc.

Gary Arnold, reviews of *Bed and Board*, *Carnal Knowledge*, *Hoa-Binh*, *A New Leaf*, *Sweet Sweetback's Baadasssss Song*, and *The Touch*, reprinted by permission of the Washington *Post*, copyright © 1971 by the Washington Post Company, Inc.

Jacob Brackman, reviews of *Carnal Knowledge*; *Drive, He Said*; *Walkabout*; and article on the rating system, reprinted by permission from *Esquire*, copyright © 1971 by Esquire, Inc.

Vincent Canby, reviews of *Bed and Board*; *Blue Water, White Death*; *Derby*; *El Topo*; *Fiddler on the Roof*; *A New Leaf*; and article "More Than a Glance at Gance," published by permission of *The New York Times*, copyright © 1971 by the The New York Times Co.

Harold Clurman, reviews of *The Sorrow and the Pity* and *Viva La Muerte*, reprinted by permission of *The Nation*, copyright © 1971, 1972 by The Nation, Inc.

Jay Cocks, reviews of *Derby*; *Drive, He Said*; and *Taking Off*, reprinted by permission from *Time*, copyright © 1971 by Time, Inc.

CONTENTS

7

AN EDITORIAL NOTE

This anthology, now in its fifth consecutive year, does not pretend to offer a comprehensive critical account of the movies of 1971; in fact, it covers roughly one out of nine movies released in New York during the year. Like the editors of previous volumes I have chosen reviews and essays on the most important and controversial films, the films that try something new or display a new talent, and the films which inspire the best in the critics who make up the National Society of Film Critics. There's no point in reprinting reviews of *shlock* material which hardly anyone went to see and which excited little more from the critics than a rumble of irritation and impatience. Of course we could be wrong, individually and collectively, and I could be excluding the wrong things from this book. Fortunately, critical error can't kill an interesting film—it finds its audience without critical help or it returns on television, at revival houses or on the programs of college film societies. In a reverse process, an overestimated film shows up less and less frequently and eventually ceases to be a presence in the consciousness of moviegoers. Thus some of these estimates will stand up for some time, while others will quickly fall to the wayside; in either case they were written as a primary stimulus to that sort of excited debate which almost all moviegoers adore as an essential part of the moviegoing experience.

Besides the twenty-one contributors to this volume, the National Society of Film Critics includes several inactive members (Joseph Morgenstern, Brad Darrach, Robert Kotlowitz) who have, for the time being, switched to activities other than film criticism. Should they return to the fold their work will appear in future volumes.

DAVID DENBY

THE AWARDS

THE NATIONAL SOCIETY OF FILM CRITICS, in its sixth annual awards, voted *Claire's Knee* the best picture of 1971. The Society named Bernardo Bertolucci as the best director of the year for *The Conformist*. Jane Fonda won the best actress award for her performance in *Klute*, while Peter Finch was chosen best actor for his work in *Sunday, Bloody Sunday*.

The Society also picked Bruce Dern as best supporting actor for his performance in *Drive, He Said* and Ellen Burstyn as best supporting actress for her work in *The Last Picture Show*.

The best screenplay award was given to Penelope Gilliatt for the original screenplay of *Sunday, Bloody Sunday*.

Vittorio Storaro received the best cinematography award from the Society for his accomplishments as director of photography in *The Conformist*.

One special award was given: to *Le Chagrin et la Pitié* (*The Sorrow and the Pity*), directed by Marcel Ophuls, as "a film of extraordinary public interest and distinction."

Participants in the voting included Hollis Alpert of *Saturday Review*; Gary Arnold of the Washington *Post*; Jacob Brackman of *Esquire*; Vincent Canby of *The New York Times*; Harold Clurman of *The Nation*; Jay Cocks of *Time*; David Denby of *The Atlantic*; Philip T. Hartung of *Commonweal*; Molly Haskell of *The Village Voice*; Pauline Kael of *The New Yorker*; Stefan Kanfer of *Time*; Stanley Kauffmann of *The New Republic*; Andrew Sarris of *The Village Voice*; Richard Schickel of *Life*; Arthur Schlesinger, Jr., of *Vogue*; John Simon of *The New Leader*; Bruce Williamson of *Playboy*; and Paul D. Zimmerman of *Newsweek*.

VOTING FOR 1971 AWARDS— THE NATIONAL SOCIETY OF FILM CRITICS

Each critic was asked to vote for three candidates in each category. The first choice was worth three points, the second two, the third one, and a simple plurality established the winner.

BEST PICTURE

HOLLIS ALPERT:	*Claire's Knee; A Clockwork Orange; The Conformist*
GARY ARNOLD:	*Fiddler on the Roof; McCabe & Mrs. Miller; The Last Picture Show*
JACOB BRACKMAN:	*The Conformist; Claire's Knee; Walkabout*
VINCENT CANBY:	*Claire's Knee; A Clockwork Orange; The Last Picture Show*
HAROLD CLURMAN:	*Hoa-Binh; Murmur of the Heart; The Garden of the Finzi-Continis*
JAY COCKS:	*The Conformist; Minnie and Moskowitz; A Clockwork Orange*
DAVID DENBY:	*The Last Picture Show; Murmur of the Heart; McCabe & Mrs. Miller*
PHILIP T. HARTUNG:	*Claire's Knee; A Clockwork Orange; Sunday, Bloody Sunday*
MOLLY HASKELL:	*Claire's Knee; Deep End; Le Boucher*
PAULINE KAEL:	*The Conformist; McCabe & Mrs. Miller; Fiddler on the Roof*
STEFAN KANFER:	*A Clockwork Orange; Sunday, Bloody Sunday; The Clowns*

16 FILM 71/72

STANLEY KAUFFMANN: *The Hour of the Furnaces; Claire's Knee; Desperate Characters*

ANDREW SARRIS: *Claire's Knee; The Taira Clan; Deep End*

RICHARD SCHICKEL: *Taking Off; Murmur of the Heart; The Last Picture Show*

ARTHUR SCHLESINGER, JR.: *Claire's Knee; The Conformist; The Go-Between*

JOHN SIMON: *Hoa-Binh; Murmur of the Heart; The French Connection*

BRUCE WILLIAMSON: *The Conformist; One Day in the Life of Ivan Denisovich; Carnal Knowledge*

PAUL ZIMMERMAN: *The Last Picture Show; A Clockwork Orange; Sunday, Bloody Sunday*

BEST DIRECTOR

HOLLIS ALPERT: Stanley Kubrick (*A Clockwork Orange*); Eric Rohmer (*Claire's Knee*); William Friedkin (*The French Connection*)

GARY ARNOLD: Robert Altman (*McCabe & Mrs. Miller*); Bernardo Bertolucci (*The Conformist*); Norman Jewison (*Fiddler on the Roof*)

JACOB BRACKMAN: Bernardo Bertolucci (*The Conformist*); Eric Rohmer (*Claire's Knee*); Nicolas Roeg (*Walkabout*)

VINCENT CANBY: Eric Rohmer (*Claire's Knee*); Bernardo Bertolucci (*The Conformist*); Stanley Kubrick (*A Clockwork Orange*)

HAROLD CLURMAN: Raoul Coutard (*Hoa-Binh*); Louis Malle (*Murmur of the Heart*); William Friedkin (*The French Connection*)

JAY COCKS: Bernardo Bertolucci (*The Conformist*); John Cassavetes (*Minnie and Moskowitz*); Stanley Kubrick (*A Clockwork Orange*)

DAVID DENBY: Robert Altman (*McCabe & Mrs. Miller*); Bernardo Bertolucci (*The Conformist*); Peter Bogdanovich (*The Last Picture Show*)

PHILIP T. HARTUNG: Eric Rohmer (*Claire's Knee*); John Schlesinger (*Sunday, Bloody Sunday*); Stanley Kubrick (*A Clockwork Orange*)

MOLLY HASKELL:	Eric Rohmer (*Claire's Knee*); Jerzy Skolimowski (*Deep End*); Claude Chabrol (*Le Boucher*)
PAULINE KAEL:	Bernardo Bertolucci (*The Conformist*); Robert Altman (*McCabe & Mrs. Miller*); Louis Malle (*Murmur of the Heart*)
STEFAN KANFER:	Stanley Kubrick (*A Clockwork Orange*); Raoul Coutard (*Hoa-Binh*); Bernardo Bertolucci (*The Conformist*)
STANLEY KAUFFMANN:	Fernando Ezequiel Solanas (*The Hour of the Furnaces*); Eric Rohmer (*Claire's Knee*); Frank D. Gilroy (*Desperate Characters*)
ANDREW SARRIS:	Eric Rohmer (*Claire's Knee*); Kenji Mizoguchi (*Utamaro and His Five Women*); Jerzy Skolimowski (*Deep End*)
RICHARD SCHICKEL:	Louis Malle (*Murmur of the Heart*); Vittorio De Sica (*The Garden of the Finzi-Continis*); Ken Russell (*The Boy Friend*)
ARTHUR SCHLESINGER, JR.:	Eric Rohmer (*Claire's Knee*); Stanley Kubrick (*A Clockwork Orange*); Bernardo Bertolucci (*The Conformist*)
JOHN SIMON:	Raoul Coutard (*Hoa-Binh*); Louis Malle (*Murmur of the Heart*); William Friedkin (*The French Connection*)
BRUCE WILLIAMSON:	Bernardo Bertolucci (*The Conformist*); Peter Bogdanovich (*The Last Picture Show*); Mike Nichols (*Carnal Knowledge*)
PAUL ZIMMERMAN:	Bernardo Bertolucci (*The Conformist*); Stanley Kubrick (*A Clockwork Orange*); Peter Bogdanovich (*The Last Picture Show*)

BEST ACTOR

HOLLIS ALPERT:	Gene Hackman (*The French Connection*); Malcolm McDowell (*A Clockwork Orange*); Jean-Louis Trintignant (*The Conformist*)
GARY ARNOLD:	Topol (*Fiddler on the Roof*); Peter Finch (*Sunday, Bloody Sunday*); Peter Bonerz (*Funnyman*)

JACOB BRACKMAN:	Peter Finch (*Sunday, Bloody Sunday*); Jean-Louis Trintignant (*The Conformist*); Jack Nicholson (*Carnal Knowledge*)
VINCENT CANBY:	Peter Finch (*Sunday, Bloody Sunday*); Jean-Claude Brialy (*Claire's Knee*); Malcolm McDowell (*A Clockwork Orange*)
HAROLD CLURMAN:	Michael Higgins (*Wanda*); George C. Scott (*The Hospital*); Gene Hackman (*The French Connection*)
JAY COCKS.	Peter Finch (*Sunday, Bloody Sunday*); Malcolm McDowell (*A Clockwork Orange*); Gene Hackman (*The French Connection*)
DAVID DENBY:	Peter Finch (*Sunday, Bloody Sunday*); Malcolm McDowell (*A Clockwork Orange*); William Tepper (*Drive, He Said*)
PHILIP T. HARTUNG:	Peter Finch (*Sunday, Bloody Sunday*); Malcolm McDowell (*A Clockwork Orange*); Jean-Claude Brialy (*Claire's Knee*)
MOLLY HASKELL:	Peter Finch (*Sunday, Bloody Sunday*); Jean Yanne (*Le Boucher*); Warren Beatty (*McCabe & Mrs. Miller*)
PAULINE KAEL:	Jean-Louis Trintignant (*The Conformist*); Topol (*Fiddler on the Roof*); Malcolm McDowell (*A Clockwork Orange*)
STEFAN KANFER:	Peter Finch (*Sunday, Bloody Sunday*); Malcolm McDowell (*A Clockwork Orange*); (no third choice)
STANLEY KAUFFMANN:	Oliver Reed (*The Devils*); George C. Scott (*The Hospital*); Kenneth Mars (*Desperate Characters*)
ANDREW SARRIS:	Peter Finch (*Sunday, Bloody Sunday*); George C. Scott (*The Hospital*); Ian Holm (*A Severed Head; Nicholas and Alexandra*)
RICHARD SCHICKEL:	Gene Hackman (*The French Connection*); George C. Scott (*The Hospital*); Tom Courtenay (*One Day in the Life of Ivan Denisovich*)
ARTHUR SCHLESINGER, JR.:	Malcolm McDowell (*A Clockwork Orange*); George C. Scott (*The Hospital*); Thommy Berggren (*Joe Hill*)

JOHN SIMON: Peter Finch (*Sunday, Bloody Sunday*); Gene Hackman (*The French Connection*); Malcolm McDowell (*A Clockwork Orange; Long Ago, Tomorrow*)

BRUCE WILLIAMSON: Jean-Louis Trintignant (*The Conformist*); Tom Courtenay (*One Day in the Life of Ivan Denisovich*); Gene Hackman (*The French Connection*)

PAUL ZIMMERMAN: Peter Finch (*Sunday, Bloody Sunday*); Jean-Louis Trintignant (*The Conformist*); Malcolm McDowell (*A Clockwork Orange*)

BEST ACTRESS

HOLLIS ALPERT: Dominique Sanda (*The Conformist*); Bibi Andersson (*The Touch*); Gena Rowlands (*Minnie and Moskowitz*)

GARY ARNOLD: Jane Fonda (*Klute*); Vanessa Redgrave (*The Trojan Women*); Renée Taylor (*Made for Each Other*)

JACOB BRACKMAN: Ellen Burstyn (*The Last Picture Show*); Dominique Sanda (*The Conformist*); Béatrice Romand (*Claire's Knee*)

VINCENT CANBY: Béatrice Romand (*Claire's Knee*); Cloris Leachman (*The Last Picture Show*); (no third choice)

HAROLD CLURMAN: Dominique Sanda (*The Conformist*); Ann-Margret (*Carnal Knowledge*); Glenda Jackson (*Sunday, Bloody Sunday*)

JAY COCKS: Jane Fonda (*Klute*); Gena Rowlands (*Minnie and Moskowitz*); Glenda Jackson (*Sunday, Bloody Sunday*)

DAVID DENBY: Jane Fonda (*Klute*); Bibi Andersson (*The Touch*); Lea Massari (*Murmur of the Heart*)

PHILIP T. HARTUNG: Glenda Jackson (*Sunday, Bloody Sunday*); Gena Rowlands (*Minnie and Moskowitz*); Bibi Andersson (*The Touch*)

MOLLY HASKELL: Bibi Andersson (*The Touch*); Jane Asher (*Deep End*); Dyan Cannon (*Such Good Friends*)

PAULINE KAEL: Lea Massari (*Murmur of the Heart*); Jane Fonda (*Klute*); Bibi Andersson (*The Touch*)

STEFAN KANFER: Jane Fonda (*Klute*); Glenda Jackson (*Sunday, Bloody Sunday*); Dominique Sanda (*The Conformist*)

STANLEY KAUFFMANN: Glenda Jackson (*Sunday, Bloody Sunday*); Irene Papas (*The Trojan Women*); Barbara Loden (*Wanda*)

ANDREW SARRIS: Jane Asher (*Deep End*); Béatrice Romand (*Claire's Knee*); Bibi Andersson (*The Touch*)

RICHARD SCHICKEL: Jane Fonda (*Klute*); Gena Rowlands (*Minnie and Moskowitz*); Lea Massari (*Murmur of the Heart*)

ARTHUR SCHLESINGER, JR.: Jane Fonda (*Klute*); Dominique Sanda (*The Conformist*); Shirley MacLaine (*Desperate Characters*)

JOHN SIMON: Jane Fonda (*Klute*); Bibi Andersson (*The Touch*); Lea Massari (*Murmur of the Heart*)

BRUCE WILLIAMSON: Bibi Andersson (*The Touch*); Lea Massari (*Murmur of the Heart*); Jane Fonda (*Klute*)

PAUL ZIMMERMAN: Jane Fonda (*Klute*); Gena Rowlands (*Minnie and Moskowitz*); Béatrice Romand (*Claire's Knee*)

BEST SUPPORTING ACTOR

HOLLIS ALPERT: Bruce Dern (*Drive, He Said*); Warren Oates (*Two-Lane Blacktop*); Michael Higgins (*Wanda*)

GARY ARNOLD: Bruce Dern (*Drive, He Said*); Leonard Frey (*Fiddler on the Roof*); Jerry Houser (*Summer of '42*)

JACOB BRACKMAN: Bruce Dern (*Drive, He Said*); Michael Higgins (*Wanda*); Ben Johnson (*The Last Picture Show*)

VINCENT CANBY: Alan Webb (*King Lear*); Michael Higgins (*Wanda*); Bruce Dern (*Drive, He Said*)

HAROLD CLURMAN: Michael Higgins (*Wanda*); Roy Scheider (*The French Connection*); Romolo Valli (*The Garden of the Finzi-Continis*)

JAY COCKS: Warren Oates (*Two-Lane Blacktop*); Val Avery (*Minnie and Moskowitz*); Ben Johnson (*The Last Picture Show*)

DAVID DENBY: Warren Oates (*Two-Lane Blacktop*); Jerry Houser (*Summer of '42*); Lou Gossett (*The Skin Game*)

PHILIP T. HARTUNG: Ben Johnson (*The Last Picture Show*); Leonard Frey (*Fiddler on the Roof*); Anthony Sharp (*A Clockwork Orange*)

MOLLY HASKELL: Roy Scheider (*The French Connection*); Max von Sydow (*The Touch*); Murray Head (*Sunday, Bloody Sunday*)

PAULINE KAEL: Warren Oates (*The Hired Hand*); Bruce Dern (*Drive, He Said*); Alan Webb (*King Lear*)

STEFAN KANFER: Warren Oates (*Two-Lane Blacktop*); Roy Scheider (*The French Connection*); Ben Johnson (*The Last Picture Show*)

STANLEY KAUFFMANN: Alan Webb (*King Lear; Nicholas and Alexandra*); Ben Johnson (*The Last Picture Show*); Gerald O'Loughlin (*Desperate Characters*)

ANDREW SARRIS: Warren Oates (*Two-Lane Blacktop*); James Coco (*Such Good Friends*); Roy Scheider (*The French Connection*)

RICHARD SCHICKEL: Bruce Dern (*Drive, He Said*); Warren Oates (*Two-Lane Blacktop*); Ben Johnson (*The Last Picture Show*)

ARTHUR SCHLESINGER, JR.:   Bruce Dern (*Drive, He Said*); Anthony Sharp (*A Clockwork Orange*); Roy Scheider (*The French Connection*)

JOHN SIMON: Max von Sydow (*The Touch*); Ian MacShane (*Villain*); Dominic Guard (*The Go-Between*)

BRUCE WILLIAMSON: Alan Webb (*King Lear*); Ben Johnson (*The Last Picture Show*); Bruce Dern (*Drive, He Said*)

PAUL ZIMMERMAN: Ben Johnson (*The Last Picture Show*); Bruce Dern (*Drive, He Said*); Warren Oates (*Two-Lane Blacktop*)

BEST SUPPORTING
ACTRESS

HOLLIS ALPERT:	Stefania Sandrelli (*The Conformist*); Dominique Sanda (*The Conformist*); Glenda Jackson (*The Boy Friend*)
GARY ARNOLD:	Béatrice Romand (*Claire's Knee*); Stefania Sandrelli (*The Conformist*); Cybill Shepherd (*The Last Picture Show*)
JACOB BRACKMAN:	Gwen Welles (*A Safe Place*); Ellen Burstyn (*The Last Picture Show*); Stefania Sandrelli (*The Conformist*)
VINCENT CANBY:	Béatrice Romand (*Claire's Knee*); Stefania Sandrelli (*The Conformist*); Cloris Leachman (*The Last Picture Show*)
HAROLD CLURMAN:	Dominique Sanda (*The Conformist*); Stefania Sandrelli (*The Conformist*); Cloris Leachman (*The Last Picture Show*)
JAY COCKS:	Ellen Burstyn (*The Last Picture Show*); Julie Adams (*The Last Movie*); Dominique Sanda (*The Conformist*)
DAVID DENBY:	Ellen Burstyn (*The Last Picture Show*); Béatrice Romand (*Claire's Knee*); Stefania Sandrelli (*The Conformist*)
PHILIP T. HARTUNG:	Cloris Leachman (*The Last Picture* Show); Béatrice Romand (*Claire's Knee*); Ellen Burstyn (*The Last Picture Show*)
MOLLY HASKELL:	Cloris Leachman (*The Last Picture Show*); Verna Bloom (*The Hired Hand*); Cybill Shepherd (*The Last Picture Show*)
PAULINE KAEL:	Ellen Burstyn (*The Last Picture Show*); Stefania Sandrelli (*The Conformist*); Béatrice Romand (*Claire's Knee*)
STEFAN KANFER:	Cloris Leachman (*The Last Picture Show*); Dominique Sanda (*The Conformist*); (no third choice)
STANLEY KAUFFMANN:	Margaret Leighton (*The Go-Between*); Verna Bloom (*The Hired Hand*); Ellen Burstyn (*The Last Picture Show*)
ANDREW SARRIS:	Diana Rigg (*The Hospital*); Margaret Leighton (*The Go-Between*); Peggy Ashcroft (*Sunday, Bloody Sunday*)
RICHARD SCHICKEL:	Ellen Burstyn (*The Last Picture Show*);

	Cloris Leachman (*The Last Picture Show*); Katherine Cassavetes (*Minnie and Moskowitz*)
ARTHUR SCHLESINGER, JR.:	Dominique Sanda (*The Conformist*); Stefania Sandrelli (*The Conformist*); Béatrice Romand (*Claire's Knee*)
JOHN SIMON:	Ellen Burstyn (*The Last Picture Show*); Eileen Brennan (*The Last Picture Show*); Xuan Ha (*Hoa-Binh*)
BRUCE WILLIAMSON:	Dominique Sanda (*The Conformist*); Milena Dravic (*Adrift; WR-Mysteries of the Organism*); Ellen Burstyn (*The Last Picture Show*)
PAUL ZIMMERMAN:	Ellen Burstyn (*The Last Picture Show*); Cloris Leachman (*The Last Picture Show*); Béatrice Romand (*Claire's Knee*)

BEST SCREENPLAY

HOLLIS ALPERT:	Eric Rohmer (*Claire's Knee*); Woody Allen and Mickey Rose (*Bananas*); Paddy Chayefsky (*The Hospital*)
GARY ARNOLD:	Penelope Gilliatt (*Sunday, Bloody Sunday*); Louis Malle (*Murmur of the Heart*); Larry McMurtry and Peter Bogdanovich (*The Last Picture Show*)
JACOB BRACKMAN:	Eric Rohmer (*Claire's Knee*); Larry McMurtry and Peter Bogdanovich (*The Last Picture Show*); Penelope Gilliatt (*Sunday, Bloody Sunday*)
VINCENT CANBY:	Penelope Gilliatt (*Sunday, Bloody Sunday*); Eric Rohmer (*Claire's Knee*); Larry McMurtry and Peter Bogdanovich (*The Last Picture Show*)
HAROLD CLURMAN:	Penelope Gilliatt (*Sunday, Bloody Sunday*); Louis Malle (*Murmur of the Heart*); Vittorio Bonicelli and Ugo Pirro (*The Garden of the Finzi-Continis*)
JAY COCKS:	Elaine May (*A New Leaf*); Woody Allen and Mickey Rose (*Bananas*); Larry McMurtry and Peter Bogdanovich (*The Last Picture Show*)
DAVID DENBY:	Louis Malle (*Murmur of the Heart*); Eric

Rohmer (*Claire's Knee*); Woody Allen and Mickey Rose (*Bananas*)

PHILIP T. HARTUNG: Penelope Gilliatt (*Sunday, Bloody Sunday*); Eric Rohmer (*Claire's Knee*); (no third choice)

MOLLY HASKELL: Eric Rohmer (*Claire's Knee*); Penelope Gilliatt (*Sunday, Bloody Sunday*); Larry McMurtry and Peter Bogdanovich (*The Last Picture Show*)

PAULINE KAEL: Louis Malle (*Murmur of the Heart*); Penelope Gilliatt (*Sunday, Bloody Sunday*); Larry McMurtry and Peter Bogdanovich (*The Last Picture Show*)

STEFAN KANFER: Penelope Gilliatt (*Sunday, Bloody Sunday*); Woody Allen and Mickey Rose (*Bananas*); Larry McMurtry and Peter Bogdanovich (*The Last Picture Show*)

STANLEY KAUFFMANN: Octavio Getino and Fernando E. Solanas (*The Hour of the Furnaces*); Eric Rohmer (*Claire's Knee*); Barbara Loden (*Wanda*)

ANDREW SARRIS: Eric Rohmer (*Claire's Knee*); Larry McMurtry and Peter Bogdanovich (*The Last Picture Show*); Penelope Gilliatt (*Sunday, Bloody Sunday*)

RICHARD SCHICKEL: Louis Malle (*Murmur of the Heart*); Woody Allen and Mickey Rose (*Bananas*); Paddy Chayefsky (*The Hospital*)

ARTHUR SCHLESINGER, JR.: Eric Rohmer (*Claire's Knee*); Paddy Chayefsky (*The Hospital*); Stanley Kubrick (*A Clockwork Orange*)

JOHN SIMON: Louis Malle (*Murmur of the Heart*); Bryan Forbes (*Long Ago, Tomorrow*); Raoul Coutard (*Hoa-Binh*)

BRUCE WILLIAMSON: Louis Malle (*Murmur of the Heart*); Penelope Gilliatt (*Sunday, Bloody Sunday*); Larry McMurtry and Peter Bogdanovich (*The Last Picture Show*)

PAUL ZIMMERMAN: Penelope Gilliatt (*Sunday, Bloody Sunday*); Louis Malle (*Murmur of the Heart*); Larry McMurtry and Peter Bogdanovich (*The Last Picture Show*)

BEST
CINEMATOGRAPHY

HOLLIS ALPERT: Vittorio Storaro (*The Conformist*); Billy Williams (*Sunday, Bloody Sunday*); Ennio Guarnieri (*The Garden of the Finzi-Continis*)

GARY ARNOLD: Vilmos Zsigmond (*McCabe & Mrs. Miller*); Gerry Fisher (*Man in the Wilderness*); Vittorio Storaro (*The Conformist*)

JACOB BRACKMAN: Vittorio Storaro (*The Conformist*); Billy Williams (*Sunday, Bloody Sunday*); Robert Surtees (*The Last Picture Show*)

VINCENT CANBY: Robert Surtees (*The Last Picture Show*); Vittorio Storaro (*The Conformist*); Nestor Almendros (*Claire's Knee; Bed and Board*)

HAROLD CLURMAN: Vittorio Storaro (*The Conformist*); Ennio Guarnieri (*The Garden of the Finzi-Continis*); Robert Surtees (*The Last Picture Show*)

JAY COCKS: Greg Sandor (*Two-Lane Blacktop*); Vittorio Storaro (*The Conformist*); Gerry Fisher (*The Go-Between; Man in the Wilderness*)

DAVID DENBY: Robert Surtees (*The Last Picture Show; Summer of '42*); Vittorio Storaro (*The Conformist*); Vilmos Zsigmond (*McCabe & Mrs. Miller*)

PHILIP T. HARTUNG: Billy Williams (*Sunday, Bloody Sunday*); John Alcott (*A Clockwork Orange*); Nestor Almendros (*Claire's Knee*)

MOLLY HASKELL: Robert Surtees (*The Last Picture Show; Summer of '42*); Vittorio Storaro (*The Conformist*); Charley Steinberger (*Deep End*)

PAULINE KAEL: Vilmos Zsigmond (*McCabe & Mrs. Miller*); Vittoria Storaro (*The Conformist*); Gerry Fisher (*Man in the Wilderness*)

STEFAN KANFER: Billy Williams (*Sunday, Bloody Sunday*); John Alcott (*A Clockwork Orange*); Vittorio Storaro (*The Conformist*)

STANLEY KAUFFMANN: (Abstained)

ANDREW SARRIS: Nestor Almendros (*Claire's Knee*); (no second and third choice)

RICHARD SCHICKEL: Vilmos Zsigmond (*McCabe & Mrs. Miller*); Billy Williams (*Sunday, Bloody Sunday*); Robert Surtees (*The Last Picture Show*)

ARTHUR SCHLESINGER, JR.:   Gil Taylor (*Macbeth*); Peter Davidsson and Jorgen Persson (*Joe Hill*); Vittorio Storaro (*The Conformist*)

JOHN SIMON: Tonino delli Colli (*The Decameron*); Tony Imi (*Long Ago, Tomorrow*); David Watkin (*The Boy Friend*)

BRUCE WILLIAMSON: Vittorio Storaro (*The Conformist*); Giuseppe Rotunno (*Carnal Knowledge*); Sven Nykvist (*The Touch*)

PAUL ZIMMERMAN: Vittorio Storaro (*The Conformist*); Vilmos Zsigmond (*McCabe & Mrs. Miller*); Robert Surtees (*The Last Picture Show*)

Voting Tabulation (1st choice = 3 points, 2nd choice = 2 points, 3rd choice = 1 point)

BEST PICTURE 1971

22 POINTS	*Claire's Knee*
15 POINTS	*The Conformist*
12 POINTS	*A Clockwork Orange*
9 POINTS	*The Last Picture Show*
8 POINTS	*Murmur of the Heart (Le Souffle au Coeur)*
6 POINTS	*Hoa-Binh*
5 POINTS	*McCabe & Mrs. Miller*
4 POINTS	*Fiddler on the Roof*
4 POINTS	*Sunday, Bloody Sunday*
3 POINTS	*Deep End*
3 POINTS	*The Hour of the Furnaces*
3 POINTS	*Taking Off*
2 POINTS	*Minnie and Moskowitz*
2 POINTS	*The Taira Clan*
2 POINTS	*One Day in the Life of Ivan Denisovich*
1 POINT	*Le Boucher (The Butcher)*
1 POINT	*Carnal Knowledge*

1 POINT	*The Clowns*
1 POINT	*Desperate Characters*
1 POINT	*The French Connection*
1 POINT	*The Garden of the Finzi-Continis*
1 POINT	*The Go-Between*
1 POINT	*Walkabout*

BEST DIRECTOR 1971

23 POINTS	Bernardo Bertolucci (*The Conformist*)
21 POINTS	Eric Rohmer (*Claire's Knee*)
13 POINTS	Stanley Kubrick (*A Clockwork Orange*)
8 POINTS	Robert Altman (*McCabe & Mrs. Miller*)
8 POINTS	Raoul Coutard (*Hoa-Binh*)
8 POINTS	Louis Malle (*Murmur of the Heart*)
4 POINTS	Peter Bogdanovich (*The Last Picture Show*)
3 POINTS	William Friedkin (*The French Connection*)
3 POINTS	Jerzy Skolimowski (*Deep End*)
3 POINTS	Fernando Ezequiel Solanas (*The Hour of the Furnaces*)
2 POINTS	John Cassavetes (*Minnie and Moskowitz*)
2 POINTS	Vittorio De Sica (*The Garden of the Finzi-Continis*)
2 POINTS	Kenji Mizoguchi (*Utamaro and His Five Women*)
1 POINT	Claude Chabrol (*Le Boucher*)
1 POINT	Frank D. Gilroy (*Desperate Characters*)
1 POINT	Norman Jewison (*Fiddler on the Roof*)
1 POINT	Mike Nichols (*Carnal Knowledge*)
1 POINT	Nicolas Roeg (*Walkabout*)
1 POINT	Ken Russell (*The Boy Friend*)

BEST ACTOR 1971

33 POINTS	Peter Finch (*Sunday, Bloody Sunday*)
17 POINTS	Malcolm McDowell (*A Clockwork Orange* and *Long Ago, Tomorrow*)
11 POINTS	Gene Hackman (*The French Connection*)
11 POINTS	Jean-Louis Trintignant (*The Conformist*)
10 POINTS	George C. Scott (*The Hospital*)
5 POINTS	Topol (*Fiddler on the Roof*)
3 POINTS	Jean-Claude Brialy (*Claire's Knee*)

3 POINTS	Tom Courtenay (*One Day in the Life of Ivan Denisovich*)
3 POINTS	Michael Higgins (*Wanda*)
3 POINTS	Oliver Reed (*The Devils*)
2 POINTS	Jean Yanne (*Le Boucher*)
1 POINT	Thommy Berggren (*Joe Hill*)
1 POINT	Peter Bonerz (*Funnyman*)
1 POINT	Warren Beatty (*McCabe & Mrs. Miller*)
1 POINT	Ian Holm (*A Severed Head* and *Nicholas and Alexandra*)
1 POINT	Kenneth Mars (*Desperate Characters*)
1 POINT	Jack Nicholson (*Carnal Knowledge*)
1 POINT	William Tepper (*Drive, He Said*)

BEST ACTRESS 1971

27 POINTS	Jane Fonda (*Klute*)
15 POINTS	Bibi Andersson (*The Touch*)
11 POINTS	Dominique Sanda (*The Conformist*)
10 POINTS	Glenda Jackson (*Sunday, Bloody Sunday*)
9 POINTS	Gena Rowlands (*Minnie and Moskowitz*)
8 POINTS	Lea Massari (*Murmur of the Heart*)
7 POINTS	Béatrice Romand (*Claire's Knee*)
5 POINTS	Jane Asher (*Deep End*)
3 POINTS	Ellen Burstyn (*The Last Picture Show*)
2 POINTS	Ann-Margret (*Carnal Knowledge*)
2 POINTS	Cloris Leachman (*The Last Picture Show*)
2 POINTS	Irene Papas (*The Trojan Women*)
2 POINTS	Vanessa Redgrave (*The Trojan Women*)
1 POINT	Dyan Cannon (*Such Good Friends*)
1 POINT	Barbara Loden (*Wanda*)
1 POINT	Shirley MacLaine (*Desperate Characters*)
1 POINT	Renée Taylor (*Made for Each Other*)

BEST SUPPORTING ACTOR 1971

21 POINTS	Bruce Dern (*Drive, He Said*)
20 POINTS	Warren Oates (*Two-Lane Blacktop* and *The Hired Hand*)
14 POINTS	Ben Johnson (*The Last Picture Show*)
10 POINTS	Alan Webb (*King Lear* and *Nicholas and Alexandra*)

9 POINTS	Roy Scheider (*The French Connection*)
8 POINTS	Michael Higgins (*Wanda*)
5 POINTS	Max von Sydow (*The Touch*)
4 POINTS	Leonard Frey (*Fiddler on the Roof*)
3 POINTS	Jerry Houser (*Summer of '42*)
3 POINTS	Anthony Sharp (*A Clockwork Orange*)
2 POINTS	James Coco (*Such Good Friends*)
2 POINTS	Ian McKellan (*Villain*)
2 POINTS	Val Avery (*Minnie and Moskowitz*)
1 POINT	Dominic Guard (*The Go-Between*)
1 POINT	Lou Gossett (*The Skin Game*)
1 POINT	Murray Head (*Sunday, Bloody Sunday*)
1 POINT	Gerald O'Loughlin (*Desperate Characters*)
1 POINT	Romolo Valli (*The Garden of the Finzi-Continis*)

BEST SUPPORTING
ACTRESS 1971

23 POINTS	Ellen Burstyn (*The Last Picture Show*)
15 POINTS	Cloris Leachman (*The Last Picture Show*)
15 POINTS	Stefania Sandrelli (*The Conformist*)
14 POINTS	Dominique Sanda (*The Conformist*)
13 POINTS	Béatrice Romand (*Claire's Knee*)
5 POINTS	Margaret Leighton (*The Go-Between*)
4 POINTS	Verna Bloom (*The Hired Hand*)
3 POINTS	Diana Rigg (*The Hospital*)
3 POINTS	Gwen Welles (*A Safe Place*)
2 POINTS	Eileen Brennan (*The Last Picture Show*)
2 POINTS	Milena Dravic (*Adrift* and *WR-Mysteries of the Organism*)
2 POINTS	Cybill Shepherd (*The Last Picture Show*)
2 POINTS	Julie Adams (*The Last Movie*)
1 POINT	Peggy Ashcroft (*Sunday, Bloody Sunday*)
1 POINT	Katherine Cassavetes (*Minnie and Moskowitz*)
1 POINT	Glenda Jackson (*The Boy Friend*)
1 POINT	Xuan Ha (*Hoa-Binh*)

BEST SCREENPLAY
1971

26 POINTS	Penelope Gilliatt (*Sunday, Bloody Sunday*)
23 POINTS	Eric Rohmer (*Claire's Knee*)
21 POINTS	Louis Malle (*Murmur of the Heart*)
11 POINTS	Larry McMurtry and Peter Bogdanovich (*The Last Picture Show*)
9 POINTS	Woody Allen and Mickey Rose (*Bananas*)
4 POINTS	Paddy Chayefsky (*The Hospital*)
3 POINTS	Bryan Forbes (*Long Ago, Tomorrow*)
3 POINTS	Octavio Getino and Fernando E. Solanas (*The Hour of the Furnaces*)
3 POINTS	Elaine May (*A New Leaf*)
1 POINT	Vittorio Bonicelli and Ugo Pirro (*The Garden of the Finzi-Continis*)
1 POINT	Raoul Coutard (*Hoa-Binh*)
1 POINT	Stanley Kubrick (*A Clockwork Orange*)
1 POINT	Barbara Loden (*Wanda*)

BEST
CINEMATOGRAPHY 1971

28 POINTS	Vittorio Storaro (*The Conformist*)
13 POINTS	Robert Surtees (*The Last Picture Show* and *Summer of '42*)
12 POINTS	Billy Williams (*Sunday, Bloody Sunday*)
12 POINTS	Vilmos Zsigmond (*McCabe & Mrs. Miller*)
5 POINTS	Nestor Almendros (*Claire's Knee* and *Bed and Board*)
4 POINTS	John Alcott (*A Clockwork Orange*)
4 POINTS	Gerry Fisher (*The Go-Between* and *Man in the Wilderness*)
3 POINTS	Tonino delli Colli (*The Decameron*)
3 POINTS	Ennio Guarnieri (*The Garden of the Finzi-Continis*)
3 POINTS	Greg Sandor (*Two-Lane Blacktop*)
3 POINTS	Gil Taylor (*Macbeth*)
2 POINTS	Peter Davidsson and Jorgen Persson (*Joe Hill*)
2 POINTS	Tony Imi (*Long Ago, Tomorrow*)
2 POINTS	Giuseppe Rotunno (*Carnal Knowledge*)
1 POINT	Sven Nykvist (*The Touch*)
1 POINT	David Watkin (*The Boy Friend*)
1 POINT	Charley Steinberger (*Deep End*)

SPECIAL AWARD 1971 TO *LE CHAGRIN ET LA PITIÉ*
(THE SORROW AND THE PITY)

FOR A FILM OF EXTRAORDINARY PUBLIC INTEREST
AND DISTINCTION—by unanimous vote.

RECOMMENDED FILMS

THE NATIONAL SOCIETY OF FILM CRITICS recommended the following films during 1971:

Une Femme Douce
Claire's Knee
The Garden of Delights
Taking Off
The Conformist
The French Connection
The Go-Between
The Last Picture Show
Sunday, Bloody Sunday

A recommendation requires a majority of the membership voting in favor after abstentions have been deducted from the total number of members. If more than one-fourth of the members abstain, the film does not receive a recommendation.

I:

THE YEAR'S FILMS

I
MASCULINE FEMININE

CARNAL KNOWLEDGE

Jacob Brackman

A few months back, writing about *Summer of '42*, I hinted at a dark underside to nostalgia for our bygone sexual "naïveté." I've put quotes around "naïveté" because it sounds nice and bouncy, like we *should* feel nostalgia for it. But we could as well choose more somber catchwords to remind us of attitudes, about pleasuring and being pleasured, which began to break down in this country during the past decade. In certain respects, we had it better than today's teenagers. Certainly we required less stimulation to thrill us through to the marrow. That deserves missing, I expect. But the intensity of our excitement owed itself, largely, to ignorant prohibitions. To a cold, unloving, unmerging experience of sexuality. Until the life-style transformations of the Sixties, such experiences may have been close to universal among educated white Americans. Now things have loosened up. Some. We can begin talking aloud, and in films, of how selfish, dirty-minded, uptight we were back then—and, for the most part, remain.

A first step: to acknowledge what sneaky sex maniacs we were through our teens. *Summer of '42* makes this acknowledgment. But it also detaches us from the era (and from adolescence itself) by inserting a mellow narrator—the tremulous Hermie of the movie, now grown—between us and the action. We can assume that grown-up Hermie's reminiscence arises from the perspective of an enlightened adult sex life.

Mike Nichols' *Carnal Knowledge* takes up several years after the Summer of '42, like a further installment. Back during that fateful initiation summer, the Jack Nicholson character, Jonathan, doubt-

35

less would have been urging his pals on to bolder night beach play. Prying for the gory details afterward. ("Did you get into her bra? *Yeah?* Did you get her bra *off?*") Showing around the trusty rubber he carried always, lest an "emergency" catch him unequipped. Talk about nostalgia! The protective tinfoil smudged with three dozen fingerprints! Back then, the Arthur Garfunkel character, Sandy, doubtless would have been swooning, hourly, over some far-off older woman of twenty-two.

It's as if, for both of them, all of life turned out to be the Summer of '42, over and over again. None of the sentimentality—for where Mulligan is mushy, Nichols is brittle and satirical—but that level of obsession, confusion, frustration. Humiliation. As if sex remained the one tormenting issue forever. As if neither hero ever made the slightest progress toward figuring out what girls were really for. We can sense their bewilderment extending out beyond the movie's end. Beyond prostate conditions. Beyond sterility. *Carnal Knowledge* implies that one doesn't outgrow so easily.

We first meet Nicholson and Garfunkel as Amherst undergraduates, roommates, in the Forties. In regard to love, each is as ignorant and lost as the other. Nicholson's self-assurance, his braggadocio, lets him define where they both stand on intimate matters. Who wonders why he's always soaping himself down in the shower? He seems to have more information about girls, particularly about how you can best maneuver them into giving you what you want. Moreover, he is charming—charismatic even—arrogant and crude. With minor misgivings, Garfunkel—a shy, earnest boy who might have turned idealistic under nobler influences—is prepared to accept him as mentor. To embrace his vision of the male-female game. Of course, no more pathetic model than Nicholson could be found anywhere. The blinder leading the blind. Then again, thousands upon thousands of equally wrong-minded and misleading guides could be found anywhere. Garfunkel doesn't just learn from the Nicholson character, you see; Nicholson is the perfect embodiment, emblem, mouthpiece of the prevailing vision of the Game. The Game's object consists mainly in scoring off lots of women without caring deeply. Without allowing oneself to be *ensnared* by any one of them.

Candice Bergen, whom the two roommates spot wallflowering at a genteel social, turns out to play the coed's side of this same Game. Object: to put out strategically. To parlay the competition for her favors into a home in the suburbs. Candice, with lipstick red as a fire truck, is practically a loose woman for the period, loose, anyway, for the Heavenly Seven Sisters Schools. Wily, too, behind her moral qualms and crocodile tears. Calculating. Garfunkel starts taking her out first. Nicholson insists on a nightly play-by-play. Shortly, impressed with his slow roommate's fast progress, he takes up with Candice himself, on the sly. He manages to get her to go all the way before Garfunkel does. Soon they're both bedding her down, and Nicholson torments himself over the sharing. Stews over the details of her affair with his roommate. Now he longs for exclusivity! He pressures Candice with "ultimatums." She can't bring herself to tell Garfunkel. Nicholson threatens to reveal all, but he can't either. Suddenly she opts for security over magnetism, for more trust than she deserves.

By the conspicuous omission of any further reference to her two-timing, we presume that Garfunkel, who marries her, never discovers he's been cuckolded. Cuckolded in advance, no less, by his best friend. This collegiate cuckolding turns out to be crucial, however, considerably more so than Garfunkel's short-lived marriage, crucial by virtue of its never coming up.

The movie goes on to show us some interchanges snatched from the course of the next twenty-five years. Their work (Garfunkel becomes a doctor, Nicholson a tax lawyer) recedes to seem arbitrary, peripheral. What counts then? We come to understand that women pass clear through their lives, leaving no more than an aftertaste. We see nothing of their play except as it touches on hungry "love" maneuvers. During a tennis match, Nichols withholds even a glimpse of the actual tennis, as though he were staging for the stage. Because what counts is not the tennis but the *double date*. Games within games, devious and blind at once. Their lives contain no personal cumulation, nothing solid or sustained apart from the friendship between them.

Yet even that friendship was contaminated at its source by the secret of Nicholson's betrayal. Not that it's any insurmountable sin to sneak off with your best friend's girl. Nicholson's bird-dogging was so palpably an attempt—albeit misunderstood, thwarted—not to take something away from Garfunkel, but to get close to him. The men never touch each other (God forbid!) but at least they can both spend time in the same place. Inside Candice. This theme—the friends' longing for each other and their inability to get genuinely together except by sharing the same pussy—informs their relationship throughout. Their misplaced mutual envy; each always wanting what the other's got. Their intimate confessions. Their titillation at the prospect of setting each other up or, better yet, *swapping*. But neither can be honest with himself, much less with the other, so they *never* make true contact. Continually looking for fulfillment from mere fornication, never understanding the erotic as a metaphor for one's deeply felt connectedness, each is doomed to fall short of satisfaction forever.

Fourteen- or fifteen-year-old boys unwholesomely preoccupied with carnal knowledge can strike us as humorous, warm, nostalgia-provoking. Even if sex affords them mainly torture, still, that's what adolescence is about, isn't it? And even if their confusion persists half a dozen years more into college, no cause yet for concern. These are years, after all, for experimentation, for testing out, right? For playing the field and sowing wild oats. We can still laugh easily at phony come-ons, missed connections, gratuitous intrigues, graceless or traumatic love play. Chalk them all up to experience. Our popular mythology—especially the movies' sentimental lies—leads us to expect resolution. Immature followed by mature. Failures at love crowned with a match made in heaven. Stormy courtships blossoming into happily-ever-afters. In real life, one's early patterns cling more tenaciously. Things tend not to get better. Which is almost the same as saying, since we're all the while growing older, they get worse. The exact sexual foolishness we find amusing in a boy of fifteen can seem bathetic in a man of thirty, near-tragic in a man of forty-five. This is why *Carnal Knowledge* is so unsettling, finally, so sad for all its funniness, so bloody sad.

What is strongest, by far, in Mike Nichols' movies is his reconstruction of waking nightmares people sometimes find themselves lost in. He shows exactly "what's so bad." In *Who's Afraid of Virginia Woolf?*, how a husband and wife, adroitly yet casually, needlessly, can turn their home into a poison den. In *The Graduate*, how a promising young man, on the threshold of every reward to which young men are supposed to aspire, can despise the life he's about to inherit. In *Catch-22*, how a man caught in war, no longer able to depend upon his leaders, his friends, his own reason, can be reduced to fearful, crazed helplessness. And here, in *Carnal Knowledge*, how men can pass through their entire lives without ever making any real connection with a woman. Nor even, for that matter, with another man.

But until now, Nichols has made disturbing movies with reassurances tacked on. In *Virginia Woolf*, Burton and Taylor embrace at the dawn, make up, having got through another long night's journey into day, their terrible compromise intact. In *The Graduate*, the focus shifts first from Dustin Hoffman's confusion over his future to confusion over his destructive affair with Mrs. Robinson. Then from anguish to adventure. The distressing questions it raised early on get mislaid well before the chase which brings the boy-gets-loses-gets-girl part of the picture to a rousing finale. In the last hundred feet, when we'd just about forgotten the impasse Benjamin had reached about his future, some echo of that impasse reasserts itself. The scene's high spirits quaver. He's snatched his girl from the altar of a disastrous marriage. Yet instead of ending on a note of jubilant getaway, Nichols had the two of them stare blankly at the camera. A quizzical shot. "So? What happens now? What have we really solved?" In *Catch-22*, the harrowing sense of Alan Arkin's isolation and dislocation—interrupted, repeatedly, by a Beetle-Baileyish genre of Service Comedy. Nichols eases up on us. Dissipates the pressure. Asks us to laugh in ways we've often been asked to laugh. In the end, Arkin makes a mad dash for freedom. The camera pulls back slowly, further, further, into one of those god's-eye, *Bridge on the River Kwai*-type fade-outs. In the expanse of background, a platoon marches off the airstrip in drill formation. On the track, a triumphant martial air. Arkin, now a tiny dot in the center of the screen, has set out to sea in a life raft. His escape! Futile, absurd, but heroic as well. Again, the ending undercuts the severity of what has gone before—but, again, undercuts only halfway.

It's easy to imagine that Mike Nichols did not really believe an escape existed for any of his characters—not in any of these movies. Or perhaps, if there *was* an escape, then his particular characters *couldn't* escape. For when they *do* escape in the end, there's no conclusive, wholehearted spirit of victory, just an uneasy truce. As if some imaginary mogul had demanded happily-ever-afters from him—"Hollywood endings"—and Nichols had delivered them as ordered. Except he'd stuck a subversive little twist on each one. A twist the mogul might not even get. *Carnal Knowledge* offers no reassurance, no resolution, and therefore needs no subversive final twist. It is uncompromised subversion from the beginning. When the traps are inside, there's no way out. Icily, but courageously, Nichols has pressed that disturbingness all the way home.

GARY ARNOLD

That Joseph E. Levine certainly is a caution. For the past several months he's been stringing the film press along on his latest production, *Carnal Knowledge*, implying that the content was so original and candid that it had to be classified information. The only approved leak was a skeletal plot synopsis of forty words.

Now the movie has arrived, and the truth can be told: the cat is out of the bag, so to speak, and he turns out to be one famished cat. One discovers that the skeletal synopsis is a product of abject necessity rather than masterful concision; it's skeletal because the story is skeletal and the characterization is skeletal. This is, in fact, one of the leanest and least nourishing artistic bones an American movie audience has ever been encouraged to gnaw on.

Somehow, most of the critics have refused to catch on to Levine's little joke; they've been acting as if a mightily impressive work of art was not just in the wings but upon and among us. My hunch is that *Carnal Knowledge* will prove itself almost exclusively with impressionable critics, who will find its streamlined look and its clinical treatment of sterile people easy to praise, just the sort of classy clichés that demonstrate we can do it too, that director Mike Nichols doesn't have to take a back seat to the Antonioni of ten years ago.

However, paying customers are going to have their problems. These won't stem in most cases from any particular erotic candor in the action and dialogue; they will stem from the fact that the material is sketchy, uncompassionate and fundamentally anti-erotic. Nichols and writer Jules Feiffer are ferocious, if newfangled, puritans: they don't even permit the characters a measure of real passion or pleasure—any intensity or spontaneity of feeling—when they're college kids, supposedly in the process of falling in love and/or discovering sex for the first time.

Anyway, I wouldn't mind having a nickel for every moviegoer who walks out of *Carnal Knowledge* feeling cheated and despondent. The basic problem with the film is that it's the artistic equivalent of the sort of thing it purports to be satirizing and abhoring; it's a cold, calculating, unfeeling view of cold, calculating, unfeeling relationships. The soullessness of the characters finds its analogue in the style of the artists, who function rather more like disinterested lab technicians or statisticians or coroner's assistants than artists. One more collaboration like this one and Nichols and Feiffer can be hailed as our foremost contrivers of zombie movies.

In an unfortunate way Feiffer really gets even with the critics who keep saying that his characters seem like cartoon figures. The people in *Carnal Knowledge* make one long for the simple humanity and extra dimensions of some of his cartoon people. Art Garfunkel, for example, is cast as such a dreary, unmitigated nebbish that one is reminded of what a lively, *conscious* nebbish Feiffer once had in the figure of Bernard Mergendeiler.

The screenplay attempts to trace the friendship and sexual attitudes of two men—one, played by Jack Nicholson, a bastard; the other, played by Garfunkel, a dope—over the course of a generation. It begins when the men are college classmates at Amherst in the late Forties and ends in the present, with the bastard, a prosperous tax lawyer, even more of a selfish bastard and the dope, a prosperous doctor, even more of a stodgy dope.

The plot outline could be developed comedically or dramatically, but Feiffer's conception is sewed up tight right from the start, a narrow, sour brief against his own generation, which is symbolized as emptyheaded and coldhearted. It's difficult to share his generational self-hatred, particularly on the kind of flimsy evidence asserted here. It might be possible to argue that these people don't deserve sympathy, but if not, why is a serious artist calling our attention to them in the first place and why is he so systematic about depriving them of feeling and personality and intelligence?

The conception is essentially undramatic and insufferable. One can respond to characters who have values to lose or feelings to hurt, like the protagonists of *The Group*, but Feiffer's targets don't have *anything* to lose. They're empty to begin with, and all we do is watch them get older.

Nichols' detached, antiseptic style of direction simply underlines the defects—instead of being expanded or humanized, the material is rendered even more cramped and mechanical and inhuman. For instance, Nicholson and Garfunkel encounter Candice Bergen, who will become the former's first mistress and the latter's first wife, at what must be the most sparsely attended mixer in collegiate history. Miss Bergen is unattended. Garfunkel approaches her, and they begin speaking satirical cant dialogue in flat, affectless voices. The scene feels false and expedient and ineffective in every respect, an overstylization of a wrongheaded idea. It would be easier to take the setting as a lounge in a mental institution and the interlocuters as lobotomized patients.

The effects and overtones have a way of being perverse without being truly witty or revealing, and often they backfire. For example, the "clever" conceit of underscoring a copulation scene between Nicholson and Ann-Margret with a recording of Frank Sinatra singing "Dream" and a squabble between the same pair with a recording of Dick Powell singing "I'll String Along with You" results in a desire to hear more of Sinatra and Powell and less of the people at hand. Similarly, the way Nicholson suggests an evil incarnation of Lon McCallister and Candy Bergen a frigid incarnation of Barbara Bel Geddes makes one feel dangerously nostalgic about—and offended on behalf of—the originals.

Carnal Knowledge may appeal to people who confuse pitilessness with integrity. In theme and tone it's reminiscent of the John Cassavetes pictures *Faces* and *Husbands* and tries to pass off the same banalities as profundities. The method is different—Cassavetes counts on actors agonizing their way to the foregone conclusion that prosperous, middle-aged Americans are soulless, while Nichols and Feiffer construct fastidious little vignettes to illustrate and reiterate the point—but it's the same nagging, aggressive, dubious message. If you can't get enough of it, this single-minded, mean-spirited film should hold you for some time to come.

The View from Mr. Nichols' Bridge

RICHARD SCHICKEL

Carnal Knowledge is a sexual history of two men we are supposed to understand as modern American archetypes. It traces their intertwined yet contrasting stories from the time they shared a room—and a Smith girl—at Amherst in the late 1940s until the present moment, when Jonathan (Jack Nicholson), who has always seen women as objects and used them selfishly, pays for his sins with virtual impotence and Sandy (Arthur Garfunkel), the more romantic of the pair, practices Consciousness III by taking as his mistress a spaced-out hippie chick.

The script is by Jules Feiffer and, as you might expect, it takes the form of a series of dialogues and monologues that, as in those he features in his cartoons, truly capture the sound of our daily miseries and mysteries. The direction is by Mike Nichols and, again as you might expect, he has given us a beautifully performed film, achieving special miracles with Candice Bergen as the Smithy and with pneumatic Ann-Margret as a not quite bright but touching TV manikin who goes to suicidal lengths to bring Nicholson to the altar.

For all of that, however, I can't say that I like *Carnal Knowledge* very much. To borrow a phrase Mr. Garfunkel made famous, it seems to me a sort of bridge over troubled waters. One has a sense of director and writer perched on it, safely high and dry, observing those thrashing about in the water beneath, making what seem to them appropriately comic and compassionate comments on the struggle down there, but unsure how it began and what it may mean, unwilling to take a nervy, truly exploratory plunge into the depths.

Therefore we never do get a satisfactory explanation of why two reasonably promising, reasonably engaging youths don't come to a somewhat better end. We see that to some degree each is victimized by misunderstanding his own nature and desires. Jonathan—had he allowed himself to try—might have made a better go of marriage than Sandy, whose temperament—if only he had understood it more clearly—might actually have been better suited to a swinging bachelor's existence. But this is only a little irony, not the beginning of a satisfactory study in character—let alone the end. We need to know what their creators think makes these characters exemplary, why they are deemed to be of general significance. We never do find out.

What we get instead is the implication that they, and by extension all of us, are inescapably corrupted by the wretched values of a materialistic society. But it is only an implication and one we are most circumspectly directed to, in part by the unrelenting emphasis of script and direction on the banality of the language, ideas, fashions and popular cultural artifacts of the last quarter century and in part by the absence of any clues that would lead us to a more complex understanding of other forces that might have shaped the fate of the film's leading characters.

In the end one feels cheated. The comedy in the piece is all based on securing the most primitive recognitions of the sillier aspects of our shared history and it comes to seem cold, superficial, manipulative. The sense of tragedy with which it alternates is attenuated, a form of show-biz big think—flashy on occasion but neither sustained nor truly harrowing. The trick here lies in blending these two elements "realistically," imparting to us the illusion that the full work is terribly, bitterly true and very important (for which purpose Mr. Nichols abandons the overstated Fellini-ism of *Catch-22* and here goes for Godard-like visual understatement—long pieces of dialogue done in a single shot, for example).

But the work, being a kind of sneak attack on our sensibilities, launched by men unsure of their targets and afraid to expose much of themselves in the process, lacks the joyful ferocity of Godard's (or Buñuel's) more open assaults—and their simple relish in the perversity of humankind.

SUNDAY, BLOODY SUNDAY

Middles and Muddles

PAUL D. ZIMMERMAN

From the beginning, movies have embraced the all-or-nothing conventions of romantic fiction. What, after all, can be more dramatic than beautiful, doomed lovers driven by the grandest of passions to shoot the moon or each other? For the same reason, films have been a good deal less interested in liaisons that are incomplete or inadequate, although such muted, difficult, often unworkable attachments make up, after all, the stuff of most people's lives.

British director John Schlesinger and his screenwriter, Penelope Gilliatt, understand that life is not beginnings and endings so much as middles that don't measure up, and they know too that happiness often depends on how people come to terms with the pale reflections of their own dreams. Their brilliant collaboration, *Sunday, Bloody Sunday*, inspects the value of such incomplete and partial loves, and it does so without recourse to the usual pieties about impossible relationships.

Their trio of lovers never quite becomes a triangle, each side coming up a bit short. Daniel Hirsh, as played by Peter Finch, moves between the most reputable and disreputable of identities, a respected doctor and a pillar of the London Jewish community on the one hand, a covert homosexual on the other. He gives the private side of himself to Bob, a pretty, young pop sculptor (newcomer Murray Head), who only half responds to his ardor, reserving the rest of his feeling for Glenda Jackson as Alex, a divorced office girl, who looks to the young man to provide a center and direction for her stagnant life.

In repudiating the hyperboles of romance, Schlesinger (*Darling, Midnight Cowboy*) works through the small events and telling textures of apartments, recorded music and kitchen routines that describe the daily life of his characters and, indeed, of us all. There are no scenes or suicides, merely embraces insufficiently answered, fantasies of escape entertained, future plans unspoken, fears of loss hidden, all caught with a sensual, alert eye by the brilliant cinematographer Billy Williams. Schlesinger's probe is irony, used with a refinement that never compromises his compassion. His trio is connected by a common answering service as well as a common lover. But the switchboard ganglion of wires that forms a bizarre nervous system is no mean-spirited joke, for in relaying muddled messages and mediating missed connections it underscores the isolation of souls in modern London and mirrors the breakdown of communications between the lovers themselves.

In the same way, the weekend in which Alex and Bob sit for the five wild children of friends represents more than a jaundiced comment on the insanity of permissive child rearing—the kids move back and forth between high-spirited play and anarchy. It also establishes a mood of familial displacement. The oldest child, at six, is more responsible and instinctively maternal than the surrogate mother, Alex. The disjointed domestic setting locates the trio beyond the bounds of family, where it must endure without roots, history or social cement.

But Schlesinger wisely avoids calling this futureless love folly or making his characters play the fool. Hirsh, as the accomplished, leonine Finch plays him, is a touching mixture of master and mortal—a father confessor and potentate to his patients, a soft, acquiescent lover, and an urbane, unruffled public figure whose vulnerability is only glimpsed in the trembling of his hands or in brows knitted from a pain rooted in his gut. Glenda Jackson invests Alex with an arch intelligence that can perceive the inadequacies of her situation without repairing them. Tears betray her at those very moments when necessity dictates indifference. Murray Head is the weak link, conveying a passivity and deficiency of feeling that hardly recommend him as a love object.

At one point, Peggy Ashcroft, as Alex's mother, tells her that, in love, "there is no whole thing." And, in an ending full of departures and promises to return that will never be kept, Schlesinger affirms the rarity of ongoing, constant love. But his conclusion, as voiced by Finch in a sudden, startling direct address, is that the half loves, the carings that never fully flower, have their value too and that happiness is feathered with such bits and pieces. Fitting them into a whole life is what counts.

Bundle from Britain

JOHN SIMON

Sunday, Bloody Sunday has all the surface glitter a film or a candy wrapping could amass. The plot itself seems dazzlingly new: a young career woman has an affair with a very young sculptor who is also having an affair with a middle-aged Jewish doctor. It is all very sophisticated. Alex Greville is an upper-class divorcée working in executive placement and leads a moderately swinging life among leftist-liberal friends while keeping a superiorly sloppy house for herself. Dr. Daniel Hirsh is a respectable general practitioner from a wealthy Orthodox family who lives neatly, graciously, and with warm appreciation of the arts. As for Bob Elkin, he is upward-mobile, which describes his sculpture almost as well as his psychosocial status, and swings merrily both ways, with latchkeys to both Alex's and Daniel's flats.

So, you see, it is really a trisexual triangle: one heterosexual, one homosexual, one bisexual—something for every taste and every type of self-identification. And whomever you identify yourself with, you can feel smugly superior to your compeers and kinfolk: Daniel is so ahead of his business-and-synagogue-oriented family; Alex is so emancipated from her parents' civil-service background; and Bob, though lower-class, has soared so high above his origins on the wings of his pop art. (Or op, or slop, or whatever art it is.) And everyone is aware of everything: Alex is jealous of Daniel but also respectful of him—for they both frequent that family of jolly radicals where the small children smoke pot and follow their elders' love affairs; Daniel, for his part, is downright concerned with how

Bob may be treating her. Alex's parents are on excellent terms with her ex-husband, and Daniel and Alex even share the same telephone answering service, as they discover to their amusement.

In other words, this is updated Noël Coward or, better yet, Freddie Lonsdale, with lots of good furniture, the biggest and most sumptuous bar-mitzvah celebration this side of the Queen's Ball, good-looking cars and children, and sorrows, in the main, gallantly stifled. There are bad moments—like the divorcée's concluding that there are times when nothing is better than something, or the doctor's learning that his lover will not accompany him on an Italian vacation. But it all has a way of being absorbed by those multiple layers of civilized amorality, and the bittersweet final encounter between Alex and Daniel, both abandoned by Bob, has such genteel, fastidious solicitude about it as to make upper-middle-class melancholy look like a positive badge of merit.

Surely, you say, there must be more. A bisexual involved with a socially, culturally and perhaps intellectually superior man and woman, manipulating them both though also having some genuine feeling for them—this must make for a searching character study. Not in a film by John Schlesinger, with a script by Penelope Gilliatt, it doesn't. The young man is the least examined figure of the three, a mere type, used as a counter to elicit reactions from the others. As he is presented by the film-makers, and nonacted by Murray Head, nothing inside him is revealed, not even what his lovers could see in him, except perhaps youth, cockiness, and *nostalgie de la boue*. But, then, maybe the feelings of Alex and Daniel are thoroughly scrutinized? No. Incidents are there—Daniel being embarrassed by the inopportune reappearance of one of his former pickups, Alex allowing herself to be swept into a one-night stand with one of her unhappy, aging, suddenly jobless executive clients. Yet I never truly had a sense of what Alex wants from life, or of how Daniel got to be what he is. Or why I should care about either of them.

What Schlesinger and Miss Gilliatt are very good at is conveying the outer shapes of existences, the little rugosities and slicknesses of the contours. The dialogue is crisp enough, and the images even crisper in the color cinematography of Billy Williams, who does better, because less flashily, here than in *Women in Love*. Nevertheless, gimmicks are everywhere. I don't believe that on a gloomy night drive through the center of London Daniel would encounter a swarm of roller skaters racing down Piccadilly, that innocent kids would be regaled by the sight of young hoodlums vandalizing parked cars, that a doctor would be so humiliatingly disbelieved by a clerk in an all-night drugstore. While such miseries do occur in life, in this film they take on a peculiarly smart-aleck, contrived air—perhaps because the whole movie seems to rely on, consist of such footling cleverness.

There are awkwardnesses, too, like a flashback to Alex's childhood that remains totally unintegrated and unhelpful, or a final soliloquy of Daniel's that is stilted in its efforts to avoid grandiloquence. Or the device of superimposing the days of the week on the image with which each new day begins—it looks portentous but adds nothing. In fact, the Tuesdays are just as bloody as the Sundays; if the point is the very uniformity and barrenness of all the days, that does not come across very compellingly either.

Actually, these lives are rather too glamorous to justify any great sympathy from the viewer. But the acting, except from Mr. Head, is so good as to jerk unearned sympathy. I am always overjoyed to see that wonderfully solid, no-nonsense actor, Peter Finch, who imbues whatever he does with exquisite tact and grace. And, in smaller roles, I greatly admired Tony Britton and Peggy Ashcroft, among many fine others. Glenda Jackson is a powerful actress, but everything about her, including her walk, is just a little too ugly for my taste. And is it in her contract that every film she appears in must also feature that wretched, scrawny bosom of hers? At least Schlesinger gives it mercifully short shrift.

The director, I repeat, is a dextrous, facile proto-artist. I suspect that it is from Elio Petri that he has learned how to make the furnishings of a place literally act, and it is surely from Truffaut's *Stolen Kisses* with its *pneumatique* cables that the idea of giving the telephone wires a juicy cameo role was derived. Allow me to describe one typical Schlesinger shot: Bob is seen adjusting a wall clock; he is framed by the top fifth of the wide-screen image, the lower four-fifths blotted out by what turns out to be the back of a large armchair. Presently the chair swings around, and we see Alex's head in it in large close-up, with Bob hovering up there in the background. Later, the chair swings back again. It is a sequence during which Alex voices her *de profundis*, but we are much more aware of the camera setup and directorial trickiness than of what is said or felt. Still, let us not minimize the film's ingenuity, especially in such scenes as the death of the dog. Only let us not confuse cleverness with depth.

Sophisticated Interiors

Molly Haskell

Even though no less an ex-sexist than Dr. Spock is prepared to see them topple, Eric Erikson's building-block discoveries (girls build houses; boys build towers and the concept of inner space) are borne out by much of world literature, especially the modern American branch. Women writers, to the extent that they are not expatriates from their gender, have been more concerned with interiors, with people, with reality, with the everyday transactions of relationships, whereas male writers have extended themselves further into fantasy, action, myth, allegory. Compare the latest fiction of Joan Didion, Sandra Hochman, Mary McCarthy, Shirley Ann Grau, for example, with John Hawkes, John Gardner, Barth, Gass, *et al.* Men reject authority, are suspicious of reality, and build superstructures to escape the ordinary, while women burrow furiously into the ordinary in search of smaller miracles.

Of course, by now we accept the mixture of male and female properties in all of us, and a writer's sensibility is more androgynous than the ordinary person's, but to the extent that one predominates (female in Proust, male in Gertrude Stein) certain characteristics can be said to follow.

When we talk of women's directors we are often talking about directors who are good with actors in general, directors who are attuned to people, who are sensitive to relationships, to shadows of suggestion and behavior. (In a sense this is what movies are all about and what all directors have to be.)

It is interesting to see what happens when a man directs a woman's screenplay. Frank Perry seems to have done better with Eleanor Perry, finding local exteriors appropriate to her psychological interiors. But Fritz Lang could have done without the services of his screenwriter wife, Thea von Harbou. In that case, Frau von Harbou's unnecessarily complicated love interests cluttered the clean line and momentum of Lang's melodrama. Lately Frank Gilroy has taken Paula Fox's *Desperate Characters* and used them as pawns in an aesthetic chess game, staples of atmosphere in a mood piece.

John Schlesinger, on the other hand, seems to have been perfectly suited to direct Penelope Gilliatt's original screenplay in the film *Sunday, Bloody Sunday* (bloody as in boring and beastly rather than corpses and catsup). He has proved his talent with actors—Julie Christie, Tom Courtenay, Dirk Bogarde, Laurence Harvey, Alan Bates, Peter Finch, Dustin Hoffman and Jon Voigt—and his feeling for a certain kind of sophisticated sensationalism. Here his affinity for the material—a wise and wistful comedy of manners about a woman (Glenda Jackson) and a man (Peter Finch) in love with the same young man—is what makes the film so effective without taking it to that other level (where it doesn't want to go, anyway) of formal complexity or mystery or myth which would make you want to see it again for new revelations. If you do see it a second time, you'll be doubly impressed with certain things: with Schlesinger's tact and subtlety. Except for a few sociological forays into drugs and vandalism, and the overextended bar mitzvah, his direction is the height of tact. He handles the shock of Finch's homosexuality, which lies in his emotional rather than sexual vulnerability, with delicate timing and tenderness. And you'll appreciate more than ever the details—harried, work-filled lives, interrupted by telephones, filled with the small gratifications of human encounters; and the wickedly comical picture of a progressive, children-tyrannized family (friends of both Finch and Glenda Jackson). But you will be disappointed if you expect even these two great performances to yield new insights.

It is a very grown-up screenplay, charged with the kind of impossibly adult common sense I associate with Germaine Greer. And Penelope Gilliatt. (And which sometimes makes me, I'm ashamed to say, want to talk baby talk back.) It's the kind of film that can poke fun at the mother of the precocious, pot-smoking child-monsters who says, "We think it's very important not to pretend," while basically pursuing her philosophy.

Peter Finch, as Dr. Daniel Hirsh, general practitioner with an Orthodox Jewish background, an unorthodox sex life, and a gentle, cultivated, masculine manner, and Glenda Jackson as Alex Greville, a well-brought-up and well-educated, cerebral and searching divorcée, are the picture's brilliant left hand and right hand. Murray Head (Judas on the recording of *Jesus Christ Superstar!*) is perfect as Bob Elkin, the designer of kinetic sculptures as elusive and free-floating and pragmatic as his own young heart. He is the love object of whom neither will ever get enough because "that's all there is." His performance has been underrated, perhaps, for being seamless and unanalyzable. He is like a one-cell creature in this context, a character on a lower rung of the evolutionary ladder.

He is the foil, the occasion for a contrast (or a coming together) of these two wonderfully individualized human beings with detailed existences, who, although they never meet until the very end, seem almost to be playing to each other instead of to Head. Except for one being fastidious (Finch, of course) and one sloppy, one heterosexual and one homosexual, they have more in common than either has with him. In addition to a lover and an answering service (manned, or womaned, with impersonal inefficiency by the remarkable Bessie Love), they share certain generational and intellectual attitudes: a feeling for privacy, possessiveness (people and things), professionalism, humor, and all the clashes of ego and superego by which they have come to define their identities.

Are they not, in a sense, self-fulfilling people, who need only a nominal, sometime partner for the outlet for their romantic feelings, for sex, for the contemplation of their misery, the exercise of regret, for the exquisitely refined understanding that in loving a lesser being on a part-time basis, they are not selling themselves short but reveling in the dual satisfaction of abasement and superiority. Glenda Jackson protests the sharing, the fragments of love. But she reminds me of certain friends in "impossible relationships" who say, "This can't go on," not as a genuine ultimatum but to experience new permutations of agony and create movement within stasis. For the only activity more absorbing than being happy in love is being miserable in love. Whereas happiness graciously takes to the wings for other activities, generously giving them a secret halo, misery insists on center stage, usurping all thoughts and emotions in its useless, selfish, luxurious wastefulness. Its celebration amounts to a quasi-religious experience like the heartbreakingly beautiful Terzettino from *Così fan tutte* which forms the musical theme of the film.

What's missing in *Sunday, Bloody Sunday* is the exploration and discovery which comes from a genuine sense of tragedy. The insights are predigested, the facts of life too well understood. Elkin's departure for America, abandoning both his lovers, is far from being tragic and inevitable. Its timing is arbitrary, and his fate is incidental to the rich reflection of sorrow it occasions.

Bruce Williamson

Watching *Sunday, Bloody Sunday* is apt to leave the viewer with the impression that he has been had by a band of consummate professionals whose talents inflate the enterprise somewhat beyond its intrinsic worth. The drama's thinness is disguised by a kinky triangular plot concerning a young mod Londoner (played with casual unisexual aplomb by movie newcomer Murray Head), an AC/DC fellow who is into kinetic sculpture and into bed with either a middle-aged Jewish doctor (Peter Finch) or an articulate young divorcée (Glenda Jackson). Both are in love with him, each knows about his affair with the other, and from this odd situation *Sunday, Bloody Sunday* generates quite a lot of emotional steam about the compromises accepted by people when they grow up enough to realize that they may need to settle for less than perfect love. Director John Schlesinger (*of Midnight Cowboy* and *Darling* fame), generally drawn to extraordinary types in circumstances too bizarre for your average Jane and Joe, here also chooses a flashy filmic style that draws attention to itself, with hyped-up editing and provocative compositions by ace cinematographer Billy Williams (who filmed *Women in Love*). Much can be read between the lines of acrid dialogue penned by English author and film critic Penelope Gilliatt, whose brisk scenario devotes a lot of footage to the telephone—as if those miles of cable and eager hearts just missing each other through an answering service were a fair measure of the quality of human communication most of us achieve.

CLAIRE'S KNEE

Andrew Sarris

Eric Rohmer's *Claire's Knee* is the first indisputably great film of 1971 and, as such, deserves the attention of every serious student of film. We have been hearing for a long time that the narrative in film is dead and that it was all for the best in this newest and most backward of all art forms. Henceforth, the argument went, we would be entering an era of themes rather than plots, ideas rather than intrigues. Indeed, movies would become so profound that they could be screened in telephone booths for all the audience they would attract.

But what about *Airport* and *Love Story?* the philistines wailed. Doesn't that prove that people still love plots to a fare-thee-well? Perhaps. But to this bemused observer, *Airport* and *Love Story* seem too high a price to pay for the preservation of the plot in cinema. Aimless, brainless formulas hardly seem the cure for the current disease of fictional debilitation in film. What we need are new initiatives and inspirations, and these we have suddenly received from an unexpected source: Eric Rohmer, a French director past fifty with seven films to his credit, five of which are described as moral tales, each a variation on a situation of moral and sexual choice common to all.

I have now seen three of the moral tales, *Ma Nuit chez Maud* (3), *La Collectionneuse* (4), and *Claire's Knee* (5), and I find the variations more striking than the repetitions. For one thing, the casts change completely from film to film down to the most marginal characters. The locations change also and the class structure as well. In each instance, however, the male protagonist must face the temptation of a disruptively emotional experience before returning to the pattern of a too carefully, too cerebrally planned life. It is Rohmer's happy inspiration, especially in *Maud* and *Claire* to take us past the point of decision before we can recognize its fatal irrevocability, and he does so by a clever trick of psychological displacement by which we are drenched with and then deprived of the sensibility of the dark-haired representative of complete womanhood (Françoise Fabian in and as *Maud*, Béatrice Romand as Laura in *Claire*) before being stuck with the superficially romantic illusionism of Rohmer's blondes to whom there is invariably less than meets the eye.

But the last thing I want to do is to suggest that Rohmer's films are afflicted with a schematic rigidity. *Claire's Knee* differs from *My Night at Maud's* as sharply as day differs from night, as summer differs from winter, and as self-deceiving lechery differs from self-deceiving fatalism, and fittingly enough as the manipulatively womanizing persona of Jean-Claude Brialy differs from the wistfully masochistic persona of Jean-Louis Trintignant. And in both instances, Eric Rohmer has rejuvenated the movie narrative at a time when too many prestigious directors—Godard, Bergman, Antonioni, Fellini, *et al.*—have renounced it.

Claire's Knee takes place around the vacation vistas (lake and mountain) of Talloires and Annecy near the Swiss border. The characters are all vacationers and hence function at that tempo of leisure and boredom at which the most trivial incidents can erupt into the most tremendous events. Nonetheless, the tendencies of summer vacations toward triteness (lost innocence, lost illusions, lost virginity, end of summer equals end of youth or end of life or end of love, the Schell games with *First Love* or the Perrys' pyrotechnics with *Last Summer*) are all resisted strenuously by Rohmer. The director ultimately transcends reality by respecting its inhuman intransigence scrupulously. His camera belongs to no character's feverish subjectivity but rather to the objective spectacle unfolding before it. Rohmer lets us look at Claire's knee not so much as if we were Jérôme (Jean-Claude Brialy) looking at the knee of Claire (Laurence de Monaghan) but rather as if we were witnessing the transformation of an image into an idea, sensuality into sensibility, a bit of furtive voyeurism into an obsessive illusion, and, most important of all, a suggestion of fetishism into a surge of feeling.

But what is so remarkable about Claire's knee? Certainly not the knee itself, nor even the manner in which it is presented as lecherous *mise-en-scène* back beyond the memory of the medium to the memory of the race in that first terrifying glimpse of a girl's legs on a ladder, the male's eyes sneaking upward toward paradise and perdition at the same time. Claire's knee is exciting simply because the title of the movie has alerted us to its pivotal role in the development of the narrative. It is the visible evidence of the protagonist's folly and of ours as well and of cinema's most of all. For is it not the fundamental folly of cinema to depend on surfaces for the expression of essences? And is not the comely but otherwise ordinary knee of Claire more beguiling visually and cinematically than the exquisite soul of Laura (Béatrice Romand)? But that is what summer vacations are for, after all—to develop a preference for the glamorous counterfeit over the gloriously real thing. To be bedazzled by the sun and consoled by the cool waters. To play God a little and crawl like a snake a little. To mark time, to kill time, and finally to use time as an alibi.

Some reviewers consider *Claire's Knee* a castigation of the intellectually manipulative Jérôme, a ridiculous creature floundering in the intuitive morass of desire. They point to the fact that Jérôme fails to break up the romance of Claire and Gilles (Gerard Falconetti) as if that were the whole point of his campaign. Quite the contrary, I think. His whole summer had dribbled down to a desire to stroke Claire's knee, and he succeeded in that desire without ever feeling the loss of an entire human being seen for the last time in a spasm of beautiful rage and sorrow at a distance behind the windshield of a car. This last shot of Laura, unobtrusive, perhaps even undistinguished by any dynamic principles of the medium, represents one of the glories of the narrative cinema. What we see ultimately in *Claire's Knee* is a spiritual misadventure unfolding discreetly against the background of nature, cruel and indifferent in its breathtaking beauty. Claire too is breathtaking in the smug complacency of her sensuality, but Laura is heart-stopping in the harshness of her emotional intelligence. And it is to emotional intelligence that Rohmer's cinema is ultimately dedicated, and what a relief in this age of the barbarians.

Gem from France

Hollis Alpert

I'm going to have to toss that word "masterpiece" around again. We've heard it often enough before. Rex Reed manages to find a film worth the accolade every other week. I tend to be more cautious; every two or three years I drag out the word on behalf of a favorite film. Last year I nearly used it for *My Night at Maud's*, a film that impressed me with its literate, witty and intelligent dialogue and its spare, clean direction. But I held back because of faint reservations. But now the same director and screenwriter, Eric Rohmer, has overcome my disinclination to employ the term with his new effort, *Claire's Knee.*

It's the kind of film that each viewer should discover and savor for himself. But, all right, it's about a thirty-five-year-old Frenchman (Jean-Claude Brialy) who spends most of a summer on Lake Geneva and encounters a family across the lake that includes two delightful young girls. Staying with the family is an old acquaintance of his, a woman novelist, and she's something of a beauty, too. She's also trying to work out the narrative of her new novel, and her absorption in her literary problems leads her to use the

Frenchman as a sort of guinea pig. She tells him that one of the girls, Laura, is in love with him.

Engaged, ready to marry and settle down, the Frenchman, fairly sated with affairs and sexual encounters, is nevertheless intrigued enough to explore the girl's feelings for him. But soon he has a new object to intrigue him: Laura's sister Claire, an extraordinarily pretty little teenager, slim, supple and coltishly involved with her young boyfriend. It is Claire who becomes a curious kind of obsession for the Frenchman. And what obsesses him most about her is her knee. I believe it's her right knee, but it might have been her left, or perhaps both. At any rate, he has this idiotic desire to caress that knee. And, since he is in the habit of discussing matters of this kind with his novelist friend, and since both are frank and have lively minds, the ensuing conversations sparkle with wit, have a tinge of eroticism, and lead to revelations that are surprising, thought-provoking, and, though kept in a subdued key, dramatic.

Rohmer has announced *Claire's Knee* to be the fifth in a series he calls "Six Moral Tales," and he declares all six to be thematically related. There probably is a spine of theme that relates *Maud* to *Claire's Knee*, but the latter stands beautifully by itself. It is distinguished, too, by the mellow color photography of Nestor Almendros. Claire appears to flower and grow lovelier. As she seems to ripen sexually, so does the Frenchman seem to decline in his powers, and, while Claire's nice little knee is not precisely a fetish, nor even a hitherto unnoticed erogenous zone, there is distinctly apparent a poignant contrast between fresh and jaded sexuality.

But there are other nuances to be found in the film, which is fresh and new because of intelligence and subtleties that are more common to the novel than the cinema. The actors are perfect in that they perform perfectly and are cast with precision. Yes, it has to be said: *Claire's Knee* is a masterpiece.

Knee-Deep in Profundities

JOHN SIMON

Preconized by our most powerful *auteurist* publication, *The New York Times*, Eric Rohmer's *Claire's Knee* is enjoying an improbable popularity. Some of the box-office onslaught can be explained by the success of Rohmer's previous film, *My Night at Maud's*, likewise puffed way beyond its slender deserts by the two resident *auteur* critics of the *Times*. *Ma Nuit chez Maud* was a well-meaning, amateurish film with painfully four-square camera placements and movements, literal-minded throughout, and with certain intellectual aspirations in the dialogue meant to compensate for the meager, contrived plot and the lack of development in the characters.

Yet *Maud* did at least have one devastating performance by Françoise Fabian, and there was a measure of reality in the hero's basic problem, even if the sophomoric philosophizing on the sound track served only *pour épater les bourgeois*. In *Claire's Knee*, however, the central theme is quirky, elusive, and finally quite trivial. This is still another of Rohmer's "Six Moral Tales," in each of which a man seemingly slated for one woman flirts or dallies with another, only to end up with the first. I am not sure that the subject, including its permutations, is worthy of a hexameron; in Rohmer's hands it achieves a lack of urgency comparable only to the question of whether a fly will succumb to the flypaper or the fly swatter.

Jérôme, the thirty-fivish French consul to Stockholm, is spending a summer month at the Lac d'Annecy in Haute-Savoie near the Swiss border, an Alpine paradise for the leisured and sometimes bored. He is selling his delicious villa and, next month, will go back to Sweden to marry Lucinde, a woman journalist he has been living with happily for some time. He discovers that Aurora, a Rumanian novelist and old friend of his, is vacationing at a neighboring villa, where the proprietress, Mme Walter, lives with her sixteen-year-old daughter, Laura. Aurora has an unfinished short story about an older man and a very young girl; to provide it with an ending, she encourages Jérôme to get involved with Laura, who, it seems, has a crush on him.

There are numerous conversations among Aurora, Mme Walter, Laura and Jérôme about love and marriage and family relations. Aurora and Jérôme, in particular, chatter endlessly about love, and conduct a kind of platonic *amitié amoureuse*. Laura is allowed to go on a two-day excursion into the mountains with Jérôme; when, finally aroused, he kisses her, her infatuation has already waned, and there are no further developments. There is more quasi-profound chitchat with Aurora about indulgence and abstinence. Finally, Claire, Laura's somewhat older half-sister, arrives.

Claire is an extrovert and happily in love with Gilles, another extrovert roughly her age. Jérôme now has further talks with Vincent, a somewhat girlish classmate of Laura's, who seems to nurture an unrequited love for her. Laura goes off to England on a vacation, and Jérôme gets more and more excited by Claire—particularly, as he confides in Aurora, Claire's knee, which he must fondle. Caught in a storm with Claire (who, generally, ignores him), he tells her about a peccadillo of Gilles's with another girl, rather exaggerating it. He makes the girl weep and, by way of consolation, is able to caress her knee. (Why she lets him do it is not made clear, but otherwise there wouldn't be even this much of a story.) His summer holiday ending, and with Claire and Gilles reconciled, Jérôme feels his craving allayed. He bids adieu to Aurora, who, it emerges, is engaged to a man in Geneva. Jérôme leaves for Sweden and the somewhat ambiguous prospect of marriage to Lucinde.

If this synopsis suggests the heights of inconsequence, it is nothing compared to the same material strung out to feature length. But Rohmer's triviality is unlike anyone else's. On the one hand, it is shot through with unprepossessing little kinkinesses; on the other, it demands to be taken seriously, as though it were full of subtle perceptions and grave pronouncements. Not only is that whole knee business presented as if fraught with existential significance, but the very details of dialogue attitudinize themselves into a sort of hysterical pregnancy.

Take Aurora's reply to Jérôme's concern over her "zero" love life: "I'm like you, *mon cher*. Chance offers you a woman, so you take her. Chance offers me nothing, so I take nothing. Why try to fight destiny?" The fact that Aurora has a man stashed away in Geneva would seem to give the lie to the remark, but let that pass. More to the point, to take someone and to take nothing are not at all the same thing. And why would chance make such distinctions between two worldly persons? Or is Aurora foolishly blaming on chance a matter of temperament? Yet Aurora is presented as wise. And how do we get from chance to destiny, as if the two were really identical? The film is full of such pseudophilosophical non-aphorisms, but people are so impressed with anything that pretends to be Thought coming at them from the screen that they fall over backward in wonderment.

Undeniably, the film has minor assets. The Savoyard landscape is sumptuous, the living in it gracious, and even nugatory word-mongering can garner some prestige from such elegant settings. Nestor Almendros' color cinematography is accomplished and provides Rohmer with the flattened-out backgrounds he wanted, presumably to suggest theatrical backdrops. Theatrical, in fact, is what Rohmer's films usually are; but in an age that wants its films as "filmic" as possible, you can always count on a certain *éclat* by going squarely against the current. Béatrice Romand, as Laura, conveys the Gallic *gamine* to perfection, down to the smugness that gives the charm a bitter aftertaste. As her mother, Michèle Montel exudes mellow womanly understanding.

The rest are less convincing. While Jean-Claude Brialy makes Jérôme engaging, he fails to suggest any depth in the man. As Claire, Laurence de Monaghan contributes a trim little figure and not much else—even her knee seems hardly worth genuflecting to. Worse yet is Aurora Cornu, as the novelist. A real-life Rumanian poet-novelist, she speaks with an accent that is an insult to French, although Rumanians used to be famous for speaking it almost better than the natives! She looks frowzy and bovine and cannot act at all: repeatedly her eyes emit S.O.S. signals in the direction of the cue cards. This is too bad because Aurora and Jérôme are meant to embody that sophisticated, playful, satisfied but not satiated relationship between cultivated ex-lovers—an easy affection that can go toward intimate friendship or fleshly intimacy with equal unconstraint. Miss Cornu is a total loss where Annie Girardot or Françoise Fabian would have made luminous sense.

Still, if anything can genuinely attract American audiences to this flimsy film, it is that relationship, as well as the faintly perverse one with Laura, who discusses her "love life" with a kind of Simone de Beauvoirishness no American girl her age could approach. For the cultists, to be sure, there are all kinds of idiot's delights, ranging from the film's unfolding as pages from the hero's diary—with a handwritten date preceding each uneventful episode—all the way to that photograph of Lucinde that Jérôme shows his friends: a picture of Jeanne Moreau. But for all its philosophizing, *Claire's Knee* remains dullish: not much patina on that patella.

LA COLLECTIONNEUSE

PENELOPE GILLIATT

La Collectionneuse was written and directed by Eric Rohmer before the hypnotizing *My Night at Maud's*. The story of the non-night with the sumptuous Maud is a droll masterpiece, wonderful about the way old friends talk, true and fresh about a very European attitude that treats flesh as if it were a buffoon of a companion to have through a life. The picture is highbrow to a degree, but amused by that, and tender. *La Collectionneuse* hasn't a very sure sense of the ridiculous, or much love, and Rohmer's command of a wry style all his own hasn't yet gathered itself to a point. The film was actually made to be the third in his "Six Moral Tales," with *My Night at Maud's* following it, then *Claire's Knee*, and with *Love in the Afternoon* still to come. "Six Contes Moraux" rings less offputtingly in French; in English it offers nothing very much to buoy anyone up—like a birthday present from a vicar that turns out to be a book of his own sermons called "A Sunday for Every Day of the Week."

La Collectionneuse is sealed in a world of time off. It moves with the tread of a very long summer holiday, spent with three characters who seem already to have been on holiday all year. It makes you long very much for an island, and then, even more strongly, for the next flight out—the effect of Cyril Connolly's *The Rock Pool*, but not as well executed. Swimming, bare feet, dazing sun, underwater plants waving like the tails of grudging cats, the insomnia that comes of having nothing particular to do at any particular time, sexual moves contemplated and discarded like chess in the head, high-flown books read in a spirit of guerrilla war against some combatant's even loftier choice not to read but to spend the next half hour tapping his espadrilles on the tiles. For all the ravishing studies of brown legs and crooks of elbows and backs of knees, lust isn't here. There can never have been a film of so many limbs that don't thrash. Rohmer is showing us a landscape of eroticism where the erotic has stalled. It tickles him to show us sensuality with the nerve of longing removed, bookish people privately discontent to know that they are learning nothing new, stinginess in prodigal circumstances, feasts looked at without appetite, the heresy of losing one's hunger for the possible. Rohmer is a religious man.

The structure that interests him in this film is much the same as the one he made for *My Night at Maud's*. In the middle, there is a quizzically seen prig with the body of a male model, called Adrien. On his right, Daniel, a much more attractive character, because he isn't in Adrien's state of catatonic absorption in his own looks: an alert, witty man with the pointed face of some famous rattle of eighteenth-century society. (There is a wonderful scene, absolutely French, in which Adrien rouses himself to be bitchy to a trusting boy who believes him when he says that he is an oculist and that the boy's sunglasses are going to wreck his eyes; Daniel looks on, and his entertained mind seems the most vivid thing in the frame.) Circling around the two men, flouncing about in a bikini as big as a couple of belts, there is a German-souled girl called Haydée, indifferent, lush, impervious, with the huge mouth of the newborn and impulses that are pre-moral. Adrien is an egoist who cultivates his egoism rigorously. A flicker of care for anyone else would tincture its purity. He tells us that he never wears a watch or looks at a calendar. His idea of courage is dandyism on no money, and he manages it; the emotional cost is great, but not to him. He is thinking of starting a gallery in the autumn. In the meantime he has nothing to do, and he decides to excel in this nothing. He observes his fragile, stalemated impulses of thought or love quite vacantly, as if they were waving seaweeds and he a lidless trout. Daniel is his friend, but friendship impinges on his aesthetic of unflawed nullity. So does his interest in Haydée, who is Daniel's girl when she can be bothered. For his own punitive reasons, Adrien manages to sour the possible conviviality in Daniel and the possible fun in Haydée, choosing instead to pickle himself in a state of sulky monkishness for the sake of a girl whom we saw him with at the very start of the picture. The girl wanted to be with him, wanted him to go with her to London. He prefers misery. The film is about a man intent on refining his natural accidie, his grand systematization of sloth and grumps, as though personality were an *objet d'art*. Rohmer now and then gives him voice-over comments on himself, delivered in high solemnity, as if he were a televised monarch in an abbey and marrying himself. The film is in French,

but Adrien's unseen voice speaks English; the switch is ventrilo-
quial and makes you jump.

The title of the film is a pun. There is a mannered art buyer in it
who knows how many degrees centigrade an ancient Chinese pot-
tery elephant's ears were baked at, and there is also Haydée, who
collects men. One of Rohmer's points is that any collector of a
series of possessions misses the essence that is in a single one. The
idea would be jubilant if you ever saw his central character with
the one.

PHILIP T. HARTUNG

Even poets as good as Byron and Shelley and Keats had
their off days and not-so-good poems, so I suppose we shouldn't
feel too surprised or let down that the latest Eric Rohmer film to
arrive on our shores is somewhat of a disappointment. *La Collectionneuse* was made in 1967; I saw it then (at the Berlin Film
Festival) and was rather impressed with its unusual story and
lovely color photography of the country around Saint-Tropez. I'm
sorry it was not shown here at that time. Since then two Rohmer
gems have appeared and *La Collectionneuse* is only a forerunner to
My Night at Maud's and *Claire's Knee*—and, alas, not nearly as
good as either of those films.

Being one of director-writer Rohmer's "Six Moral Tales," *La
Collectionneuse* follows the plot pattern used in them all—and already familiar to us from *Maud* and *Claire*. This time, Adrien, a
young dealer in antiques, refuses to go with his mistress to London
and intends to spend the summer alone at a friend's villa in Saint-
Tropez. On arrival, he discovers he will be sharing the place with
Daniel, a painter friend and an extremely attractive, empty-headed
girl, Haydée. Adrien is determined not to get involved with Haydée, who has quite a reputation for sleeping around and is in fact a
collector of men. What happens when Adrien is finally attracted to
Haydée is only mildly interesting—especially since Rohmer's plot
pattern will demand that Adrien scurry off to London to return to
his first love. The main trouble with *La Collectionneuse*, however,
is that its characters aren't very interesting. Haydée is attractive to
look at, Daniel is clever and amusing, but Adrien, himself, is a
rather dull, self-centered prig. Rohmer's admirers will run to *La*

Collectionneuse; others will see *Maud* again or wait till next year for the sixth "Moral Tale," *Love in the Afternoon.*

MURMUR OF THE HEART

Louis Malle's Portrait of the Artist as a Young Dog

PAULINE KAEL

Murmur of the Heart is mellow and smooth, like a fine old jazz record, but when it's over it has the kick of a mule—a *funny* kick, which sends you out doubled over grinning. Assured and unflamboyant in technique, it is yet an exhilarating film—an irresistible film, one might say if one had not heard word of some resistance, especially by the jury at Cannes, which chose to ignore it, managing even to pass over Lea Massari's full-scale portrait of the carelessly sensual mother of a bourgeois brood of sons in favor of Kitty Winn's drab, meager-spirited performance in *The Panic in Needle Park.* Massari's Clara is a woman without discretion or calculation; she's shamelessly loose and free, and she's loved by her sons because of her indifference to the bourgeois forms, which they nevertheless accept—on the surface, that is. What makes this movie so different from other movies about bourgeois life is that the director, Louis Malle, sees not only the prudent, punctilious surface but the volatile and slovenly life underneath. He looks at this bourgeois bestiary and sees it as funny and appalling and also —surprisingly—hardy and happy. It is perhaps the first time on film that anyone has shown us the bourgeoisie *enjoying* its privileges.

From the way Malle observes the sex education of the youngest, brightest son of the family, fourteen-year-old Laurent (Benoit Ferreux), one knows that the movie is a portrait of the artist as a young dog. It comes after a succession of Malle films, but in its subject, and in the originality and the special surefootedness that the director (who also wrote the script) brings to the material, it is, clearly, the obligatory first film. The picture is set in Dijon—also the setting for Malle's *The Lovers*—in 1954, at the time of Dien Bien Phu (which must have been only a few years after the director's schoolboy days), and before the children of the bourgeoisie became radicalized. Though the film itself reveals the sources of Malle's humor, this story probably wouldn't have been nearly so funny or, perhaps, so affectionate if Malle had told it fifteen years ago. It is a film by someone who doesn't have to simplify in order to take a stand, who no longer needs to rebel; he has come a distance, and the story is additionally distanced by the changes in French student life that Godard recorded in *Masculine Feminine* and *La Chinoise*. In 1954, the sons of the successful gynecologist (Daniel Gélin) and the Italian-born Clara could still enjoy their wealth as their due. Seen with the vivacity of fresh intelligence, they're a family of monsters, all right, but normal monsters—no more monstrous than other close-knit families—and they're happy hypocrites.

I'm not sure how the picture was sustained and brought off so that we see the stuffiness and snobbery of the privileged class on the outside and the energetic amorality underneath, but the story moves toward its supremely logical yet witty and imaginative conclusion so stealthily that the kicker joke is perfect. Advance word had suggested that the picture was a serious, shocking view of incest, but the only shock is the joke that, for all the repressions these bourgeois practice and the conventions they pretend to believe in, they are such amoral, instinct-satisfying creatures that incest doesn't mean any more to them than to healthy animals. The shock is that in this context incest *isn't* serious—and that, I guess, may really upset some people, so they won't be able to laugh.

I can't remember another movie in which family life and adolescence have been used for such high comedy. The details are as singular, as deeply rooted in the period and the place, as the details in Truffaut's *The 400 Blows*, and the picture has that kind of candor. But no one in the film requires sympathy. Malle's approach has some of Buñuel's supple objectivity and aberrant humor. Malle satirizes the family from inside as Buñuel satirizes Catholicism from inside. The boys casually loot their own home, turn the dining room into a tennis court with a ball of spinach. Members of the family tease and squabble, but they enjoy the squabbling, because it is part of their intimacy and their security. Home is chaos; the three boys are not subdued even when there are guests. The vinegar-face father, severe and disgusted, though in a sort of ineffectual, ritualistic way, is tolerant—perhaps even, like the old family servant, proud that his boys are such irresponsible, uncontrollable *boys*. They're expensive pets, expected to commit outrages, and also expected to shape up eventually. In a poor environment, the boys would be brats, or even punks and delinquents; here they're the young masters. Papa's distaste is amusing, and the boys goad him; the grumblings of a put-upon father are a reassuring sound. And when you're furious with a brother, he's still a brother, and you have the pride and safety in that that you can never feel when you quarrel with those outside the family. This movie catches the way people care about each other in a family, and the feeling of a household in which there's no discipline. Which I think is probably generally the case but is something that movies like to lie about. The mixture of contempt and affection that the boys feel toward the old servant is so accurate—even if one has never been near a fuddy-duddy family retainer—that it sweeps away all those false, properly respected movie servants.

The only quality common to the films of Louis Malle is the restless intelligence one senses in them, and it must be this very quality that has led Malle to try such different subjects and styles. A new Chabrol or a Losey is as easily recognizable as a Magritte, but even film enthusiasts have only a vague idea of Malle's work. Had Malle gone on making variations of almost any one of his films, it is practically certain he would have been acclaimed long ago, but a director who is impatient and dissatisfied and never tackles the same problem twice gives reviewers trouble and is likely to be dismissed as a dilettante. Malle, though he is still under forty, predates the New Wave and has made amazingly good films in several styles. Born in 1932, he was co-director with Cousteau of *The Silent World*, then assistant to Bresson on *A Man Escaped,* and then, in 1957, at twenty-five, he made his first film, the ingenious, slippery thriller *Lift to the Scaffold* (also called *Frantic*), with Maurice Ronet and Jeanne Moreau, and a Miles Davis score. The following year, he had his biggest American success—*The Lovers*, with its flowing rhythms and its Brahms, the message of woman's desire for sexual fulfillment and the wind rippling through Moreau's white chiffon. It was facile movie-poetry but erotic and beautifully made. In 1960, he did a flipover to *Zazie dans le Métro*, from the Queneau novel—a fiendishly inventive slapstick comedy about a foul-mouthed little girl, which was too fast and too freakish for American tastes, so that Americans did not credit Malle with the innovative editing, and later gave the credit instead to Tony Richardson's *Tom Jones* and to Richard Lester and others. *Zazie*, a comedy that owed a debt to Tati but carried Tati's dry, quick style to nightmarish anxiety, included satirical allusions to *La Dolce Vita* and *The Lovers*. After the wild *Zazie* came *Vie Privée*, with Brigitte Bardot and about her life as a sex-symbol star. *Le Feu Follet*, in 1963, the film that first convinced me that Malle was a superb director, shows the influence of Bresson but is without the inhuman pride that I think poisons so much of Bresson's later work. *Le Feu Follet* (sometimes called *The Fire Within*) has been seen by few people in this country. It received some generous reviews (especially in this magazine), and no one appears to be very clear about the reasons for its commercial failure—whether it got snarled in distribution problems or whether the film was simply "not commercial" in American terms. An elegy for a wasted life, adapted by Malle from a Thirties novel, it dealt with the forty-eight hours before the suicide of a dissolute playboy (Maurice Ronet again) who, at thirty, has outlived his boyish charm and his social credit. It is a study of despair with no possibility of relief; the man has used up his slim resources and knows it. He does not want to live as what he has become; his taste is too good. It was directed in a clean, deliberate style, with a lone piano playing Satie in the background. Genet wrote of the director, "He has effected something phenomenal this time, having turned literature into film, photographed the meaning of an unsubstantial, touching, and rather famous book, and given its tragic intention a clarity it never achieved in print." And Brendan Gill said, "Between them, Malle and Ronet have composed a work as small and vast, as affecting, and, I think, as permanent as Fitzgerald's *Babylon Revisited*." It was a masterly film, and it seemed almost inconceivable that a director still so young could produce a work about such anguish with such control. *Le Feu Follet* should have made Malle's reputation here—in the way that *L'Avventura* made Antonioni's. After that painful, claustrophobic film, Malle did another flip, to the outdoors and the New World— to the frivolous, picaresque *Viva Maria!*, set in the Latin America of La Belle Epoque, with Moreau and Bardot. At the opening, the child who will become Bardot helps her imperialist-hating father dynamite a British fortress in Ireland, and the contrast between the father's act and the child's blooming, innocent happiness as she plays in the fields planting explosives is rapturously comic. *Viva*

Maria! was lavish and visually beautiful, but the subsequent bomb-ings and shootings weren't so funny; the central conceit involved in the pairing of Bardot and Moreau didn't work out, so the slapstick facetiousness was just left there, with nothing under it. But Bardot —not because of any *acting*—has never been more enchanting than in parts of this movie. When Malle put her into boys' clothes, with a cap and a smudge on her cheek, she was a tomboy looking for fun: Zazie grown up but still polymorphously amoral. After *The Thief of Paris*, with Jean-Paul Belmondo, Malle went to India, where he shot documentaries, the most famous of which, *Calcutta*, has never opened in New York.

The director traveled a long road before looking into his own back yard; now, when he goes back to it in *Murmur of the Heart*, we can see in that gleeful, chaotic household the origins of the radiant prankishness of *Zazie* and *Viva Maria!* and of those riffs that don't stop for breath, and we can see the sources of the studied, overblown romanticism of *The Lovers*, and also of the caustic view of romanticism in the great *Le Feu Follet*. I don't think *Murmur of the Heart* is a greater film than *Le Feu Follet*, but in excluding all joy that film was a very special sort of film: getting so far inside a suicide's attitude toward himself can really wipe viewers out. This is a joyous and accessible work, and so the anguish of *Le Feu Follet* begins to seem youthful—like an early spiritual crisis that has been resolved. Although *Murmur of the Heart* is obviously semi-autobiographical, it's a movie not about how one has been scarred but about how one was formed. You can see that Malle is off the hook by the justice he does to the other characters. (The only character that seems to me a failure and no more than a stereotype is the lecherous priest, played by Michel Lonsdale.)

Lea Massari (she was the girl who disappeared in *L'Avventura*) has, as Clara, the background of a libertarian father—reminiscent of Bardot's background in *Viva Maria!* Clara says she grew up "like a savage," and when she smiles her irregular teeth show her to be a spiritual relative of the impudent Zazie. Malle's films have swung back and forth between the eroticism of the Moreau characters and the anarchic, childish humor of the Zazies; Massari's ravishing Clara combines them. Her relaxed sensuality is the essence of im-propriety. There is a moment when Clara, who has blithely re-marked to her sons as they watch her changing clothes, "I simply have no modesty," catches Laurent peeping at her in her bath. She

instinctively slaps him; he is deeply offended, and she apologizes
and says he should have slapped her back. This many-layered confusion of principle and hypocrisy and instinct and injustice is one
of the rare occasions when a movie has shown how knotted the ties
of family life really are for most of us. Clara comes alive because of
that freak bit of Zazie in her; she will never grow up and become
the mature mother of simplified fiction. She is not one of those Fay
Bainter mothers, born at forty full of wisdom and christened
"Mother."

As for Laurent—or Renzino, as Clara calls him—Benoit Ferreux
probably is only about fourteen, but, without being fey, he looks
enough like the Lauren Bacall of an earlier era to hold the camera
in a vise, and he appears to have an impeccable sense of what's
wanted. You're never quite sure how you feel about Laurent. His
musical tastes—Charlie Parker and the other jazz greats we hear on
the track—are irreproachable, and, in their irreproachability, marks
of fashion and caste. He's extraordinarily clever, but he's also an
arrogant, precocious little snot who thinks that people were put in
the world to serve him; he despises a snob Fascist boy because the
boob hasn't mastered the right tone—the acceptable amount of
snobbery. The movie is about the childhood and growing into
manhood of those who are pampered from birth, and at every step
it shows what they take for granted. It defines the ways in which
the rich are not like you and me, and the ways in which they are.
Malle resembles Fitzgerald, but a Fitzgerald with a vision formed
from the inside, and with the intelligence for perspective. His is a
deeply realistic comic view—free of Fitzgerald's romantic ruined
dreams. In pulling his different styles together in *Murmur of the
Heart,* Malle finds a new ripe vein of comedy: believable comedy;
that is to say, life seen in its comic aspects. There's a sequence in
which smart Laurent outsmarts himself: he attempts to disrupt a
meeting that his mother is having with her lover, and his intrusion
results in her going off with the lover for a few days. When it
comes to family ties and basic affections and how to lose one's
virginity, even the smart and the dumb aren't so very far apart.

ROBERT HATCH

One of the English reviewers quoted by the importers of
Louis Malle's *Murmur of the Heart* (the title should be translated

Heart Murmur, since that is what the young hero suffers in more than one sense of the term) can imagine no one, "of however delicate sensibilities, being shocked, outraged or offended by it." This assurance refers, I assume, to the climactic episode, a passage of mother-son incest, which is indeed handled with great discretion, but which nevertheless offended not my sensibilities but my understanding of psychological cause and effect.

Indeed, the whole film did that. Malle has, it would seem from his recent works, reached a stage of cynicism about human behavior that not only permits him to shrug off whatever his people do but to suppose that they will be similarly unaffected. He chuckles over their appalling mishaps—which is his privilege—but he also portrays them as chuckling, which invests his films with a disconcerting atmosphere of idiocy that I cannot imagine he intends.

Thus the fifteen-year-old youth (Benoit Ferreux) leaps purposefully from the bed of his mother (Lea Massari) after their discreet but quite explicit union and pads down the corridor of the spa hotel, where they are staying for his health, to the bedroom of a teenage girl where he supposes, quite correctly, that he will be engagingly received. In the morning he returns to the family suite, to be greeted with good-natured raillery by the whole family—father and two older brothers have arrived during the night. He looks suitably pleased with himself, and the mother gets off some such line as "We shall always remember what we did together as a precious experience, but we will never speak of it or return to it again."

For God sake! What is the use of dealing with people if they are to be shown as utterly numb to what they do and what is done to them? *Murmur of the Heart* is offered as a 1950's domestic comedy, not as a clinical study in emotional catalepsy. Incest is not the only devastating event that occurs to the young man. He is treated throughout the film, in particular by his brothers, as though he were a laboratory animal who had fallen into the hands of sadistic technicians. There is a scene in a whorehouse that is of most exquisite brutality, but again everyone treats it as a jolly joke in dubious taste, and even the victim broods over it only momentarily. The brothers, passed off as fun-loving louts, ought to be in institutions, and the whole sunny *ménage* is poisonous.

I understand about poison in the sunshine, and if Malle's intention were to contrast setting and content, I believe I would catch his purpose. On the contrary, what he appears to be saying is that life is a great joke because nobody ever gets hurt. That point of view is bad enough in Tom and Jerry cartoons; when applied to alleged human beings it becomes moronic.

BED AND BOARD

Bed and Board—but Not Bored

VINCENT CANBY

It comes as something of a shock when, toward the end of *Bed and Board*, François Truffaut's very funny new film, Antoine Doinel (Jean-Pierre Léaud), who has failed as everything from private detective to florist's assistant, reveals that he is writing an autobiographical novel about his truly terrifying childhood. It is characteristic of Truffaut that the information is initially presented as the peg for a series of gags: Antoine is talking to Césarin, *patron* of the local bar. Césarin points out that another great novelist, Baudelaire, had also begun in flowers and he goes on to suggest a title for the book, *With Neither Drum Nor Trumpet*, since there will be no drums or trumpets in Antoine's novel.

A little later, Christine (Claude Jade), Antoine's temporarily estranged wife, angrily turns on Antoine when he suggests that it's his writing that has come between them. She tells him not to bother sending her a copy of the novel, because she won't read it. "I may be ignorant," she says with the manner of someone who is convinced she isn't, "but I know one thing for certain: a work of art can't be a settling of old accounts, or it isn't a work of art."

All of this comes as a shock because it indicates that Antoine—at least the Antoine of *Bed and Board*—has been living a secret literary life off-screen. On-screen he has been the hero of a series of exuberantly comic, broadly slapstick, decently sentimental (and occasionally quite cruel) blackout sketches. It also looks as if Truffaut, in a gesture that is both cockeyed and immensely self-confident, is attempting to connect Antoine Doinel, once of *The 400 Blows*, to the real-life juvenile delinquent who grew up to become one of France's most passionate and talented film directors.

Although *Bed and Board* (whose original French title is *Domi-*

cile Conjugal) is an inextricable part of Truffaut's total work, I'm not sure that the connection between its Antoine and the one in Truffaut's first film can, at this late date, be so easily re-established. It's almost as if Truffaut, who has said that this will be the last chapter in the adventures of Antoine Doinel, had decided to kill off Antoine, not by one of those automobile accidents that so fortuitously remove soap-opera characters whose contracts have expired, but by suddenly endowing Antoine, who has always had a poetic sensibility, with a creative artist's discipline, which is something totally alien to the character.

The Antoine Doinel movie cycle is, however, nothing less than unique, representing, as it does, the collaboration of the same writer-director (Truffaut), star (Léaud) and character (Antoine) over a twelve-year period that was crucial in the emotional and artistic development of its collaborators. (In the case of Léaud, it was even a time of physical development.)

The cycle was begun in 1959 with *The 400 Blows,* Truffaut's first feature, the tight, tough, lyrical (but never sentimental) drama that introduced Antoine (played by the fourteen-year-old Léaud) and defined the end of his childhood in that memorable (and, subsequently, all too often imitated) final freeze frame. You must remember it: Antoine trapped between the sea and the reform school from which he had escaped. The cycle continued in 1962, the year after the triumph of *Jules and Jim,* with "Antoine and Colette," an episode in the *Love at 20* feature, in which Antoine, now out of reform school, falls hopelessly in love with a nice, middle-class girl, but wins only her parents.

In 1969, Truffaut, having made *The Soft Skin, Fahrenheit 451* and *The Bride Wore Black,* none of which was a great critical or financial success, returned to Antoine. In *Stolen Kisses,* which is, for me, Truffaut's loveliest film next to *Jules and Jim,* Antoine, having been judged "temperamentally unfit" for the Army (as was Truffaut), takes up his life in Paris again, pursuing a bizarre assortment of unsuccessful careers and women, before finally falling in love with Christine. *Bed and Board* is the story of their marriage.

One of the most interesting aspects of the Antoine cycle is that the films are not really sequels in the conventional sense, although they all have to do with a person named Antoine Doinel played by a young actor who has literally grown up on the screen before us and whose personality, according to Truffaut, has shaped Antoine's as much as has Truffaut's. In spite of all the references in each of the films to events in preceding films, and in spite of the continuity of the actors, *Bed and Board* has as many ties to *The Soft Skin*— say—as it does to *The 400 Blows*. Perhaps more, since both *Bed and Board* and *The Soft Skin* have to do with the resolution of marriages and are, in effect, elaborate rationales conceived by erring husbands.

Further, each film in the Antoine cycle belongs in a different time zone, to a different movie era. *The 400 Blows* is very much of its own period, the late 1950's, which, as seen through the eyes of young Antoine, can pass for the 1940's, those war years in which Truffaut lived Antoine's adventures. "Antoine and Colette" is a kind of timeless idyl, but its spirit is that of the early 1950's, when the French cinema was dominated by what Truffaut once rather sneeringly referred to as "the tradition of French quality." Its humor and irony are typically Truffaut, but it is essentially "nice."

Stolen Kisses, ostensibly set in the 1960's, is as much of the 1940's as its title song. It is a movie of almost unbearable nostalgia, though not for an era but for a love that has not yet vanished, but probably will. At the end of *Stolen Kisses*, Christine is approached by a completely humorless gentleman, "Le Type," who offers her an exemplary love and pledges never to leave her, to devote every minute of his life to her. He promises her perfection, but Christine, being human, departs with Antoine, who is only slightly more trustworthy than a tadpole.

In *Bed and Board*, Antoine turns out to be everything Le Type was offering to protect Christine against. He is self-centered and so sure of Christine's love that he is quite surprised when she seems angry about his affair with a beautiful Japanese girl, which, because this is hard-luck Antoine, quickly becomes awfully boring to him. *Bed and Board* is very much a 1930's film. Its principal setting, a Parisian court inhabited by colorful—and perhaps somewhat too representative—petite-bourgeoisie, is strictly *Sous les Toits de Paris*. The marvelously elaborate ways in which Truffaut elects to redo and disguise cliché scenes (a husband's learning that his wife is pregnant) recall the best 1930's domestic comedies that charmed not because of their original themes but because of the variations they managed to work out on seemingly exhausted themes. Truffaut's greatest affection is reserved for Renoir, but *Bed and Board* also evokes René Clair.

In his introduction to the four Antoine screenplays, published last year in France under the collective title of *Les Aventures d'An-*

toine Doinel, Truffaut pays tribute to Jean-Pierre Léaud ("the best actor of his generation") and credits Léaud with having shaped the character of Antoine into what he became in the films that followed *The 400 Blows.* Because there is no reason to doubt Truffaut's sincerity, then it does seem that Léaud must be at least partially responsible for the very mixed feelings we have toward Antoine by the time *Bed and Board* ends—with a rather sad, depressing gag that presents us with an Antoine as trapped as was the boy at the end of *The 400 Blows.*

Today there is something offputting about Léaud that I can't quite isolate, and it just may be that Léaud-the-professional-actor no longer coincides with the Truffaut surrogate represented by Antoine. Léaud has grown up, and he has grown away from Antoine, and we don't for a minute believe he could write a single sentence that would in any way be comparable to a single frame of any Truffaut film.

There is, however, enough of Truffaut in *Bed and Board* to make it not only a most appealing, entertaining film, even when it is separated from the other films, but, in conjunction with those other films, a work of deep fascination. There is a beautiful, intense moment in *Bed and Board* that illuminates the appeal of the Antoine cycle: Christine is going on, somewhat oppressively, about why they should have a telephone. If they get bored, she says, they can call their friends (of whom they actually have precious few). Antoine turns on her with real disgust and says something to the effect of: "What do you mean, bored? I don't know what boredom is. . . . There is always something to do! I can cut the pages of a book—or do a crossword puzzle—or make notes. I wish each day had thirty hours! I'm never bored! I can't wait until I'm old, so I'll only need five hours' sleep!" He turns his back on her and prepares to go into the bathroom, equipped with a flashlight, a book, a knife to cut the pages of the book, his cigarettes and a newspaper.

Truffaut, like Antoine, cannot be bored by life—which is a kind of genius.

GARY ARNOLD

According to the testimony of a friend in New York, François Truffaut's new film, *Bed and Board,* plays very well with audi-

ences, and it certainly caused an abundant early flowering of raves
among the more oft-quoted New York critics, including—he noted
cynically—a few who were chilled by *The Wild Child*. This pre-
amble is, obviously, a way of letting myself down gently, because
Bed and Board is the sort of Truffaut movie that leaves me cold.
Like all of *Mississippi Mermaid*, most of *Fahrenheit 451* and *The
Bride Wore Black* and random moments of *Stolen Kisses*, it confirms my feeling that when Truffaut sets out to do something conventionally ingratiating, he doesn't know what he's doing.

Bed and Board belongs to the romantic comedy genre of *Stolen
Kisses* and, indeed, is the sequel to *Stolen Kisses*. The French title
is *Domicile Conjugal*, and Truffaut's scenario is an episodic survey
of the first couple of years of young married life. Jean-Pierre Léaud
returns as Antoine, grown so vacant and ineffectual that he's
scarcely a shadow of his original character, the smart and resource-
ful little "delinquent" boy of *The 400 Blows*. Claude Jade returns
as Christine, his sweet and capable bourgeois bride. They're hus-
tled over and around the predictable hurdles—early housekeeping
and wage-earning, parenthood, separation, reconciliation.

By an unlucky coincidence, my wife and I were chatting about
our impending parenthood at lunch with a good friend, an hour or
so before seeing *Bed and Board*. Like thousands before us, we were
fascinated by the bottomless gulf separating obstetrics as it is experienced by ordinary, conscious human beings from obstetrics as it is
usually depicted at the movies.

Personally, I'd never been able to fathom or tolerate the customary facetious conception of expectant daddies, particularly their
convulsive astonishment when informed, by coyly smiling expectant mommies, that A Little Stranger was on the way. Convincing
portraits of more or less resigned husbands-and-fathers come readily to mind—for example, George Segal in *Loving* or Peter Sellers
in *Only Two Can Play*—but I can't recall a single instance of
psychological affinity in movie fathers-to-be. Moreover, when Hollywood gets serious about reproduction, it's likely to deliver something like *The Baby Maker*, which makes one appreciate the relative innocence of the farce conventions.

Still, Truffaut is an artist one looks to for the verification of common sense and experience and the illumination of human psychology. When he takes up a conventional form of marital comedy,
you expect a transformation of the conventional: a marital comedy

that owes more to real life than theatrical reflexes, rendering the stale miraculously fresh.

There's no miracle. Instead, one gets a peculiarly fey, halfhearted excursion through the old clichés. For example, *Bed and Board* began to alienate me for good at the point where Léaud discovers he's going to be a father: Miss Jade, smiling coyly, leaves him standing outside an office which houses a hairdresser, a gynecologist and a notary public; in the next scene we find the poor sweet boob walking past a diaper ad at a Métro station and suddenly putting two and two together so violently that even the billboard must have chuckled.

This might be a special complaint if it weren't for the fact that *Bed and Board* is overstocked with similarly inventive howlers. It's rather astonishing to see Truffaut amusing himself at this elementary *shlock* level; it's also embarrassing to note that he's rather inept and absent-minded as a *shlock* fabricator and stylist. Truffaut doesn't try to alter the traditional devices and situations of marital comedy, as one hoped he would, but at the same time he's not crude or energetic enough to see those situations through, to play them with real verve, with all the stops out.

Truffaut tends to undermine the comedy, second-rate as it is, by simply tossing problems aside with some little "touch" that is meant to be endearing or ironic but usually feels gratuitous or insensible. For instance, Miss Jade tries to punish her husband's infidelity with a Japanese girl by greeting him in Japanese costume one fine evening. It's the sort of thing Lucy might have done to Desi or Doris to Rock after jumping to conclusions. Truffaut doesn't seem to know that an idea this dumb can only be redeemed through vigor, which would probably mean the hurling of accusations and sukiyaki by the little woman. Truffaut ends the scene with a little tear running down Miss Jade's grotesquely painted cheek.

This "affecting" effect is really more grotesque than a slapstick domestic donnybrook would be. If Truffaut doesn't intend to alter the conventions, he should really respect their integrity from beginning to end. If he's up to something else, he should junk the clichés. Only inspired clowning could save material this trivial, but in blatantly commercial waters Truffaut has an uncanny way of letting the wind out of his own sails.

THE TOUCH

Bergman about Love

PENELOPE GILLIATT

Some are more mortal than others. Ingmar Bergman's new film, *The Touch*, the best about love he has ever made, is a record of a man who brings into the existence of a calmly married couple his own feeling that death is something that has to be ambushed daily. The couple, Swedish, a doctor and a housewife, are played by Max von Sydow and Bibi Andersson. Their names are Andreas and Karin, and their life is fine. The invader, whom they are each and differently devoted to, is a German-American Jew called David, played by Elliott Gould. He lives as if he were running onto the end of a blade. Who would think that Elliott Gould, whose American pictures have cast him as a gusty hell-raiser, could have the great technique and responsiveness to tip the balance for an alien director who sensed that he could play a figure of ancient trouble? The Swedes speak English to him and Swedish between themselves. The practical solution is aesthetically perfect. The hesitancies and the intimacies are precise: one closed world, known and fluent; one not mapped, and dangerous.

David's self-hatred bites his bones. This isn't the Elliott Gould we know. He even looks different in Bergman's picture, which was photographed by Sven Nykvist. The lowering, poetic head, often seen in close-up, has huge power and gentleness. The character loathes himself very confusingly for anyone fond of him. Sometimes the touch of his affair with Karin soothes him, but sometimes it drives him into a fury because he so powerfully dreads the loss of it. The dread practically makes him precipitate the loss, like a man so horrified by his own mortality that he kills himself. The two others live their lives as if everything were going to last forever; his behavior is a trap for anticipated death, laid in a rage, with him shivering behind the hedge. What is he bringing into the world of these two happy blond neutralists, this rancorous man? Elliott

Gould's acting has always had an edge of danger, and Bergman uses it wonderfully.

Karin's mother has just died. At the beginning of the film, Karin is racing to the hospital too late. No crying in the room. A nurse brings her the wedding ring. She escapes then into the dark somewhere and hides to weep. David looms into her sanctuary and puts on the lights. "Can I do something for you?" "Turn the lights down, please. Please leave me alone."

A while later, when Andreas has treated David for what is said to be some kidney trouble, David is spending an evening with the two of them. Alone with her for a few moments, he blurts out that he is in love with her. She pays no heed, it seems. Turn the lights down, please. Please leave me alone. We're *happy,* her silence yells. David persists in talking out loud. He first saw her when she was crying at the hospital, he says. Her face blocks him. Perhaps she remembers him, perhaps not. "You were sitting in the cloakroom crying. *I fell in love with you,*" he says. The affair they have later shuttles between the same extremes of concern and clamor, and always seems rooted in that moment at the hospital when Karin was unlike herself and didn't want to be seen, and when David was stirred and caught up by the sight of a fellow-sufferer. Most of his family were killed by the Nazis. He was brought up in America. Now he is an archaeologist, digging up a past that he can't leave alone. You can watch his mind sometimes wrecking the present for him by going over and over old soil. The film uncurls slowly, in time with what Karin takes in. One learns only much later that he was treated by Andreas not for kidney stones but for putting his head in a gas oven, and that he has a lethally attached sister in London who has known about Karin all the time when Karin has never heard of her.

After the first dinner, when the insurgent has left, Andreas and Karin go to bed. The intimacy between them seems exact. They are without suspicion, joking and muttering, like erotic twins. The peculiar chaos of David's presence that evening can be ignored. Andreas, an intelligent, watchful man with the outward style of someone boring, was showing home-movie slides: Karin and the children, and some studies of orchids. The orchids drove David mad. "Haven't you a picture of your wife nude?" he said, off the top of his head. The couple now forget that, for the moment.

Bibi Andersson has never before given such a performance. In the scenes between Karin and Andreas, everything is long-established and light. The attachment is feathery. No peril exists. When she goes to David's flat and begins to fall in love with him, she behaves with the same instant trust but also borrows some of his raw impulse. On the first day, he loses his nerve and can't stop talking bashfully about the weather and her clothes, which she has already changed ten times with a self-mocking and sad chagrin over what she looks like; she is the one who gets them to bed. Her legs are rather too short and her bottom is too big, she says, gabbling the most touching breakneck inventory of herself. "Shut up!" he seems to be yelling at her. "I'm a monster, don't you realize? I can't manage you if you're going to be nice." It takes him months to deal with the pure, sweet key of her feeling for him. Meanwhile, for the first time in her life, she takes on the onus of duplicity. Hard. Bergman cuts backward and forward between the couple's pretty, cultivated house and David's flat, which is near some building site with screaming buzz saws. Moments of the affair seem benedictive. The two of them live on bits and pieces of time, and he flies into rages about the bourgeois domesticity that he accuses of robbing him. For a while, she pulls him out of the mud. She hasn't an idea, this flaxen wife, of what she has taken on, and perhaps the very fact that she doesn't know it is what transforms him. He looks at her with amazing softness, unseen by her, while she reads a poem to him in Swedish, laughing at herself a bit, and then tries to translate it. What's the word? To do with fireplace. Something they had long ago. "Hearth," he says. The paradox is that she and Andreas probably have five hearths, and that it is David, the antiquarian, who is dragging her into the world of buzz saws. The film is partly about a man introducing someone he adores to the very sophistication about mortality and extinction that he loves her for not having.

The Touch is also about compacts. David gets furious with Andreas for ever mentioning again that he tried to kill himself. We agreed not to, he says, to get out of the impossibility that he is in the middle of being confronted with an Andreas talking about the major compact between himself and Karin. The most powerful of David's agreements, moving and deathly, turns out to be with the congenitally ill sister in London. Her blood runs in him in every way. "We are inseparable," she says to Karin in London at the end of the film, smoking endlessly, looking scared, clumping around in heavy shoes and an embroidered cardigan to offer a drink in a flat that she and David are in the midst of moving from. The attachment between brother and sister is the adhesion of flesh to a live electric wire. In hindsight, her possessiveness and fright have been there in David's bad moments with Karin all through the film.

Like *Persona* and *The Passion of Anna*, the two other masterpieces of this great time in Bergman's life, *The Touch* has the most subtle and complicated interest in the idea that intimates' identities pour in and out of one another. Karin sometimes wondrously manages to empty David of too much past. With Andreas, she is the vessel of their solid married life; she sees her husband changing, but she thinks it is a matter of her own changed way of looking at him—changed by secretiveness about being on the telephone, or by fear of suddenly looking incomprehensibly happy. She doesn't know that he is trying desperately not to be flooded with the blackness of David's spirit. Long before she does, we pick up that he understands what's happening. There is something unmistakable about the longing and silence of the way he hangs on to her one night when they are on their way to bed, with him looking at her achingly in the mirror while she looks at him in it and avoids noticing his expression. *The Touch* is a picture floodlit from within, sometimes halcyon, always transparently fond of its characters—people with three quite different styles of grownupness. David combats life, living on some adrenalin of grievance, rooting up old anguish in the middle of the present. How to contain the indwelling historian, how not to tot up accounts. Andreas is a classical man whose only inflexible rage is directed against the Romantic view of suffering. He is, after all, a doctor. Karin was used to being able to manage; a love without equanimity throws her off balance. Bergman's screenplay for his people is simple and expressive. Karin's hesitations in speaking English are part of the eloquence of it: "I've lost my, whatever it is, footing," she says. Her insights into what she and this difficult man could do for each other are the same as his, but they have them at different times. "Please, let me go now," she says to David when he has grabbed her out of a shop, onto the street, and she says it obviously hoping that he never will, but his hands at once fly away from cupping her face, because he is on trust to himself to pretend that it's easy. His pledges and pleas come too late, when he has returned months after leaving Sweden without a word. She had fled to his flat and found it abandoned, with her letters stacked in the only drawer that had anything in it. The film is full of acting moments that are physically miraculous, like brilliant fish drawn up on a line, like the memories of everyone. In this scene in the empty flat, she simply walks up and down very fast, as people do when they are in pain. And then she stands near a wall and props herself against it with her forehead. I once saw a great race horse do that when it was about to die, as though it only had a headache.

GARY ARNOLD

The Touch is utterly ridiculous, the probable low point of Ingmar Bergman's often trying but independent and distinguished artistic career. However, if you don't mind the giggling-in-church aspect of the evening—and there are some real lulus to giggle about —*The Touch* can be more entertaining than a lot of better Bergman films. The audience, for example, seemed rather at a loss while the picture was unreeling, but afterward, talking about how awful it was, people became quite jolly and animated.

Despite the credits and the presence of actors like Bibi Andersson and Max von Sydow, *The Touch* doesn't particularly look or feel like a Bergman picture. It's a conventional and trivial-minded adultery story, photographed in the sort of dismally chic style one would associate with a hack of the second magnitude. For better than a decade Bergman and his cameraman, Sven Nykvist, have been evolving the most intense, straightforward style of composition in movies; out of nowhere we suddenly have floral arrangements along the borders of the image, a great deal of superfluous bustle and emotional underlining (the phone looms ominously in the foreground as Miss Andersson awaits an important call), gleanings from commercial hits like *The Lovers* and *Divorce American Style,* plus the truly startling bonus of nagging, ricky-ticky "background" music.

If the style is disconcerting, it's nothing compared to the content, which is howling. Von Sydow and Andersson are a "happy" bourgeois couple, he a nice doctor and she a busy housewife and mother (of two cute adolescents). For no apparent reason she surrenders to the furry, oafish advances of Elliott Gould, supposedly an archaeologist with a troubled personality and certainly the most unattractive lover since Frank Langella in *Diary of a Mad Housewife.*

We're asked to believe that this nitwit affair endures for a couple of years. The heroine's persistence appears to alienate husband and children and produce a third child, although the outcome and paternity of the pregnancy remain two of the loose ends Bergman fails to tie up. (I, for one, would be more interested in hearing about the baby in the lovers' final parting scene, rather than the heroine's four-o'clock Italian class.) One may agree with her conclusion that Gould's rotten, unstable temper makes further association impossible, but one also wonders why she failed to wise up the first time he belted her—or upon learning of his suicidal tendencies or upon meeting his possessive, crippled sister, and so forth and so forth.

The heroine is insufferably dense and coltish, the lover obnoxious, the husband pained but patient. Such a triangle may long endure, but my patience with it is severely limited. I can't recall a more cliché situation in a Bergman film—not to mention a more cliché handling of the fundamental cliché. It's similar to the way Truffaut bungled the conventions of romantic comedy in *Bed and Board*; here Bergman, instead of transforming the conventional middle-class adultery plot through superior insight and artistry, seems to be competing, rather awkwardly, at the level of the commercial hacks, manipulating an overly familiar premise for overly familiar responses.

Both heroine and director seem to be indulging a sort of second girlhood. Andersson's housewife suggests someone catching up with the bad college love affair she never had, while Bergman gives us an idea of what things would have been like if he'd decided to hire out to Hollywood.

While it's difficult to imagine this material being very edifying in any language, *The Touch* is an English-speaking production, and the language shift could contribute in various ways, subtle and otherwise, to Bergman's problems. The exchanges between Andersson and Gould are tiltillating in the wrong way—one would swear such dialogue had been written for an old Sid Caesar–Imogene Coca or new Carol Burnett–Harvey Korman parody. The biggest problem is Gould. Even if he can't hear the oddness of Elliott Gould saying things like "I'll be preparing a series of lectures—eighteen of them" or "It hurts, physically, being without you; it's like a constant ache," doesn't Bergman notice how funny Gould *looks* burying his head in Miss Andersson's lap (sort of—he appears to be chewing the hem of her coat), how klutzy and unsympathetic his presence *is?*

Apparently not, and the result is one of the more misbegotten

actor-director collaborations of recent years. One indication of the
director's absent-mindedness is that he gives Miss Andersson not
one but two scenes in which she slowly breaks into sobs. Another is
the scene in which she and Gould are reunited after an absence of
several months. Ignoring the obvious fact that he has shaved his
scruffy beard, she greets him, tenderly, with "You've changed. You
look thinner." In *The Touch* several things have escaped Ingmar
Bergman's notice.

2
NOSTALGIA

SUMMER OF '42

DAVID DENBY

If we are honest with ourselves, our adolescent sex experiences are likely to appear in memory as pretty funny or at worst an awkward mess—no matter how intense or spiritual they may have seemed at the time. Screenwriter Herman Raucher's recollection of himself and his friends at age fifteen, *Summer of '42*, is most fully alive when it is most explicit about the fantastic energy and humor of boys on the make: the physical problem of getting your hand around a girl's shoulders at the movies and then onto her breast (and not her arm, for Christ's sake!), the terrifying trip to the drugstore for contraceptives, and all the rest. But when Raucher tries to make poetry out of first love and the loss of male innocence (his own), he shows us that he still thinks like an adolescent; the movie becomes both elevated in tone and incoherent in feeling, an exercise in soft-focus commercial nostalgia.

The male characters are sharply observed. At the center of the movie there is earnest little Hermie (Gary Grimes), the screenwriter-in-adolescence, a conventionally good-looking, all-American type of boy who falls recklessly in love with Dorothy (Jennifer O'Neill), the lovely twenty-two-year-old "adult" whose husband goes off to fight in the Second World War. Transfixed by her perfect physical wholeness and beauty, Hermie courts her with manly courage and abashed formality, completely unsure of what he should be doing or what he wants to happen. Then there's Oscy (beautifully played by Jerry Houser), the teenage sexual entrepreneur: aggressive, affectionate, gregarious, Oscy turns the rites of sexual initiation into a vast comic game in which every event is to be celebrated and enjoyed. In pursuit of his "feels" and finally his "lay," he becomes an entertainer and prod for his friends, inquiring after their progress and denouncing them as "homos" when they fail to act (not because he means it, but because the word functions as an all-purpose reproach for a friend who's fallen into behavioral limbo). Girls, on the other hand, are not quite as real as friends; they are the others, the ones talked about and acted on, and are to be approached with put-on gallantry and a thorough knowledge of the illustrated marriage manual. Finally, there is Benjie (Oliver Conant), who is skinny and has glasses and is not ready for experience; he bolts at the first sign of a girl.

These three and their families are passing a dull summer together on an underpopulated island off the coast of New England; while brothers and husbands go off to fight, the boys struggle against boredom by staging raids on the Coast Guard station, picking fights with one another, prowling the island for girls, and spying on the beautiful war bride. Not only is the movie set in the Forties, but it also has some of the feeling of a Forties movie in its over-all placidity, confidence, and emotional fullness. These teenagers seem to have time to make mistakes, to have adventures, and to learn; as characters they are more attractive and believable than the contemporary kids in Frank and Eleanor Perry's *Last Summer* (1969), who were seen moving toward a miserable, neurotic adulthood as rapidly as their creators' hysteria could impel them.

The softness and evasiveness of the Forties pictures are also evoked and kidded in the scene in which Hermie and Oscy go to the movies with two girls to see *Now, Voyager*. The fancy manners and tactful passions (the second half of *Now, Voyager* is devoted to the complicated reasons why the hero and the heroine cannot go to bed together) provide the perfect mood for some furious making out in the theater; in a wonderful piece of acting, the boys' faces struggle to hold serious expressions, receptive to the stately evasions on screen, while their hands are groping in the dark for a soft landing.

Robert Mulligan, who directed *To Kill a Mockingbird, Up the Down Staircase,* and many other films, is known for his lyrical touch, and in *Summer of '42* the lyricism works best when it is least studied. I don't think I've ever seen a movie in which characters were moving so much of the time; as Mulligan keeps his camera in motion to stay up with those hyperenergetic boys, it takes in the shabby old houses and careless beauty of the seaside landscape in a continuous, unforced flow of space. Compare the casual beach sequences here, with their hazy, salty look, to those in *Ryan's Daughter*, in which the camera spotted isolated figures from afar and then zoomed in across an immensity of gleaming white sand.

But in the scenes of Hermie's infatuation with the older girl, Raucher's script trails off into moony vagueness, and Mulligan begins working in a conventionally "sensitive" style. When the boys spy on Dorothy and her husband from a distance, she is indeed a vision of loveliness, and we can believe that Hermie is struck dumb, but then Mulligan switches to slow motion as the husband carries her into the house. This combination is repeated when the boys witness the husband going off to war: Hermie, emotional over what he sees, is again silent, and Dorothy is slowed down as she sadly walks away. Well, girls are pretty in ordinary motion, too, and that staring, silent boy isn't conveying much to the audience. The intimate scenes between these two are purposely awkward, but the awkwardness lacks tension; Raucher hasn't really created a character in Dorothy (as if he felt that giving her any distinct personality would reduce her loveliness), and Hermie's stumbling importunacy meets a rather blank response. She seems like a boy's fantasy of a real sweet lady, but the rest of the movie is told from the vantage point of adulthood, not adolescence. There's certainly no hint in these scenes of the complexity that would account for what Dorothy does later. In her struggle to find the right emphasis in an unwritten part, Jennifer O'Neill turns out to be a nervous, well-meaning young actress who winds up creating a little pocket of embarrassment around her whenever she appears.

The movie itself gets rather tongue-tied in these moments, and when Dorothy finally takes Hermie into bed, it becomes as evasive as anything from the sentimental Forties. Is anyone really initiated this way? The woman is older but still young, beautiful, freshly crying from the news of her husband's death, in need of consolation. The boy doesn't have to do anything or say a word. Shadows loom over the characters so we can't see what they might be feeling (Mulligan may have wanted to protect his inexperienced actors here), breezes sweetly blow, and in darkness and silence the moment unfolds, blessed by tears.

Afterward, Raucher's narration takes over: "For everything that we take with us, we leave something behind. In a very special way I lost Hermie forever." But what is the "very special way"? Since Hermie doesn't say a single word for the rest of the movie, we don't know whether he's appalled or thrilled or crushed by this first "adult" experience of life. He won't answer Oscy's questions or ours, and once again we're left with that staring boy (but we know that sex did not silence Raucher forever). The whole lively stream of detailed, funny, idiosyncratic reactions to experience which on balance make this a good movie suddenly runs dry, an inhibition which suggests that Raucher hasn't come to terms with that particular event even to this day. Hermie's silence represents not the maturity of his new consciousness but the author's inability to relinquish a fond, foolish fancy.

THE LAST PICTURE SHOW

The Streets of Anarene

PAUL D. ZIMMERMAN

The Last Picture Show is a masterpiece. It is not merely the best American movie of a rather dreary year; it is the most impressive work by a young American director since *Citizen Kane*. Orson Welles dazzled us with his cocksureness and the audacity of his innovations. Peter Bogdanovich, a thirty-one-year-old critic turned film-maker, works in the classic tradition of John Ford and Howard Hawks, even to the point of shooting this compassionate chronicle of small-town Texas life entirely in black and white.

The gamble pays off. With the aid of veteran cinematographer Robert Surtees, Bogdanovich gets a feeling of desolation in his ghostly gray landscapes and the grainy textures of his interiors—neglected poolrooms, oilcloth kitchens and linoleumed back bedrooms—that color could not capture.

The film is not without its flaws—its brief excursions into sentimentality, its sometimes untidy definitions of family ties. But these minor slips of an authentic and maturing talent are buried under an avalanche of positive achievements, starting with the finely tuned screenplay, adapted from Larry McMurtry's novel, by Bogdanovich and the novelist. If Robert Altman's genuis in *McCabe & Mrs. Miller* was to create in time and space the birth and burgeoning of an entire town, Bogdanovich describes with equal brilliance its decline and death.

In a narrow sense, the film is a period piece, set in 1951, when the advent of television was dissolving those communal bonds that made small towns something more than mere miniatures of the bigger cities. Even at the film's outset, Anarene, Texas, is physically moribund; its shabby stores, windswept, desolate streets and bleak main highway mark it as one of those way stations that American civilization left behind on its long push west.

But its soul has not expired, surviving in the figure of Sam the Lion, the owner of Anarene's pool hall, diner and movie house, who represents the last link to the frontier past. Sam must be perfectly cast if the film is to work. In the rugged terrain of his lived-in face, we must be able to read a recklessness now tamed, an innocence that has passed through sin into wisdom. In the cadences of his Western speech and in his right but never righteous tone, we must hear that voice of elemental justice and fair play that characterized our cowboy heroes, even though these virtues may never have existed as anything but a myth.

Bogdanovich finds the perfect actor for Sam in Ben Johnson, a veteran of Westerns from *Shane* and *Rio Grande* to *The Wild Bunch*, who indeed embodies in the honesty of his worn face an integrity and totally masculine presence that sets him apart from the mean and seedy citizens around him. When he banishes the high-school kids from his movie house for having cruelly forced the town's young mute between the legs of a two-bit whore, he speaks as the last just man, the voice of moral authority in an oasis of wayward boredom.

Johnson is but one of a brilliantly cast ensemble that includes Timothy Bottoms as an All-American teenager whose sad eyes register the slow realization that he lives and is destined always to live in a town without pity. Jeff Bridges brings the look of a young Elvis Presley to the role of Duane, Sonny's hard-nosed, dirt-poor buddy who loses the rich girl in town and chooses possible death in Korea over a dead-end destiny in Anarene.

As Jacy Farrow, Duane's oil-rich girl friend, Bogdanovich uses an untried fashion model named Cybill Shepherd and artfully draws from her a performance that embodies every crummy value in town—duplicity, hard ambition, rote obedience to every local shibboleth. Still, she retains an allure of innocence, as much victim as victimizer, her wide eyes searching out financial security in men she doesn't care about because financial security has been held up to her as life's only sure thing. In the all-too-easy way she shuffles off Duane as a bad gamble and latches onto Sonny as a possible man of property, in the calculated way she discards her virginity because it's a social liability, we feel the pathos of a girl who plays for keeps the only game in town.

The film delights with its artful observations on the frustrations and fraud of teenage romance—in a shot of Sonny kissing his gum-chomping girl friend at the movies while he stares longingly at Elizabeth Taylor on the screen; in the bored, automatic way his girl friend sheds her bra in the cab of a pickup truck and the equally automatic way she prevents his hand from breaking new ground; in the bossy way Jacy forces Duane to seduce her, in the clumsiness of his failure and his false bravado afterward; in a brilliant, erotic sequence at a nude swimming party in which a nervous, determined Jacy, seeking initiation, must strip on the diving board in return for social acceptance.

The teenagers are all vitality and aspiration. But, in Anarene, spiritual death comes at an early age. The adult community is anesthetized by television, plugging along without hopes. Ellen Burstyn, as Jacy's itchy, bored mother, creates a superb study of a woman who settled down and down and down, a mixture of wistful memories and knowing toughness. Cloris Leachman, as the neglected coach's wife who takes Sonny as a lover, tells us all we must know of the perils of such a romance in a single shot—sitting on her creaky bed in white, like an abandoned bride, waiting for the boy who will not come because Jacy has claimed him.

When Sam the Lion dies, the last vestiges of decency in Anarene die with him. Soon after, the movie house plays its last picture show, *Red River*, in which John Wayne's call to start the cattle drive reminds us how Anarene has declined from its early energies and ambitions into a mean-spirited morass of wasted lives. Bogdanovich tailors his truths to fit local speech, as in Ellen Burstyn's observation that "nothin's ever the way it's supposed to be." True of Anarene, it applies with equal justice to every American town, every American life. For, in the end, *The Last Picture Show* stands as both an elegy to the American dream and its epitaph.

Some Lessons in Growing Up

RICHARD SCHICKEL

The Last Picture Show is about adolescents trying to grow up in a small (and declining) Texas town in the early 1950's. After the usual number of experiments with sex and booze and small-scale physical and psychological violence (and a brush or two with mortality), some of them make it to what passes in this country for maturity.

Familiar stuff, the material of hundreds of novels, autobiographies, movies. And yet Peter Bogdanovich's movie seems to me a very good one. It transcends and transforms its near-banal material partly because it contains, all the way through the cast, some of the best acting you're likely to see this year, mostly because it is so sensitive to the details of time and place without insisting on showing its superiority to them through satire.

I'll admit to prejudice in this matter. I am the exact contemporary of these kids, and though I'm sure we didn't grow up in anything like a golden age, I'm equally sure, on the evidence of my own eyes, that no subsequent generation has any right to feel culturally advantaged in comparison. Mr. Bogdanovich is, in fact, at some pains to place the songs, films and TV shows of our formative years in proper perspective, using them to create a background appropriate to the particular manner in which we grew up, but not implying that the decline of American civilization can be dated from the popularity of Frankie Laine, Johnnie Ray and Patti Page. Conversely, he refuses to sentimentalize this material, impute a value to it that was never present in it. His tributes to this period are sensible ones: He quotes from two of the good movies of the time, *Red River* and *Father of the Bride*, and, cannily, chooses to shoot in black and white and in the best formal manner of John Ford. All of which is a way of saying that the director has a very clear idea of what was valuable and what was not, in a time of mixed blessings.

Bogdanovich's story has two protagonists, best friends played by Timothy Bottoms and Jeff Bridges. The latter is the high-school hero—a back on the football team, a putative make-out artist, the force around which the gang at the pool hall coalesces, a success within the values of his peer group. His problem, however, is that he can't seem to grow beyond those values. He lusts—both angrily and moonily, but always with indifferent success—after the class belle (a type whose teasing and self-absorption are definitely defined by Cybill Shepherd) and, rejected, drifts away into the oil fields and then the Army and, we understand, into a life that will lack distinction because it lacks the habit of self-examination.

In contrast, his friend, the soft-spoken boy who used to block for him on the football team, opens himself up to others, most notably to Sam the Lion (Ben Johnson), an ex-cowboy who owns the town's cultural center—that is, the pool hall, the café and "the last picture show"—and is the repository of the best male values: to Ruth Popper (Cloris Leachman), wife of his athletic coach, who initiates him not only sexually but into the enduring feminine mystery, and to Lois Farrow (Ellen Burstyn), mother of the tease and possessor of that wry worldliness we all need to find both early and gently. As has become customary in films about kids, we scarcely glimpse the boys' real parents, but the film's principals constitute what we would now call an extended family, and what the picture says, ever so softly and ever so intelligently, is that the way out of an adolescence that always carries with it the threat of becoming perpetual is through decent connections with those few adults who, whatever their other problems, have at least made this journey successfully and are willing to show and tell what it's like. The movie says what we all know—that too few adults are willing to perform these vital initiatory functions—but it adds a point that, in our present romanticizing of rebellious youth, we often forget that a youth has to reach out to them, make known in some civil way his pain and need. One cannot speak too highly of this movie's sense of style, of its affectionate but unsentimental rendering of the moods of a vanished milieu, but what grants it a claim to greatness is its precise, humane understanding of how generations succeed and fail in communicating. It is, to risk the vulgar phrase, the one "youth picture" from which all can profit, the one exercise in nostalgia that is not false in detail, in attitudes, in fundamental viewpoint or intelligence.

John Simon

Peter Bogdanovich is America's answer to the *Cahiers* phenomenon of film critic turned film-maker; yet behind every answer there is a question. In this case, how good was he as a critic in the first place? The answer is that he was never a serious critic, only an *auteurist* hero-worshiper. And how is he as a film-maker? His first film, *Targets*, handled a valid subject in a trashy way; his new one, *The Last Picture Show*, is a great hit with the reviewers, so too with the audiences, and strikes me as not bad by current standards. Inasmuch as Bogdanovich is in his very early thirties, this may augur well. But there is a "but" here, and quite a big, fat but it is, too.

The Last Picture Show takes place in the two-horse town of Anarene, Texas, in 1951, when the town's only picture show (i.e., movie theater) closed down before the onslaught of television, which brought the dream factory right into the living room. Sonny Crawford, co-captain of the high-school football team, is at the center of this one-year chronicle. We see him go from unsatisfactory pettings with his plain but busty girl friend in the back of the picture show or in the front seat of his pickup truck, to an affair with Ruth Popper, the neglected middle-aged wife of the crude football coach; thence to an unconsummated affair and promptly annulled wedding with Jacy Farrow, a classmate who is the local pretty and spoiled rich bitch.

Meanwhile Sonny's best friend, Duane Jackson, the backfield captain, goes from being Jacy's platonic boyfriend to becoming, ever so fleetingly, her lover, thence to the Army and the Korean war. Two lovable figures around town die: Sam the Lion—owner of the picture show, poolroom and eatery, the three sole recreational centers of Anarene—a fine remnant of a more romantic West; and Billy, a little idiot boy whom Sam took care of and Sonny, often inadequately, protected.

Jacy goes from fooling around with Duane to getting herself deflowered by him merely to move in on the fast, smart set of Wichita Falls, where virginity would be held against her; thrown over by one of those megalopolitan rich boys, she returns to the local talent and takes on, first, Abilene, her mother's lover, then Sonny himself, only to cast him off. On the sidelines, there are two women watching and commenting: Genevieve, the hardy, good-natured café waitress; and Lois, Jacy's jaded mother, bored and exasperated by her loveless marriage to Anarene's oil millionaire.

All this is framed by an opening shot of the picture show still functioning and a closing shot of it standing there on the town's main street, deserted. The former shows us a dry, windy, dusty, bleak day and sets the climate of the film. The latter is a super-imposition: Sonny, who has graduated and is already a forgotten outsider at the school football games, has sneaked back to see Ruth Popper, whom he so recklessly abandoned for Jacy. Ruth receives him nicely, gives him coffee, and then has her outburst: why has she always been so self-effacing, waiting on everyone, Sonny included; why has she never asserted her rights? Sonny is remorseful, Ruth's moment of rebellion passes. Now they sit there, dejected, no longer lovers and not yet friends, holding hands unhopefully as their image dissolves into that of the abandoned movie theater of a godforsaken town.

Though schematic, this doesn't sound half bad. But look at the film more closely. The locale is captured accurately by Robert Surtees' black-and-white cinematography, and the time seems indeed to be 1951, as we are told it is. Told? Clobbered with it. Just about every hit song of the period manages to hit us from radios or juke-boxes; every major television program of the time seems to be watched by someone in the film at some point or other.

Yet this is fairly easy. The lay of the land has not changed much since Larry McMurtry wrote or lived the autobiographical novel on which he and Bogdanovich based this screenplay. I got my Air Force basic training near Wichita Falls in 1944, and I can vouch for the area's being of the sort that a decade or two can barely make a dent in. The monochromatic photography is quite good, but in an era when almost everything is filmed in color, you can score easy points just by clinging to black-and-white—whether it is finally called honesty, nostalgia, or an *hommage* to your favorite directors of the period. And, certainly, the general outline of the film convinces: McMurtry lived it, wrote it almost without senti-mentality or anger, and Bogdanovich approaches the material rev-erently—all too reverently, in fact.

McMurtry, who also wrote the novel on which *Hud* was based, considers himself a minor regional novelist and at a symposium engagingly mentioned that in working on the script of *The Last Picture Show* he discovered how much better a novel could have been made from the material—and, by implication, how much bet-ter a film, had Bogdanovich not been so enamored of the published text. But as both Pauline Kael and Andrew Sarris (who have, un-like me, read the novel) pointed out, there were some minor yet not wholly insignificant changes made, adding up to a certain romanticizing of the matter. Thus the movies the kids see in the film are better than the ones in the novel (Bogdanovich even anachronistically drags in *Red River* as a tribute to one of his *auteur-*heroes, Howard Hawks); Lois is not allowed, in the film, to have sex with Sonny, whom her daughter has just betrayed; Jacy's crude sexual bout with her mother's lover on a pool table, and the young bloods having intercourse with a blind heifer are also excised.

What is kept is not always particularly persuasive, either. I cannot believe the scene where all their classmates watch Jacy's and Duane's sexual initiation from cars parked outside the motel; I do not see the need to make Lester, a two-bit operator (Randy Quaid), seem more idiotic than Billy, the real halfwit. I think it is a bad boiling down of the novel that introduces Sonny's father out of nowhere as an outcast, drops him immediately, and never tells us anything about Sonny's home life; the same goes for Duane and his family, with a mother making a belated, almost subliminal appearance. The character of Abilene, the town stud, is woefully underdeveloped; Sam the Lion is so idealized that we see him only in scenes where he can deploy generosity, righteous indignation, gracious forgiveness, or noble, homespun philosophizing. His basic, quotidian relationship to Genevieve and Billy is left completely unexamined.

The whole last part of the film proceeds by jerky, disparate lurches that do not blend into a balanced narrative, and the conclusion is so ambiguous (my interpretation, given above, is perforce quite arbitrary) as to be close to a mere effect. Worst of all, Sonny is unconvincing—whether in the writing, acting or directing, or in all three, hardly matters. We are supposedly looking, for the most part, through his eyes, and he is meant to be a reasonable enough young fellow in the process of coming of age. Yet what has he really learned, or taught us, in the end? And how can we take him seriously if he is so stupid that, when Genevieve observes the town is so small that no one can sneeze in it without other people holding out a handkerchief, he asks, "What do you mean?"

Indeed, almost all of these people are cloddish. The fact that Anarene is a cultural backwater may explain this but does not necessarily reconcile us to spending two hours with its essentially dreary denizens. True artists, of course, can illumine the simplest people—in both senses of the verb—and can make plain words take on great resonance. Though McMurtry and Bogdanovich succeed once or twice, that is hardly enough to rouse one's sympathy from its sleep.

Potentially most gripping are those unfulfilled older women: Ruth, Genevieve, Lois Farrow. But none of them quite makes it. Ellen Burstyn is very competent as Lois, yet the part is too skimpy and burdened with drippy lines like "Nothing has really been right since Sam the Lion died." Eileen Brennan's Genevieve captures the essence of the likable tough broad of the old movies, but they, rather than life, seem to be the unfortunate source of the character. As Ruth, Cloris Leachman gives a poor performance. Her weeping comes out comic, her shy love for a very young boy lacks genuine warmth and seems almost calculating, her face is usually a rather unattractive blank. She seems to be all nose and sharp bones; even a boy like Sonny might have found her no sexier than a Gillette razor blade.

Above all, Bogdanovich's direction is sheer derivativeness. To put it bluntly, it is *cinémathèque* direction. A John Ford shot is followed by a George Stevens one; a Welles shot by one out of Raoul Walsh. Even if every sequence is not as patently copied as the funeral is from *Shane*, the feeling is unmistakable that one is watching a film directed not by a young director in 1971 but by a conclave of the bigger Hollywood directors circa 1941. This may give the film visual authenticity, but of what kind? Imagine a present-day composer writing like Haydn, a painter working in the exact style of Vermeer. At best such men are epigones; at worst, forgers. At its most successful, *The Last Picture Show* rises to the heights of pastiche.

There are also serious minor problems, the most bothersome of them being unsubtlety. When Sonny and Ruth make love for the first time, the springs of the bed do not just squeak, they ululate. If this were intended as deliberate heightening from a subjective point of view, it would have to occur throughout the film, which it doesn't. Sonny has a way of fondly turning around the baseball cap on Billy's head so that the visor faces backward. He does this some half-dozen times in the film, and when *he* doesn't do it, Duane does. It becomes grating in its predictability. Or take Billy's death; the boy is run over by a truck. The scene is staged stiffly and ploddingly, and the gloom-inducing devices run amuck. Never, on those other windy days, has a shutter been banging in the poolroom; now there is one beating the Devil's tattoo. Never before has a single tumbleweed tumbled down the streets of Anarene; now there is a bunch of them doing enough tumbling for the main ring at Barnum & Bailey's.

At other times, instead of hitting us over the head, Bogdanovich does not make a point at all. When Sonny, after Billy's death, gets into his truck and drives off to leave this horrible town forever, we follow him along the empty road across scarcely less empty country until suddenly, for no visible reason, he makes a U-turn and capitulates. A reliable film-maker would have taken us inside Sonny as the resolution to escape peters out; if nothing else, he would have found an objective correlative, the tiny external factor that undermines the boy's resolve. Instead, like so many things in the film, the change of mind has to be taken simply on faith.

The acting is far from consistently good. Aside from Cloris Leachman's and Randy Quaid's unpleasant work, there are Clu Gulager's Abilene, Timothy and Sam Bottoms' Sonny and Billy, and Cybill Shepherd's Jacy to leave one unmoved. Miss Shepherd is a model (though how, with that dubious figure, I can't imagine) whose face Bogdanovich found on a teenage magazine cover. Although her face is absolutely right for Jacy, nothing else is. Ben Johnson does nicely by Sam the Lion, however, and Jeff Bridges is convincingly oxlike as Duane.

FIDDLER ON THE ROOF

A Bagel with a Bite Out of It

Pauline Kael

I can't talk about Hollywood. It was a horror to me when I was there and it's a horror to look back on. I can't imagine how I did it. When I got away from it I couldn't even refer to the place by name. "Out there," I called it. You want to know what "out there" means to me? Once I was coming down a street in Beverly Hills and I saw a Cadillac about a block long, and out of the side window was a wonderfully slinky mink, and an arm, and at the end of the arm a hand in a white suède glove wrinkled around the wrist, and in the hand was a bagel with a bite

out of it.—Dorothy Parker, in 1956, in an interview in
the *Paris Review*.

Everyone may have a different view of what that bagel represents, but if it is the symbolic ordinary Jewish food that the show-
business *nouveaux riches* cling to, it may also symbolize a vulgar
strength that repelled Dorothy Parker—and in which she did not
share. Hollywood Jews overdressed like gypsies who had to carry it
all on their backs, and they clung to a bit of solid, heavy food even
when they were no longer hungry, because it seemed like reality.
Vulgarity is not as destructive to an artist as snobbery, and in the
world of movies vulgar strength has been a great redemptive force,
canceling out niggling questions of taste. I think *Fiddler on the
Roof*, directed by Norman Jewison, is an absolutely smashing
movie; it is not especially sensitive, it is far from delicate, and it
isn't even particularly imaginative, but it seems to me the most
powerful movie musical ever made.

Musical comedy is one of the American contributions to world
theater; it is also primarily an American Jewish contribution.
There would be a theater in America without Jews, and perhaps it
would be not much worse than it is—though it would certainly be
different—but, as William Goldman has pointed out, "Without
Jews, there simply would have been no musical comedy to speak of
in America. . . . In the last half century, the only major Gentile
composer to come along was Cole Porter." What separates *Fiddler
on the Roof*, which is set in Czarist Russia, from other Broadway
shows and from such movie musicals as *West Side Story* and *The
Sound of Music* and *My Fair Lady* and *Hello, Dolly!* and *Camelot*
and *Paint Your Wagon* and *Star!* and *Doctor Dolittle* is that it is
probably the only successful attempt to use this theatrical form on
the subject of its own sources—that is, on the heritage that the
Jewish immigrants brought to this country. The only other big
movie musical of recent years with any explicit Jewish material was
Funny Girl, and although essentially a blown-up show-business bio,
it also got some of its drive from that explicitness. *Fiddler on the
Roof* finds its theme in the energy and gusto and the few remnants
of moldy traditions—the religion of the bagel—that have resulted
in such wonders as the American musical theater as well as in the
horrors of a pandering theater full of Jewish-mother jokes. But
Fiddler on the Roof is a celebration of a Jewish *father*, and Tevye,
the dairyman pulling his wagon, is a male Mother Courage, not a

male Molly Goldberg. Maybe because its means are utterly square and plain, the movie succeeds in doing what Elia Kazan, for all his gifts and despite some fine scenes, failed to do in *America America* (which dealt with the persecution of his Greek ancestors in Turkey and the dream of the new country). Though it is a musical, *Fiddler on the Roof* succeeds in telling one of the root stories of American life: As Tevye's daughters marry and disperse and the broken family is driven off its land and starts the long trek to America, Tevye's story becomes the story of the Jewish people who came to America at the turn of the century—what they left behind and what they brought with them.

It is not a movie about "little people," though it seems so in the first five minutes—a "hearty" pre-title sequence featuring the song "Tradition," which is show-business Jewish-Americana, a gruesome romp that makes one wince in expectation of more of the same. But then the credits come on, and Isaac Stern plays the theme (as he does in the solo parts throughout the movie) with startling *brio* and attack; Isaac Stern's energy and style carry us into a different realm. His harshly sweet music clears away the sticky folk stuff, and the movie takes off. It never again sinks to the little-people-at-their-simple-tasks level, because Topol's Tevye has the same vitality and sweetness and gaiety as Isaac Stern's music; he's a rough presence, masculine, with burly, raw strength, but also sensual and warm. He's a poor man but he's not a little man, he's a big man brought low—a man of Old Testament size brought down by the circumstances of oppression. The crooked, ironic grin when he gestures to God and the light in his eyes after a love song with his wife tell the story of a dogged man who can be crushed again and again and still come back.

Topol is a broad actor, but not in the bad sense of broad; Clark Gable, though incapable of registering much suffering, was a broad actor, and so is Sean Connery. I mean not an actor who lacks finer shades (although Gable certainly did, and it may turn out that Topol does, too) but, rather, an actor with a heroic presence, a man's man, an actor with *male* authority—a Raimu, a Jean Gabin. Typically, these actors play earthy, working-with-their-hands roles and look out of place when they are cast in the upper class. They are almost totally physical actors—deep-voiced men who dominate the stage or screen by energy and power, actors with a gift for projecting common emotions and projecting them to the gallery. Anna Magnani is the last woman star of this type—the actors and actresses of the people. Anthony Quinn's Zorba was a comparable large-spirited role. It's easy for small-spirited people to put down this kind of acting, but when a director has enough taste and control to keep an outsize performer within limits, the emotional effects can be satisfying and rich in a way that other kinds of acting never are. Topol (rather too broad for his role in *Before Winter Comes*) was a superb choice for the movie Tevye, because his brute vitality makes Tevye a force of nature—living proof of the power to endure. Tevye is the soul of *Fiddler on the Roof*; Topol, a giant dancing bear of a man, embodies the theme, and, big as the movie is—and it's *huge*—he carries it on his back.

Topol has a fine speaking voice, low and resonant but also cracked and playful; he can twist a word right up to a high register. The humor in Tevye's role is not only in the jokes themselves but in the playing; they don't stale, because a good performer reactivates them. Such folk humor as a man talking about a girl while the man he's talking to thinks the conversation is about a cow is so primitive one watches it ritualistically; it's the beginning of vaudeville. Perhaps because Topol is an Israeli, not an American Jew, he plays with a strength that is closer to peasant strength than to an American urban Jewish image. If his heroic strength overpowers the original qualities of the character, his backbone is what this big musical-comedy movie needs. His is a Sabra Tevye, and I suppose this may disconcert those who saw the first Broadway Tevye, Zero Mostel, who I understand was much funnier. Mostel is a brilliant, baleful, sad-eyed buffoon, weirdly inventive, and with his freak specialty—the surprise of how light he is on his toes—but on the screen he could no more embody the Jewish Everyman than W. C. Fields or Jonathan Winters could be the WASP Everyman. He is a clown, and, like many great clowns, he creates his own atmosphere. Topol is handsome, which is a blessing in movies, and, though bigger than life, he's still in the normal human range—his bigness is an intensification of normal emotions.

Norman Jewison's movie is astonishingly square—astonishing not only in how square his approach is but in how joyously square the results are. Never having seen *Fiddler* on the stage, I can't judge what has been lost, but, on its own terms, the movie has an over-all, ongoing vitality that is overwhelming. It is a show that reveals not what made Jewish writers or thinkers but what has made American Jewish show business. It is an attempt to bring joy out of basic experience; the hero is a myth-size version of a limited, slightly stupid common man. Jewison has a sound instinct for robust, masculine low comedy; he showed it in the way he handled Rod Steiger in *In the Heat of the Night* and Alan Arkin in *The Russians Are Coming, The Russians Are Coming*. (On a small scale, Arkin's Russian was a warm-up for Tevye.) The producers were probably wise—or maybe lucky—when they selected a Gentile director, because Jewison (an exotic name for a Methodist) doesn't let the movie slip into chummy Jewish sentimentality. In the movie, to be chosen for suffering is a joke that Tevye and the other Jews in the Ukrainian village are in on. The Jews are a chosen people the way blacks are beautiful. Those who suffer may need to believe there is a higher meaning in their suffering, just as those whose beauty has not been sufficiently recognized may need to rediscover it and emphasize it. The irony that the chosen of God seem to have less access to Him than others do is, in fact, the source of Tevye's comedy in the movie, as it is in the Sholem Aleichem stories on which the musical is based. Tevye is a religious man but also a realist—because he can't get God's ear. Younger members of the audience—particularly if they are Jewish—may be put off the movie if their parents and grandparents have gone on believing in a special status with God long after the oppression was over, and have tried to prop up their authority over their children with boring stories about early toil and hardship (as the superpatriot judge in *Little Murders* does). Too many people have *used* their early suffering as a platitudinous weapon and so have made it all seem fake. And I suppose that *Fiddler on the Roof* has been such a phenomenal stage success partly because it can be used in this same self-congratulatory way—as a public certificate of past suffering. And perhaps the movie can be, too. But this movie is far from a Jewish *The Sound of Music* and is infinitely less sentimental than the youth rock musicals.

Jewison treats the Jews as an oppressed people—no better, no worse than others—and this sensible attitude, full of essential good will, and yet not self-conscious, as a Jewish movie director's attitude might easily have been, keeps the movie sane and balanced, and allows it to be powerful. The movie is not a celebration of Jewishness; it is a celebration of the sensual pleasures of staying alive and of trying to hang on to a bit of ceremony, too—a little soul food. Jewison does not permit the Jewish performers to be too "Jewish"; that is, to become familiar with the audience with that degrading mixture of self-hatred and self-infatuation that corrupts so much Jewish comedy. Only one of the leads—Molly Picon, as Yente, the matchmaker—gets away from him and carries on like a stage Jew, with a comic accent. Why do Jewish performers like Molly Picon have to overdo being Jewish when they play Jews? What do they think they are the rest of the time? They're like those Hollywood actresses who, when they got past forty and the time came for them to play the parents of teenage children, did themselves up like Whistler's mother. It is an anomaly of American entertainment, in which Jews have played so major a role, that it is not the Gentiles but the Jews who have created the Jewish stereotypes, and not to satisfy any need in the Gentiles but to satisfy the mixed-up masochism of Jewish audiences. (Black performers put on comic black masks for black audiences, too; it could conceivably be argued that the comedy is in showing their own people the masks they wear for whites, but this argument certainly doesn't carry over to the Jews.) It's this kind of cheap courting of favor with the Jewish audience that one may fear when one goes to see *Fiddler on the Roof*, and Jewison keeps the movie about 99 percent pure.

As the timid tailor who loves Tzeitel, Tevye's oldest daughter, Leonard Frey is as innocent of heart and tangled in his limbs as a young Ben Blue, and as the daughter Rosalind Harris, a tall, slender young actress, looks just enough like Frey for the marriage to have been made in Heaven; they're a lunatically sweet pair of Shakespearean lovers—funny, pastoral, perfect. Paul Mann, with his winged eyebrows and ruddy, button-nose face, is a marvelous camera image—a true St. Nick. His wealthy butcher, like his rug merchant in *America America,* is a lived-in character. You look at him and you see a whole way of life—groaning boards loaded with meat, the pleasures of materialism. The butcher's and Tevye's explosions of temper at Tzeitel's wedding are possibly the truest moments of folk humor. (The movie is most false, I think, in the reaction shots of the constable when he and Tevye talk; these shots seem to come out of a Second World War movie—they make dignity-of-man points.) Michele Marsh is a bit too conventional an ingénue as the second daughter but redeems the performance with her farewell song; the third daughter, Neva Small, very young and with long red hair, has a special comic spark in her early scenes. The Golde (Tevye's wife) of Norma Crane is physically suitable, but the character, regrettably, never emerges.

The movie is highly theatrical, but it isn't stagy. Joseph Stein, who wrote the stage show, also did the movie script, and it's a serviceable adaptation. Jewison has managed to keep the whole production, including the out-of-doors scenes, somewhat stylized, so that the simple transitions in and out of the songs and dances are not jarring but just a further step in stylization. And since, as the stage show was conceived (mostly by Jerome Robbins, from all accounts), the songs and dances are meant to be not "professional" but heightened expressions of emotion by the characters, the numbers are in any case not so different from the somewhat formalized theatrical scenes they grow out of. Jewison's devices to get from one scene to the next are so naïve that they can easily be accepted, because they serve the material. The vastness of fields with only a few figures is a simple conversion from a bare stage. These fields may then be dissolved into an abstraction to end a scene, or the camera may move from the figures in a field to a landscape. Some of the devices don't serve good purposes. Though the picture seems to ride right over its own faults, it *is* irritating that the direction and editing so often go for obvious effects—a shift, say, from the candles' being lighted in one home to the candles' being lighted all over the village. Jewison fails at certain scenes because of a kind of nondenominational blandness: The revolutionary from Kiev (Michael Glaser) becomes just an attractive juvenile, and the scene in which he tries to teach radical ideas to Tevye's daughters is insipid. The third daughter's Gentile suitor (Raymond Lovelock) is a walking example of Hitler-youth-movement calendar art. However, the worst flaw in the film except for the unrealized Golde is that the best dance scenes are all but wrecked by the whirlybird attempt to create dazzle and speed with a camera amidst the figures instead of letting the dances build by choreographic means. You want to see the whole figures and the steps, not blurred faces and bits of bodies. Dance has greater power than film-makers may realize, and the wedding dance of four men with wine bottles on their heads is the high point of the film. I don't know if it's traditional or a Jerome Robbins contribution— perhaps it's a blend of both—but it's a beautiful ritual dance and beautifully performed. It comes as a gift of art, like Isaac Stern's violin songs.

I fear that people of taste have been so indoctrinated now with a narrow conception of cinematic values that a movie in a broad popular style will be subject to a snobbish reaction. But square can be beautiful, too. It can be strong in a very direct way, and the theme of *Fiddler on the Roof* justifies this large-scale (nine-million-dollar) production. One doesn't go to a big American movie musical expecting impeccable ethnic nuances or fine brushwork; that's not what this particular genre provides. What it does offer is the pleasure of big, bold strokes—and spirit. *Fiddler on the Roof* is American folk opera, commercial style. So was *Porgy and Bess*. And though the score, by Jerry Bock (the music) and Sheldon Harnick (the lyrics, functional but uninspired), isn't in the Gershwin class, it isn't *bad*. No other American folk opera (certainly not *Porgy and Bess*, which has a rather unfortunate libretto) has ever been so successfully brought to the screen as *Fiddler on the Roof*. Its great advantage on the screen is its narrative strength; the material builds and accumulates meaning, until, at the end, when the Jews who have left their homes huddle on a raft, Tevye's story becomes part of the larger story, and the full scope of the movie is achieved. Though the techniques and simplifications are those of musical comedy, when they are put to work on a large emotional theme that is consonant with the very nature of American musical comedy—is, in fact, at its heart—the effect on the large screen is of a musical epic. The music is certainly not operatic, but the movie of *Fiddler on the Roof* has operatic power. It's not a soft experience; you come out shaken.

Dorothy Parker, so apt and so funny, was also so *wrong*. She was right, of course, in seeing Hollywood as a mink-and-bagel story; that's what anyone researching movie history comes up against, and it must be what anyone researching the musical theater comes up against, too. And it's the easiest thing to patronize. But that bagel with the bite out of it should have cheered her. Imagine that arm without the bagel and you have cold money. Didn't it tell her that the woman in the mink in the Cadillac didn't quite believe in the mink or the Cadillac? Didn't it tell her that movies, like musical comedies, were made by gypsies who didn't know how to act as masters, because they were still on the road being chased? Couldn't Miss Parker, split down the middle herself—a Jewish father and a Gentile mother—see that that bagel was a piece of the raft, a comic holy wafer?

Is Fiddler More De Mille than Sholem Aleichem?

VINCENT CANBY

Because a mean spirit, as well as snobbishness, have been imputed to anyone who doesn't find *Fiddler on the Roof* the most powerful movie musical ever made, I'd like to say right off—in a friendly, humble, populist sort of way—that I hope the film, now at the Rivoli, will make pots of money for everyone connected with it. Not only is it a well-meant, if literalized, adaptation of a lovely, stylized show (which can still be seen in something like its original Broadway purity at the Broadway Theater, several blocks north of the Rivoli), but business has been so bad this year that any movie that can possibly keep the creditors away—without insulting its audience—deserves our support.

However, that doesn't necessarily mean that it deserves our blind admiration, if unfelt, or our denial of a fact of history. That is, that the decline in movie attendance over the years, the increase in the costs of production, plus the well-deserved flops of *Star!* and *Dr. Dolittle*, have just about finished the once joyful tradition of the original American film musical. It's no accident, I think, that with the possible exception of *Gigi*, none of the great original movie musicals of the 1940's and 1950's (*An American in Paris, Singin' in the Rain, Funny Face*, etc.) was conceived as a movie that had to be financially successful if the company that produced it was to survive. In that once-upon-a-time, movie musicals were no big deals. When they were good, they looked free and casual and unafraid.

Today we have what amounts to a new, mostly joyless tradition, that of the safe, artistically solemn, pre-sold musical behemoth adapted from the Broadway hit. It's a tradition that puts a terrible burden on the already reeling Broadway theater (which is now in the position to kill off film musicals forever). It also puts a dreadful strain on the imagination of the film-maker, who must decide how to preserve the original sensibility, which accounted for the Broadway success, in a medium that can show us hundreds of people, at one time, or the saliva in a man's mouth, but can simulate the excitement of the stage's person-to-person contact only through the recognition of shared emotions.

The movie *Fiddler* is superior in almost every respect to *Hello, Dolly!* and *Paint Your Wagon*, each of which had the intimate charm of the Brooklyn Bridge wired as a sound-and-light show, to *Funny Girl* and *On a Clear Day* (although it lacks their star performances and occasional moments of splendor), and to *Oliver*—largely because the source material—the libretto and the score—is superior. It's not a grossly bad movie, but it left me so untouched that several days after seeing it, I walked up the street to the Broadway Theater to see the original—which meant subjecting myself to more *Fiddler*, in a short space of time, than perhaps any non-addict need sanely do. It was, I realize, an unfair test for the cast of a show that's been running seven years and that's not exactly getting younger with each performance. Yet, miracle of miracles (comparatively speaking, anyway), the show still lives, even though a bit run-down at the heels and a bit automatic in its responses to the live audience. It is very much a Broadway show, employing the sophisticated Broadway technology that is much further removed from the world of Tevye, and the life of the Jews in a Czarist Russian *shtetl*, than Broadway is removed from Hollywood. Why, then, does the show evoke emotional responses that are left undisturbed by the movie? It should follow that if you are moved by one, then you must be moved by the other. Or does it?

Jerome Robbins, who staged the show, employed the kind of Broadway shorthand that comes close to being—in very unexpected ways—the theatrical equivalent of the Sholem Aleichem prose. The dancers soar and the singers traffic in images and melodies that are Tin Pan Alley *cum* Jewish folk, but nothing denies the direct simplicity of the narrative, which has a marvelous woeful modesty to it. The show is a fable told in highly theatrical Broadway terms, and it never makes the mistake of indicating that it knows it's an epic. Such a thought would, I'm sure, make the show's Tevye shrug with a certain embarrassment. He talks directly to God, and to us, but he lets us discover his happinesses and his sorrows discreetly.

To call the movie an epic is really to define what's wrong with it, which is to mistake Sholem Aleichem for Leo Tolstoi, and to substitute for the necessarily limited physical resources of the stage the vast physical resources of the screen. In literalizing the show, in making a big ethnic thing out of it in real landscapes and real houses, Norman Jewison, the director, and Joseph Stein, who adapted his stage book to the screen, have effectively overwhelmed not only Aleichem but the best things about the stage production. These include Mr. Robbins' breathtaking choreography, which is mostly seen on the screen in bits and pieces, either from the neck up or from the knees down, and the lovely Sheldon Harnick–Jerry Bock score, which is strong, as Broadway scores go, but which was never designed to meet the grand, operatic requirements of a literal exodus. Thus pushed beyond its limits, the music goes flat and renders banal moments that, on the stage, are immensely moving.

Perhaps because the mannerisms of the New York Yiddish theater have common philosophical roots with Aleichem, I found the single most touching performance in the film to be that of Molly Picon as the matchmaker. She is excessive and outrageous and very dear. Equally fine, though a good deal more legitimate, is Leonard Frey as Motel, the otherwise timid tailor who carries off Tevye's eldest daughter to what promises to be a life of blissful hardship.

The entire show must, however, be shouldered by the actor who plays Tevye, and this is where the movie takes its boldest step and one that is most distorting. Topol, the Israeli actor, is a fine, vigorous performer, a man with the easy, slightly calculating charm of a matinee idol, and, when he is not being upstaged by the movie's visual and aural grandeur, or by close-ups so huge that you pull back in your seat, he does shoulder the movie. However, he shoulders it as if he were a youngish Moses instead of a rueful Job, which amounts to a kind of theatrical blasphemy. It's difficult, for me, to be very much moved by a Moses figure, since I'm always aware that Moses has a hot line to God, whereas Job (and Tevye) seem often to be talking into receivers that someone has left off the hook, quite arbitrarily.

Gone—spirited away, so to speak—with the substitution of Moses for Job, is a measure of the magnificence of a certain kind of human indomitability, which is what I take Aleichem to be all about. There are hints of Aleichem throughout the film, but don't be fooled. Deep within it there beats the mechanical heart of Cecil B. De Mille's 1956 *The Ten Commandments*, which may possibly turn out to be a stroke of genius, at least for the box-office success of a very valuable property, but it diminishes *Fiddler on the Roof*.

BRUCE WILLIAMSON

The profligate screen version of *Fiddler on the Roof* opens with a violin solo by Isaac Stern, whose virtuosity adds little to the play's intrinsic value but provides a clue to the values cherished by producer-director Norman Jewison and playwright-adapter Joseph Stein. Having repeated its phenomenal Broadway success in cities throughout the world, the musical smash based on Sholem Aleichem's stories about simple, poverty-stricken peasants in Czarist Russia cannot, it seems, be treated as anything less than a blockbuster. The result of this blatantly commercial big-think is a noisy, lumpish and aggressive spectacle that crushes both the spirit of the stories and the easygoing charm of the original show. Part of the problem can be traced to director Jewison's peculiar ideas about casting—particularly his decision to bypass Zero Mostel, who created the role of Tevye onstage, in favor of Israeli star Topol, celebrated in his homeland as a youngish actor (he is thirty-four) with a knack for playing characters twice his age. To put it politely, Topol is miscast. To put it bluntly, he gives a forced and unfeeling performance, overstretching his broad smile to fill a Panavision screen the size of a football field, but seldom evoking the humanity and wisdom of a devout, delightful old Jew with five marriageable daughters on his hands. As Tevye's wife Golde, Norma Crane at best brings consistency to a cast that appears to have been recruited from one of *Fiddler*'s least-distinguished touring companies. Only Rosalind Harris as Tevye's eldest daughter, Tzeitel, and Leonard Frey as the simple tailor she loves prove capable of asserting themselves as believable individuals against the movie's intimidating pomposity. Filming on location in Yugoslavia merely heightens the flaws of Jewison's over-all conception, for the glimpses of a realistically humble peasant village, populated by actual peasants, seem strangely out of sync with a production so slick and studied that every song cue sets off an avalanche of sound—as if the Red Army Chorus were concealed in a nearby barn. *Fiddler*'s familiar score (by Sheldon Harnick and Jerry Bock) also suffers from overzealous cinematography, which reduces every big number to a lively but meaningless blur, as if cameras were invented expressly to obscure the words and music. Once again, moviedom's merchant princes have reaffirmed their faith in the perverse alchemy that transforms a great theatrical showpiece into a triumph of mediocrity.

THE GARDEN OF THE FINZI-CONTINIS

DAVID DENBY

Of all the emotions, nostalgia is one of the most treacherous and self-deluding. In so many examples of longing for the past we detect an essential fakery, an impulse to dramatize the self, to make a display of feelings that aren't truly justified by what was left behind. For instance: Do adults really value their undergraduate days, or is it only a boring pretense they act out to assuage their later disappointments and gull the young?

It is one of the many virtues of Vittorio De Sica's lovely *Garden of the Finzi-Continis* that it doesn't trouble us with doubts like these. Here is a fully sustained elegy for the past that convinces us that the things loved and lost were truly valuable; as a result we are drawn to the things themselves rather than left wondering about the emotions of the elegist.

De Sica's adaptation of Giorgio Bassani's semi-autobiographical novel of 1962 chronicles the life of two Jewish families in Ferrara, Italy, during the brutal closing days of the fascist period, 1938–43. The practical middle-class family tries to accommodate itself to anti-Semitism, while the aristocratic Finzi-Continis ignore the whole thing, but in both cases we know that their lives as Italians are over, that they must escape or face deportation to the concentration camps. As their basic rights evaporate and the atmosphere of the town takes on an increasing menace, they continue to enjoy an active Jewish family life, but behind closed doors; while recording the felicity of this life, the film moves inexorably toward its conclusion—the arrival of the secret police, followed by Tito Schipa singing a lamentation in Hebrew for the dead of Treblinka and Auschwitz.

The passivity of the Finzi-Continis is one of the givens of the movie, although it is an agony for us. We would like to reach up to the screen and shake them by the shoulders, even though there's no reason to think it would do any good. People like this were probably warned often enough; it became part of the elegance of their lives to remain completely oblivious, to trust that anti-Semitism, like bad taste, could never hurt them if it were thoroughly avoided.

The word "elegy" has two meanings—a lamentation for the dead and also a lamentation for unrequited love. In the unfulfilled longing of Giorgio, the middle-class boy (Lino Capolicchio), for young Micol Finzi-Contini (Dominique Sanda, in another stunning performance) we get a smaller elaboration on the themes of loss and ruined hope which animate the movie as a whole. Micol is abrupt, provocative, unreachable, her very remoteness a form of eroticism; she has been Giorgio's lifelong obsession. A truly noble fellow, an anti-fascist by instinct, Giorgio is nevertheless a blank for Micol; he has the dullness of virtue, and she is attracted instead to a coarser, more self-confident man.

Despite his nobility, Giorgio the lover turns into Giorgio the voyeur: In one of the screen's greatest images of sexual exclusion he steals into the garden of the Finzi-Continis to spy on her and suffers the extreme mortification of the unloved. These relationships, which would be completely absorbing in themselves, are made still more affecting by our consciousness of their fragility in the face of the general annihilation which is yet to come.

The Finzi-Continis are that rarity in European history, a family of aristocratic land-holding Jews. Their "garden" (the grounds of their huge estate) is both the geographical center of the movie—where the afternoon tennis, memories of youth, and erotic encounters take place—and also a simple metaphor for the high state of the Finzi-Continis' cultivation. Actually, their culture is, by the late Thirties, a rather languorous and decadent affair, with tuberculosis and a hint of incest in the younger generation, but it is still exquisitely accomplished and not something we may easily condescend to.

Bassani and De Sica are unabashedly in love with the accouterments of an ideal aristocracy—the sumptuous great house set in the thickly wooded park, the library of uniform editions and original manuscripts, the life of spacious leisure and casual but genuine intellectual distinction. The director makes it all extremely beautiful, but the beauty is not decorative or incidental. It is essential to the meaning of the movie. If these were ordinary Jews about to lose their lives and possessions, we might be equally moved or angry, but we wouldn't be left with the peculiar ache of despair, the mournful indignation that is the residue of this movie. In each of us, no matter how egalitarian in belief, there probably remains an impulse to admire the perfection of luxury that only great wealth can sustain and to indulge the wealthy and cultivated—however spoiled or useless—in the enjoyment of their privileges.

Only the ultimate ruthlessness of the "Final Solution" would destroy these harmless aristocrats, with their taste for minor Italian poets and Jean Cocteau and silk dressing gowns. When the unshaven, nondescript fascist agent carelessly smashes a china vase while searching the house, a perceptible shudder went through the entire audience. I imagine very few people in the theater would actually care to display that vase in their own apartments, but the act was rightly felt to be a desecration, an attack on the fitness of things. The critique of fascism from the point of view of useless and antiquated beauty is as valid as any other.

"Summer afternoon, summer afternoon . . . the two most beautiful words in the English language," Henry James is supposed to have said, and perhaps, with their universal associations of pleasure, they are the most beautiful words in any language. Like Eric Rohmer in his *Claire's Knee*, De Sica has staged most of his film during long summer afternoons, but instead of the hard-edged style of the French film, De Sica and cinematographer Ennio Guarnieri have achieved a softer tone more appropriate to elegy. Their color photography is slightly grainy and intentionally overexposed, with an occasional softening of focus. It's a style that has its dangers, and they labor to avoid sentimentality or a merely static prettiness by keeping everything in motion, adapting the superactive manner of the Sixties—with its zooms and rapid pans and fast cutting—into a smoothly meshed flow of constantly changing perspectives.

The effect is both restless and magical. When the young people bicycle through the park in their tennis whites, they literally gleam in the sun; the setting as a whole seems entirely composed in lemon and reddish brown and dark green. The overly lush titles sequence is obviously a mistake and there is still another a few minutes later—a rapid tilt up into the tall trees of the park before we have any feelings associated with the trees of the setting. At that point, one feels a willingness in De Sica to indulge in the reeling, tilting, full-of-life clichés of commercial lyricism, but it's only a momentary slip. The rest of the film is tightly shot, and the beauty of the scene is passed over lightly. We discover that beauty for ourselves and it inspires in us feelings of longing and regret not easily stilled.

3

THE DIRECTOR'S STYLE: PERSONAL FILMS

THE CONFORMIST

The Poetry of Images

PAULINE KAEL

What makes Bernardo Bertolucci's films different from the work of older directors is an extraordinary combination of visual richness and visual freedom. In a Hollywood movie, the big scenes usually look prearranged; in a film by David Lean, one is practically wired to react to the hard work that went into gathering a crowd or dressing a set. Bertolucci has been working on a big scale since his first films—*La Commare Secca*, made when he was twenty, and *Before the Revolution*, a modern story derived from *The Charterhouse of Parma*, made when he was twenty-two—and his films just seem to flow, as if the life he photographs had not been set up for the camera but were all there and he were moving in and out of it at will. Most young film-makers now don't attempt period stories— the past is not in good repute, and period pictures cost more and tend to congeal—but Bertolucci, because of the phenomenal ease of his sweeping romanticism, is ideally suited to them; he moves into the past, as he works in the present, with a lyrical freedom almost unknown in the history of movies. He was a prize-winning poet at twenty-one, and he has a poet's gift for using objects, landscapes, and people expressively, so that they all become part of his vision. It is this gift, I think, that makes *The Conformist* a sumptuous, emotionally charged experience.

Bertolucci's adaptation of the Alberto Moravia novel about the psychology of an upper-class follower of Mussolini is set principally in 1938 (Bertolucci was born in 1941), and I think it's not unfair to say that except for Jean-Louis Trintignant's grasp of the central character—it's an extraordinarily prehensile performance—the major interest is in the way everything is imbued with a sense of the past. It's not the past we get from films that survive from the Thirties but Bertolucci's evocation of the past—the Thirties made expressive through the poetry of images.

Trintignant, who has quietly come to be the key French actor that so many others (such as Belmondo) were expected to be, digs into the character of the intelligent coward who sacrifices everything he cares about because he wants the safety of normality. Trintignant has an almost incredible intuitive understanding of screen presence; his face is never too full of emotion, never completely empty. In this role, as an indecisive intellectual, he conveys the mechanism of thought through tension, the way Bogart did, and he has the grinning, teeth-baring reflexes of Bogart—cynicism and humor erupt in savagery. And, playing an Italian, he has an odd, ferrety resemblance to Sinatra. Everything around him seems an emanation of the director's velvet style—especially the two beautiful women: Stefania Sandrelli, an irresistible comedienne, as Trintignant's deliciously corrupt middle-class wife, and Dominique Sanda, with her swollen lips and tiger eyes, as the lesbian wife of an anti-fascist professor he is ordered to kill. (She's rather like a prowling, predatory stage lesbian, but she's such an ecstatic erotic image that she becomes a surreal figure, and Bertolucci uses her as an embodiment of repressed desires. She also appears, only slightly disguised, in two other roles—conceived to be almost subliminal.) The film succeeds least with its ideas, which are centered on Trintignant's fascist. I think we may all be a little weary—and properly suspicious—of psychosexual explanations of political behavior; we can make up for ourselves these textbook cases of how it is that frightened, repressed individuals become fascists. In an imaginative work, one might hope for greater illumination—for a fascist seen from inside, not just a left view of his insides. Yet though the ideas aren't convincing, the director makes the story itself seem organic in the baroque environment he has created, and the color is so soft and deep and toned down, and the texture so lived in, that the work is, by its nature, ambiguous—not in the tedious sense of confusing us but in the good sense of touching the imagination. The character Trintignant plays is by no means simple; when he says "I want to build a normal life," it's clear that he needs to *build* it because it's not normal for him. He shows a streak of bravura enjoyment as he watches himself acting normal.

Bertolucci's view isn't so much a reconstruction of the past as an infusion from it; *The Conformist* cost only seven hundred and fifty thousand dollars—he brought together the décor and architecture surviving from that modernistic period and gave it all a unity of style (even with the opening titles). Visconti used the Thirties-*in-extremis* in *The Damned*—as a form of estrangement. Bertolucci brings the period close, and we enter into it. His nostalgia is open; it's a generalized sort of empathy, which the viewer begins to share. You don't think in terms of watching a story being acted out, because he provides a consciousness of what's going on under the scenes; they're fully orchestrated. Bertolucci is perhaps the most operatic of movie directors. I don't mean simply that he stages movies operatically, in the way that other Italians—notably Zeffirelli—do, but that he conceives a movie operatically; the distinction is something like that between an opera director and an opera composer. Visconti in *The Damned* was somewhere in the middle—composing, all right, but in a single, high-pitched scale, as if the music were to be howled by wolves. *The Damned* was hysterical; *The Conformist* is lyrical. You come away with sequences in your head like arias: a party of the blind that opens with the cry of "*Musica!*"; an insane asylum situated in a stadium—a theater-of-the-absurd spectacle of madness; a confession-box satirical duet between priest and non-believer; a wedding-night scherzo, the bride describing her sins, to the groom's amusement; the two women on a late-afternoon shopping expedition in Paris; a French working-class dance hall (a *Bal Populaire*) where the women dance a parody of passion that is one of the most romantic screen dances since Rogers and Astaire, and where the crowd join hands in a farandole. The political assassination in the forest—an operatic love-death—is the emotional climax of the film; Trintignant sits in his car, impotent—paralyzed by conflicting impulses—while the woman he loves is murdered.

Two years ago, Bertolucci made *Partner*, an inventive but bewildering modernization of Dostoevski's *The Double*, in which the hero, a young drama teacher (Pierre Clémenti), had fantasies of extending the theater of cruelty into political revolution. This basic idea is shared by many young film-makers, including, probably, Bertolucci, but Clémenti never conveyed enough intellectuality for us to understand the character, who seemed to be a comic-strip Artaud. Despite the fascination of *Partner* (I recall one image in particular, in which books were piled up in heaps on the floor of a room like the Roman ruins outside), the film was shown here only at the 1968 New York Film Festival. It was a political vaudeville for the movie generation bred on Godard's *La Chinoise*; the meanings were lost in the profusion of images and tricks of his original, daring high style. Bertolucci seemed to have forgotten the story of his own *Before the Revolution*, in which his Fabrizio discovered that he was not single-minded enough to be a Communist—that he was too deeply involved in the beauty of life as it was *before* the revolution. Bertolucci, like Fabrizio, has "a nostalgia for the present." This may seem a bourgeois weakness to him (and to some others), but to be deeply involved in the beauty of life as it is is perhaps the first requisite for a great movie director. (And, far from precluding activity for social change, it is, in a sense, the only sane basis for such activity.) It's a bit ironic that the young director who has the greatest natural gifts of his generation for making movies as sensual celebrations should have sought refuge for this talent in the fascist period.

After *Partner*, Bertolucci made a television film about a plot to murder Mussolini during a performance of *Rigoletto—The Spider's Stratagem*. Based on a Borges story, it was attenuated—it didn't have enough content to justify the atmosphere of mystification. *The Conformist* is his most accessible, least difficult film from an audience point of view. I don't put that accessibility down; despite the intermittent brilliance of *Partner*, it *is* a failure, and trying to figure out what a director has in mind is maddening when it's apparent he hasn't worked it out himself. *The Conformist*, though in some ways less audacious, is infinitely more satisfying. One may wish that Bertolucci had been able to integrate some of the Godard influence, but no one has been able to do that; Bertolucci has simply thrown the discordant notes out of his system and gone back to his own natural flowing film rhythm. (Is it perhaps an in-joke that the saintly bespectacled professor who is murdered faintly resembles Godard?) In this film, one knows that Bertolucci knows who he is and what he's doing; young as he is, he's a master director. Except for the unconvincing and poorly staged concluding sequence, the flaws in *The Conformist* are niggling. It's very tempting for young film-makers, through cutting, to make their films difficult; the film-makers look at their own footage so many times that they assume an audience can apprehend connections that are barely visible. Bertolucci uses an organizing idea that puts an unnecessary strain on the viewer: The film begins with the dawn of the assassination day, and the events that led up to it unfold while Trintignant and a fascist agent are driving to the forest. The editing at the outset is so fast anyway that cutting to and from that car is slightly confusing, but as one gets caught up in the imagery that slight confusion no longer matters. In a Bertolucci film, in any case, there are occasional images that have no logical explanation but that work on an instinctive level—as surreal poetry, like the piles of books in *Partner* or the desk here, in a fascist's office, that is covered with neatly arranged walnuts. However, I don't think *The Conformist* is a great movie. It's the best movie this year by far, and it's a film by a prodigy who—if we're all lucky—is going to make great films. But it's a triumph of style; the substance is not sufficiently liberated, and one may begin to feel a little queasy about the way the movie left luxuriates in fascist decadence.

One of the peculiarities of movies as a mass medium is that what the directors luxuriate in—and what we love to look at—has so often been held up as an example of vice. Except for the sophisticated comedies of the past and occasional thrillers about classy crooks, we get most of our views of elegance under the guise of condemnation. Our desire for grace and seductive opulence is innocent, I think, except to prigs, so when it's satisfied by movies about fascism or decadence we get uncomfortable, because our own enjoyment is turned against us. One wants modern directors to be able to use the extravagant emotional possibilities of the screen without falling into the De Mille–Fellini moralistic bag. There are some sequences in *The Conformist* that suggest the moralistic extremism of *The Damned*—that party of the blind, for example, and the blue light on Trintignant's and Sanda's faces in the cloakroom of a ballet school.

The old puritanism imposed on movie-makers is now compounded by the puritanism of the left which coerces film-makers into a basically hypocritical position: They begin to deny the very feelings that brought them to movies in the first place. The democratic impulse that informed the earliest screen masterpieces was to use the new medium to make available to all what had been available, through previous art forms, only to the rich and aristocratic. It was the dream of a universalization of the best work that could be done. As this dream became corrupted by mass culture produced for the lowest common denominator, the young film-makers had to fight to free themselves from mass culture, and the fervor of the earlier democratic spirit was lost. Most young American film-makers, in college and after, now think of themselves as artists in the same way American poets or painters do—and the poets have long since abandoned Whitman's dream of the great American audience. Film-makers often talk as if it were proof of their virtue that they think in terms of a minority art. American movies have now reached just about the place the American theater did a decade or so back, when, except for the rare big hits, it had dwindled into a medium for the few.

The radicalized young are often the most antidemocratic culturally, and they push radical film-makers to the point where no one can enjoy their work. Any work that is enjoyable is said to be counter-revolutionary. The effect may be to destroy the most gifted film-makers (who are also—not altogether coincidentally—mostly left) unless the young left develops some tolerance for what the pleasures of art can mean to people. These issues become central when one considers a Bertolucci film, because his feeling for the sensuous surfaces of life suggests the revelatory abandon of the Russian film poet Dovzhenko. If anyone can be called a born movie-maker, it's Bertolucci. Thus far, he is the only young movie-maker who suggests that he may have the ability of a Griffith to transport us imaginatively into other periods of history—and without this talent movies would be even more impoverished than they are. The words that come to mind in connection with his work—sweeping, operatic, and so on—describe the talents of the kind of movie-maker who has the potential for widening out the appeal of movies once again. But movies—the great sensual medium—are still stuck with the idea that sensuality is decadent. If Bertolucci can break all the way through this barrier—and he has already broken through part way—the coast is clear. But if he uses his talent—as "commercial" directors so often do—at half-mast, and somewhat furtively, to celebrate life under the guise of exposing decadence, he'll make luscious, fruity movies. When "period" becomes more important than subject, the result is often decorator-style—as in the worst of Minnelli. Bertolucci has such a feeling for detail that one fears he could go this route into empty, gorgeous film-making. That would be one more devastating blow to the art of motion pictures; sensuality is what they have lost. Except for *The Conformist* (and *Claire's Knee*), the new movies in New York have—for what I think must be the first time in decades—sunk below the level of the theater season (which happens to be an unusually good one).

THE CONFORMIST 117

People say you have to psych yourself up to go to a movie these days, and that's not far from the truth.

ROBERT HATCH

I find myself somewhat nonplused by *The Conformist*, Bernardo Bertolucci's mannered portrait of an Italian fascist gunman. Taken from a novel by Alberto Moravia, the film recounts the history of Marcello (Jean-Louis Trintignant), who had been seduced at the age of twelve by his family's chauffeur and who had then shot the man with his own gun. Marcello's driving motivation ever since has been to prove to others, and especially to himself, that he is an utterly normal man. This has led him, by the time of the picture, to marry an utterly banal girl and to undertake, while on honeymoon in Paris, to eliminate an expatriate professor (Marcello had been his student) who has been irritating the Mussolini hierarchy.

So far, good enough. A pre-adolescent seduction accompanied by manslaughter might well dispose a man to obsessive preoccupation with conformity, and forty years ago blind obedience to Il Duce's interests could well be the form it would take. Moreover, Marcello's character is given higher relief because he manifestly finds the role of assassin more congenial than the act of assassination (he falls into Shakespeare's "second murderer" category) and because he has been able to normalize everything in his life except his sexual proclivities.

However, Bertolucci's method strikes me as excessively complex. I find no fault with narrative manipulation when it enhances insight, but in this case the process seems to open a good many cinematic opportunities without enriching one's understanding of, or interest in, a character who is in any case nonevocative by definition. It is plausible that people who seek the anonymity of compliance are most disposed to do repression's dirty work, but I don't see that the film does more than state this.

The story is told almost entirely in a flashback, beginning when Marcello, with a fascist bully in an Orson Welles hat at the wheel, sets out in pursuit of the professor and his wife through a snowy and very beautiful French countryside. As they drive, Marcello, half dreaming, recalls the past. This permits the director to edit with elliptical flexibility and to vary his approach from approximate realism to photogenically elegant fantasy. But it also makes it difficult to know how to "take" the proceedings. For example, during much of the picture I was inclined to see Marcello's tough companion as a comic extravagance—particularly since, in one shot, his face looms up near an old Laurel and Hardy handbill. In the dénouement, he turns out to be anything but a joke.

Furthermore, it strikes me that Marcello is remembering more than he has experienced—in one case, details of a lesbian infatuation between his wife and the wife of the professor; if Bertolucci is cutting into and out of the flashback without signaling his turns, the complexity is getting out of bounds. And further still, this mixture of memory and dreams leaves facts in limbo. Was the professor really surrounded in his Paris flat by a band of six or eight young muscle men, and if he was that cautious, why did he encourage intimacy with Marcello, of whom he was obviously suspicious, and then take off on that lonely ride? If the professor's wife really thinks Marcello a fascist trigger man, as she states with disgust, why does she attempt to seduce him? Perhaps to protect the professor, perhaps to get at the other wife? You can't tell through all that gauzy manner. A film that is a fabric of ambiguities is one thing, and very compelling it can be; but a film that shows a tendency to go ambiguous at the turning points leaves the viewer with no base for his understanding.

I suspect that *The Conformist* will be admired principally by those who prefer cinema to film. It obliges you to watch very closely and it achieves some striking effects, but I cannot persuade myself that two hours spent with so dull a fellow as Marcello is time well spent, and I wonder whether Moravia gave him more substance. The intellectual level of the picture is not very aspiring. Plato's myth of the cave runs through it as a kind of motif, and the hero's best friend is a blind fascist theoretician. If the work needs allegory, which I doubt, allusions a bit less pat would have grated less.

MCCABE & MRS. MILLER

Pipe Dream

PAULINE KAEL

McCabe & Mrs. Miller is a beautiful pipe dream of a movie—a fleeting, almost diaphanous vision of what frontier life might have been. The film, directed by Robert Altman, and starring Warren Beatty as a small-time gambler and Julie Christie as an ambitious madam in the turn-of-the-century Northwest, is so indirect in method that it throws one off base. It's not much like other Westerns; it's not really much like other movies. We are used to movie romances, but this movie is a figment of the romantic imagination. Altman builds a Western town as one might build a castle in the air—and it's inhabited. His stock company of actors turn up quietly in the new location, as if they were part of a floating crap game. Altman's most distinctive quality as a director here, as in *M*A*S*H*, is his gift for creating an atmosphere of living interrelationships and doing it so obliquely that the viewer can't quite believe it—it seems almost a form of effrontery. He has abandoned the theatrical convention that movies have generally clung to of introducing the characters and putting tags on them. Though Altman's method is a step toward a new kind of movie naturalism, the technique may seem mannered to those who are put off by the violation of custom—as if he simply didn't want to be straightforward about his storytelling. There are slight losses in his method— holes that don't get filled and loose ends that we're used to having tied up—but these losses (more like temporary inconveniences, really) are, I think, inseparable from Altman's best qualities and from his innovative style.

There's a classical-enough story, and it's almost (though not quite) all there, yet without the usual emphasis. The fact is that Altman is dumping square conventions that don't work anymore: the spelled-out explanations of motive and character, the rhymed plots, and so on—all those threadbare remnants of the "well-made" play which American movies have clung to. He can't be straightforward in the old way, because he's improvising meanings and connections, trying to find his movie in the course of making it—an incredibly risky procedure under modern union conditions. But when a director has a collaborative team he can count on, and when his instinct and his luck both hold good, the result can be a *McCabe & Mrs. Miller*. The classical story is only a thread in the story that Altman is telling. Like the wartime medical base in *M*A*S*H*, the West here is the life that the characters are part of. The people who drop in and out and the place—a primitive mining town—are not just background for McCabe and Mrs. Miller; McCabe and Mrs. Miller are simply the two most interesting people in the town, and we catch their stories, in glimpses, as they interact with the other characters and each other. But it isn't a slice-of-life method, it's a peculiarly personal one—delicate, elliptical. The picture seems to move in its own quiet time, and the faded beauty of the imagery works a spell. Lives are picked up and let go, and the sense of how little we know about them becomes part of the texture; we generally know little about the characters in movies, but since we're assured that that little is all we need to know and thus all there is to know, we're not bothered by it. Here we seem to be witnesses to a vision of the past—overhearing bits of anecdotes, seeing the irrational start of a fight, recognizing the saloon and the whorehouse as the centers of social life. The movie is so affecting it leaves one rather dazed. At one point, cursing himself for his inability to make Mrs. Miller understand the fullness of his love for her, McCabe mutters, "I got poetry in me. I do. I got poetry in me. Ain't gonna try to put it down on paper . . . got sense enough not to try." What this movie reveals is that there's poetry in Robert Altman and he *is* able to put it on the screen. Emotionally far more complex than *M*A*S*H*, *McCabe & Mrs. Miller* is the work of a more subtle, more deeply gifted—more mysterious—intelligence than might have been guessed at from *M*A*S*H*.

The picture is testimony to the power of stars. Warren Beatty and Julie Christie have never been better, and they *are* the two most interesting people in the town. They seem to take over the screen by natural right—because we want to look at them longer and more closely. Altman brings them into focus so unobtrusively that it's almost as if we had sorted them out from the others by ourselves. Without rigid guidelines, we observe them differently, and as the story unfolds, Beatty and Christie reveal more facets of their personalities than are apparent in those star vehicles that sell selected aspects of the stars to us. Julie Christie is no longer the androgynous starlet of *Darling*, the girl one wanted to see on the screen not for her performances but because she was so great-looking that she was compelling on her own, as an original. She had the profile of a Cocteau drawing—tawdry-classical—and that seemed enough: Who could expect her to act? I think this is the first time (except, perhaps, for some of the early scenes in *Doctor Zhivago*) that I've believed in her as an *actress*—a warm and intense one—and become involved in the role she was playing, instead of merely admiring her extraordinary opaque mask. In this movie, the Cocteau girl has her opium. She's a weird, hounded beauty as the junky madam Mrs. Miller—that great, fat underlip the only flesh on her, and her gaunt, emaciated face surrounded by frizzy ringlets. She's like an animal hiding in its own fur. Julie Christie has that gift that beautiful actresses sometimes have of suddenly turning ugly and of being even more fascinating because of the crossover. When her nose practically meets her strong chin and she gets the look of a harpy, the demonstration of the thin line between harpy and beauty makes the beauty more dazzling—it's always threatened. The latent qualities of the one in the other take the character of Mrs. Miller out of the realm of ordinary movie madams. It is the depth in her that makes her too much for the cocky, gullible McCabe; his inexpressible poetry is charming but too simple. An actor probably has to be very smart to play a showoff so sensitively; Beatty never overdoes McCabe's foolishness, the way a foolish actor would. It's hard to know what makes Beatty such a magnetic presence; he was that even early in his screen career, when he used to frown and loiter over a line of dialogue as if he hoped to find his character during the pauses. Now that he has developed pace and control, he has become just about as attractive a screen star as any of the romantic heroes of the past. He has an unusually comic romantic presence; there's a gleefulness in Beatty, a light that comes on when he's on-screen that says "Watch this—it's fun." McCabe pantomimes and talks to himself through much of this movie, complaining of himself to himself; his best lines are between him and us. Beatty carries off this tricky yokel form of soliloquy casually, with good-humored self-mockery. It's a fresh, ingenious performance; we believe McCabe when he says that Mrs. Miller is freezing his soul.

A slightly dazed reaction to the film is, I think, an appropriate one. Right from the start, events don't wait for the viewers' comprehension, as they do in most movies, and it takes a while to realize that if you didn't quite hear someone's words it's all right—that the exact words are often expendable, it's the feeling tone that matters. The movie is inviting, it draws you in, but at the opening it may seem unnecessarily obscure, perhaps too "dark" (at times it suggests a dark version of Sam Peckinpah's genial miss *The Ballad of Cable Hogue*), and later on it may seem insubstantial (the way Max Ophuls' *The Earrings of Madame de . . .* seemed—to some —insubstantial, or Godard's *Band of Outsiders*). One doesn't quite know what to think of an American movie that doesn't pretend to give more than a partial view of events. The gaslight, the subdued, restful color, and Mrs. Miller's golden opium glow, Leonard Cohen's lovely, fragile, ambiguous songs, and the drifting snow all make the movie hazy and evanescent. Everything is in motion, and yet there is a stillness about the film, as if every element in it were conspiring to tell the same incredibly sad story: that the characters are lost in their separate dreams.

The pipe dreamer is, of course, Robert Altman. *McCabe & Mrs. Miller* seems so strange because, despite a great deal of noise about the art of film, we are unaccustomed to an intuitive, quixotic, essentially impractical approach to movie-making, and to an exploratory approach to a subject, particularly when the subject is the American past. Improvising as the most gifted Europeans do has been the dream of many American directors, but few have been able to beat the economics of it. In the past few years, there have been breakthroughs, but only on sensational current subjects. Can an American director get by with a movie as personal as this—personal not as in "personal statement" but in the sense of giving form to his own feelings, some not quite defined, just barely suggested? A movie like this isn't made by winging it; to improvise in a period setting takes phenomenal discipline, but *McCabe & Mrs. Miller* doesn't look "disciplined," as movies that lay everything out for the audience do. Will a large enough American public accept American movies that are delicate and understated and searching —movies that don't resolve all the feelings they touch, that don't aim at leaving us *satisfied*, the way a three-ring circus satisfies? Or do we accept such movies only from abroad, and then only a small group of us—enough to make a foreign film a hit but not enough to make an American film, which costs more, a hit? A modest picture like *Claire's Knee* would probably have been a financial disaster if it had been made in this country, because it might have cost more than five times as much and the audience for it is relatively small. Nobody knows whether this is changing—whether we're ready to let American movie-makers grow up to become artists or whether we're doomed to more of those "hard-hitting, ruthlessly honest" American movies that are themselves illustrations of the crudeness they attack. The question is always asked, "Why aren't there American Bergmans and Fellinis?" Here is an American artist who has made a beautiful film. The question now is "Will enough people buy tickets?"

ANDREW SARRIS

I happen to admire Robert Altman's *McCabe & Mrs. Miller* even though many people whose opinions I respect don't like the movie and many people whose opinions I suspect do. Furthermore the main anti-argument (pretentiousness) strikes a more responsive chord in my critical temperament than does the main pro-argument (realism). *McCabe & Mrs. Miller* is photographed through a test-pattern haze of pea soup, and much of the dialogue is thrown away so hard it bounces. The star turns of Warren Beatty and Julie Christie trip and fall over the most cluttered *mise-en-scène* since the days of De Mille's jungle salons for slinky Swanson. I've heard tell that Altman was already over budget before he finished building a set more woody than Hollywoody and that he fits almost too neatly into the slot of sorehead directors like Stroheim, Brown and Peckinpah.

No matter. *McCabe & Mrs. Miller* confirms the impression of striking originality that goes beyond the Beetle Bailey mechanics of *M*A*S*H* to the more controlled horror and absurdism of *That Cold Day in the Park* and *Brewster McCloud*. It is true that a large part of Altman's originality is more peculiar than effective, particularly the squashed jokes with the predictably deadpan reaction shots as if the joke had not been heard, or if heard, not understood, or if understood, not appreciated, or if appreciated, not acknowledged. By the time every character and every situation is run through this wringer of non-reaction, the audience may begin to yawn with American Antoniennui.

Hence, I don't expect *McCabe* to be any more successful than

Brewster with the trendsy public. Nonetheless, *McCabe* succeeds, like *Brewster*, almost in spite of itself, with a rousing finale which is less symbolic summation than poetic evocation of the fierce aloneness in American life. I can't remember when I have been so moved by something which has left me so uneasy to the marrow of my aesthetic. Unlike so many of his contemporaries, Altman tends to lose battles and win wars. Indeed, of how many other films can you say that the whole is better than its parts? Beatty's reluctant hero and Christie's matter-of-fact $5 whore are nudged from bumptious farce through black comedy all the way to solitary tragedy imbedded in the communal indifference with which Altman identifies America. However, Altman neither celebrates nor scolds this communal indifference, but instead accepts it as one of the conditions of existence. In this way his stock company never degenerates into a chorus line, but remains an anarchic agglomeration of lumpy loners. Lumpy but never too stony. There is give and take and need as when McCabe rushes upstairs to Mrs. Miller, now suddenly the last great love of his scheming life, and is told casually that she is occupied with a customer, and he stops awkwardly in his tracks, weighs the news with studied calmness on his swaying shoulders, all the while disguising the lover's face with the businessman's mask, but without bitterness or malice or wounded pride in any way diminishing the love he feels for a woman as open as he.

I disagree with those detractors of *McCabe* who argue that Altman imposes an anti-Establishment aura on the climactic gunfight. In my view Altman transforms what might have been parochial politics into universal poetics by shifting keys between the satire and the violence. I also disagree, however, with those defenders of *McCabe* who see Altman's achievement as the final nail in the coffin of the Western genre. Quite the contrary. The best moments in *McCabe* owe their majestic splendor to the moral integrity and psychological implacability of the Western genre. Ultimately, *McCabe & Mrs. Miller* shapes up as a half-baked masterpiece with a kind of gutsy grandeur. It's personal as all-get-out, and I thought that's what everyone had been screaming for all these years. Not more factory fakery like *Love Story* and *Airport*.

The Sense of Period
DAVID DENBY

The Western genre, usually quite conservative in its aesthetic and political values, has yielded some fascinating exceptions in recent years. I would guess that these are indirectly due to the war in Vietnam: The impossibility of telling the truth about the war in large-scale Hollywood films (which are financed by banks that are wary of political controversy) has produced a general desire among serious film-makers to tell the truth about the past, to discover a past which may be ugly but which is true. And so we have the phenomenon of the tendentious Western, films like Abraham Polonsky's *Tell Them Willie Boy Is Here* and Arthur Penn's *Little Big Man*—both half-crazed with disgust for treacherous, lying America and its myth-building popular culture. But for directors like Sam Peckinpah and now Robert Altman the past is not a field for simplified political-moral accusations or for analogies to the present. Instead, they are bringing to the Western genre a more complex sensibility and a more accurate feeling for period than we have ever seen before.

Altman's *McCabe & Mrs. Miller* is so unusual that it seems to have confused many people. Warner Brothers began by treating it as a failed mass entertainment and was astonished to discover that they had on their hands a successful minority movie, a work of movie art; some of the early reviews, however, were wildly hostile—the reviewers couldn't understand what Altman was up to and wrote about things that were in their own heads, not in the movie.

Like so many Westerns, *McCabe & Mrs. Miller* begins typically with a stranger riding into town, but everything else is different. The town is not the usual dusty outpost in the Southwest or the Plains, but a cold, sloppy, half-built clearing in the Northwestern wilderness near the Canadian border. The period is later than usual (1902), well after the heroic settling of the West, so the possibility of glamorous adventure has vanished and only the endless hard work is left. Finally, McCabe is not the conventionally taciturn gunfighter or ex-marshal, but a garrulous poseur who keeps his undistinguished past thoroughly obscured in order to create a mystique around himself while he carries out his small-time business ambitions.

As McCabe (Warren Beatty) moves through the low-ceilinged, smoky, buzzing little saloon, the viewer may recall the atmosphere of Altman's M*A*S*H. The mining town of Presbyterian Church is another rough, uncomfortable society, nearly all male, whose inhabitants work hard and take their pleasures when they can. The film is permeated with the special melancholy of minor physical discomfort—the feeling of never being quite warm enough or clean enough or well fed enough or surrounded by enough friendly people. The solace of such an existence lies in the rituals of male sociability: solemn poker games, cheap whiskey, endless, lunatic swearing, and the repetition of old stories and gossip. Besides these things a man hopes for an occasional bit of sex. In M*A*S*H the doctors' revenge against the hifalutin' nurse was so exactingly nasty because her snobbishness broke the circle of inclusive camaraderie and casual sex which formed the only defense against madness and loneliness. In the new film McCabe ministers to the health of the mining town and also makes money by establishing a whorehouse. The Western whorehouse has provided the occasion for considerable rib-poking whimsy in recent movies, but Altman is too smart for such a dull game. For the miserable little town the half dozen whores are a godsend, and the whorehouse becomes the center of affection, playfulness, and loyalty. The men are immensely grateful and treat the women well, and the women—lewd, half ugly, humorous—don't seem too unhappy in their service. Altman's point seems to be that in this semiwilderness, where the law and schools haven't arrived and family life is virtually impossible, there's not much "honest" work for a woman to do. The brothel scenes are rowdy but not brutal; with disapproval and self-consciousness both in abeyance, the concept of "sin" disappears into thin air and everyone has a vulgar good time. It is only McCabe who wants love, and his desire is tragic.

The conversation of men who work together in an office, a factory, or on a construction crew invariably falls into patterns of joking, complaining, and mock belligerency—talk which may not be necessary to the job but which creates the atmosphere of companionship that allows the job to get done. In this movie we often catch the fragments of such relationships; at first we may strain to hear more, but we soon realize that Altman doesn't want us to understand the specific words so much as he wants to convey the tenor of sociability, the non-purposive chatter, that gets people through the day. Rather than emphasize every bit of speech with close-ups, Altman generally holds the camera back from the actors, letting them improvise within a basic mood; since they have been living and working together for some time, a network of relationships has already been established which allows them to improvise without getting stuck or wandering off into non sequiturs. We get the feeling of a casual but definite familiarity among the characters, and this can't be done with a written-out script in which every line has its ineluctable dramatic function; nor can it be done in completely hang-loose situations (like Norman Mailer's films), in which a group of friends get together for a good time and hope that something will come out on the screen (usually it's a mess).

There is a central story in this thick texture of relationships, but we must work to get a hold on it; and even then we may find it elusive and subtle. The story concerns the sad affair between Warren Beatty as McCabe, the whorehouse proprietor, and Julie Christie as Mrs. Miller, his smart, tough madam. McCabe enters the film in great mystery, commandeers a saloon table with the authority of a born gambler, and immediately loses his money. He's a faker and a bumbler, a man who adopts the manner of some famous or legendary character of the old West, but who actually has the imagination and humor of a second-rate traveling salesman. Through most of the film he is stumbling around half drunk, dogged by his fantasies, and by reality, too, which finally closes in on him. It could be an ugly role, but Warren Beatty has the sense to make McCabe tremendously likable, restraining the mockery in his performance and giving the character genuine dignity in his passion and death.

It is the unfortunate fate of this limited man to fall in love with a woman much smarter than himself who constantly reminds him of his failure. But who could blame him? Julie Christie has one of the greatest movie faces since Garbo or the young Joan Crawford, and she brings an amazing intensity to a difficult part. Her Mrs. Miller is clever and hardheaded about practical affairs, but she is also preoccupied with an interior mental life that McCabe is not allowed to see. She is amused and touched by him, possibly she even loves him, but her feelings are waylaid by some mysterious inner assassin, and she cannot bring them out in the open; in the end, her love is cruelly inaccessible to McCabe. Trying to impress her with his boldness, he blunders into a deadly encounter with three hired killers, and unlike the sentimental finale of *High Noon*, his woman is not there to help or even to witness his courage—she gets stoned on opium to avoid the worst, and McCabe dies alone in a blizzard.

A large part of the emotional coloring of this movie is provided by Vilmos Zsigmond's photography and Altman's rugged outdoor compositions. Many movies have condescended to the past with an overly placid and perfect pictorialism that gives the audience the impression of quaintness. Here we get the impression of active and disorderly life. The movie is full of rough movement and physical sloppiness—rain, snow, mud, junk piles, and wooden buildings only half completed. It has the scraggy lyricism, the true lyricism of great nineteenth-century photographs, in which you feel the pathos of a country which is young and beautiful and already despoiled. In one stunning scene, McCabe rides slowly into town with three ugly prostitutes he has acquired for his whorehouse, and the sequence is lit from the back by the intensely orange-gold light of the early sun streaming through the trees. Unshaven, slovenly men come pouring out of structures whose freshly cut wooden frames are bright orange-gold in the sun, and they ogle at the girls, finally pulling them down from their horses. What might have been sentimental or merely harsh in Altman's film is saved by his juxtaposition of odd elements: The impassive physical loveliness and human warmth afford his "low" content a grave and permanent beauty.

DEEP END

ANDREW SARRIS

Jerzy Skolimowski has finally put it all together in *Deep End*: passion without hysteria, intelligence without derision, and compassion without special pleading. *Deep End* is the best of Godard, Truffaut and Polanski, and then some—nothing less, in fact, than a work of genius on the two tracks of cinema, the visual and the psychological. The title, for example, is poetically apt both as a still living figure of speech for the mental state of the fifteen-year-old protagonist (John Moulder-Brown) and as a literal description of the operative milieu in which the protagonist's mental state achieves its fatal expression. More important, the title reflects also Skolimowski's audacity in diving head-first into the deepest part of his own psyche. The film begins as if it might lead into the ant-in-a-jar sociological irony of Olmi's *Il Posto* or to a Grand Guignol of repression à la Polanski's *Repulsion*. But the very first bits of business between John Moulder-Brown's lower-class bathhouse attendant and Jane Asher's more experienced but no less vulnerable co-worker place us in the presence of a desire so fierce and so obsessive that no pat sociological or sexological formulas can be applied. Whereas *Carnal Knowledge* tries to tell us that every sexual encounter is the same old thing, *Deep End* reminds us that no two encounters are ever alike. Consequently, there is a marvelous give-and-take in *Deep End*, whereas in *Carnal Knowledge* it is all take and no give, all aggression and deception without the slightest trace of self-submergence or self-realization.

Still, too many of the reviewers have both misunderstood and underrated *Deep End* because of traditional bugaboos about mixed moods: not the studied alternations of pathos and whimsy in Chaplin and Fellini so much as the impetuous leaps from vaudeville to death in Renoir's *The Rules of the Game*, Truffaut's *Shoot the Piano Player*, Godard's *Pierrot le fou*, and, now, Skolimowski's *Deep End*. Part of the problem is a kind of suppressed class snobbery among supposedly humanistic film critics. Thus though the characters in *Deep End* have very real difficulties with money, these difficulties are in no way emotionally decisive, and, hence, the people involved cannot be reduced to problems for the liberal conscience. What the lack of money does is to force them into grotesque situations through which their passions flow unchecked. I don't want to describe these grotesque situations in any detail because they involve sight gags and visual rhythms and impulsive splashes of color and movement that should be experienced without detailed and diagrammed anticipation.

Skolimowski has always had the talent and humor for a *Deep End*. What he always seemed to lack was stylistic cohesion. After working on the script for Polanski's *Knife in the Water*, he made two films with himself in the lead: *Walkover* (knockabout fighter) and *Rysopis* (student draft dodger). I saw both movies at the Pesaro Film Festival in 1964 or 1965, and Skolimowski was there himself, speaking absolutely no English. Jean Douchet and some of the other French critics were very high on Skolimowski, but I really couldn't see why. I kept forgetting that he was Polish; his movies looked more like shaggy-dog pseudo-Kafkaesque exercises from the Czech cinema of that era. Skolimowski displayed nothing of Wajda's very formal expressionism, Has's theatrical grace, Munk's hard-potato irony, or Polanski's prankish absurdism. Thinking back, I suppose that his work must have had some kind of anarchic quality, although, of course, one critic's anarchy is another critic's chaos.

Of his two subsequent films, the Polish-made *Bariera* has always struck me as more appealing and accomplished than the Belgian-made *Le Depart* with that Truffaut–Godard troll, Jean-Pierre Léaud, in the lead. Although more fantastic on the surface, *Bariera* struck me as more realistic and necessity-ridden at the core. But his theme of anti-socialistic man lusting for the forbidden joys of the flesh and the senses has remained constant from the beginning. There was never really any place in the gray new world of Eastern Europe for a sybaritic temperament like Skolimowski's. He had to come west to the Free World where men and women create their own hells under the benign neglect of the System. Their own hells and their own rapturous downfalls.

Skolimowski is well served not only by Jane Asher and John Moulder-Brown but by Karl Michael Vogler as a multi-faceted sportsman, Erica Beer as a middle-aged bundle of repressed hostility and sensuality, Christopher Sandford as a cuckold before marriage and Diana Dors as a frightening reminder of what Marilyn Monroe might look like if she were alive today. Indeed, the behavioral resilience and resourcefulness of all the characters turns potentially embarrassing scenes into revelations of character. Also, the movie is marvelously original. You've seen whores, for example, with hearts of gold. And you've seen whores (yawn) without hearts of gold. But when, I ask you, have you ever seen a whore with a cast on her leg?

THE GO-BETWEEN

STANLEY KAUFFMANN

Some novels are remembered chiefly for their opening lines. Muriel Spark's *The Girls of Slender Means:* "Long ago in 1945 all the nice people in England were poor, allowing for exceptions." Even more memorable, L. P. Hartley's *The Go-Between:* "The past is a foreign country: they do things differently there." (Note that both these lines are nostalgic!) The latter is also the opening utterance, by an unseen speaker, in Joseph Losey's film of Hartley's novel.

And that's the most rewarding aspect of the film, its visit to a foreign country in which "we" once lived. That country is the summer of 1900—the time is the real geography. But the physical locality is a stately home in the English countryside near Norwich. Losey exploits so many details of costume and custom so well that we are plunged into the scale and rhythm and airiness of that home's upper-class life, so eternally secure for such a short eternity.

The story is of a doomed love affair as witnessed by a thirteen-year-old boy whose experience conveys the requisite information to us but who doesn't himself understand the matter until much later. The boy goes to stay with a school chum in the great house and is employed as a secret "postman" between the chum's older sister and a young farmer. The two are having an affair, despite the fact that the sister is engaged, to a lord.

Losey, like Visconti, whom he evidently admires, is good at crystalizing detail: the croquet, the hammock, the Sunday bell-ringers, the Sunday prayers in the household with the servants, the village cricket match, the Norwich market. It's an almost palpable re-creation of a past environment, and that environment is the film's real achievement, not the drama enacted within it. In fact, the "feel" is so fine that it increases our eventual disappointment: The picture comes at last to so little that we become a bit resentful of (let's call it) the build-up. If style and form are to be the content, very well; but then why pretend to content?

A great deal of nonsense has been written about Harold Pinter's screenplay. As a Pinter admirer I deplore his getting praise—as well as blame—he doesn't deserve. The dialogue has been garlanded with compliments for its rhythmic sensitivity, lyricism, and flavor. By my estimate, about 98 percent of the dialogue comes directly from Hartley's book. Pinter's job has been principally to select and compress in a manner no better or worse than several dozen other professionals might have done. The one exceptional touch is the way he has handled the narrator—the adult "today" who was the boy then. Hartley begins and ends with him; Pinter begins with the man's voice only, then slips in quick flashes of him, in the present, on a pilgrimage to his past. These flashes gradually become longer and more explicit, the man's face eventually becomes visible (Michael Redgrave), and at the end he has a brief scene with the heroine, now very old.

This is hardly an original device. Just one instance: Griffith used something like it in *Way Down East* (1920) to fix the point toward which his story was traveling before it got there. Here Pinter uses it very adroitly, making sure that all stops are pulled out for the *temps perdu* diapason.

Yet this adroitness, too, only adds to the ultimate thinness. What is this film about? Are we to be wrung by the stupidity of class barriers? Today? If the novel had been written by Henry Green or I. Compton-Burnett—let alone Lawrence or James—the resonance might have been immense; here it is shallow. Is it the *frisson* of the schoolboy "curse"? (The boy has a passion for witchcraft and concocts a curse. At the end the aged heroine says that her grandson, who is also the grandson of the farmer, seems to think he's under a curse.) But that's just a cheap vaudeville "snapper"—third-rate Saki.

There is only one small resolution for the story. The narrator is today an emotionally withered man, unmarried, presumably because of the events he witnessed as a child. ("You flew too near the sun and you were scorched.") Here Losey italicizes what Hartley left implicit and what Pinter simply took from Hartley in his (published) screenplay. In the film the discovery of the lovers *in flagrante delicto* is flagrant indeed. But what does *that* come to? Is this whole intricate story simply the explanation of the narrator's trauma? This gives it the specific gravity of any Hitchcock psycho-pathic film about a Liebes-trauma.

Most of the time Losey has directed it well, with much of his characteristic feline rhythm. He falls for the old pastoral cliché shots through waving grass in the foreground—but generally the camera moves and perceives with a kind of easy tension. Gerry Fisher's cinematography appreciates the materials, except for the sunny skies, which sometimes come out white, as in amateur snap-shots.

Margaret Leighton is first-class as the lady of the great house, filled with well-bred suspicion of her daughter, then with ire. As the father, Michael Gough is amusingly Olympian. Dominic Guard, the boy, has a nice homely face and is engaging. Alan Bates has sturdy composure as the farmer, though not much character. Also, he wears side whiskers and sometimes looks like Ringo Starr.

Julie Christie is the heroine and fails to supply the needed magic. First, she is prematurely losing her looks. Second, unlike Gough and Leighton and others in the film, she gives no conviction of gentility—that subject so dear to the working-class Pinter and the American Losey. If Leighton were young enough to play her own daughter, it would have been a more satisfactory film. (Leighton was originally scheduled for the role when the film was first planned by others, back in the mid-Fifties.) And Leighton, in her last scene as her aged self, would not have needed to have her voice dubbed by someone else, which I assume is what they did with Christie.

Still I wouldn't want to leave a last impression that this film is not worth looking at and listening to. At his best, in such films as *The Servant* and *Accident* and this one, Losey makes all the right artistic decisions except the fundamental ones. As the old joke has it, don't expect much and it won't disappoint you.

WALKABOUT

Jacob Brackman

Walkabout is the sort of spare, mythic tale people call "deceptively simple." They mean something more like *deeply* simple, for what lies beneath has less to do with complexity than with elemental configurations, wishes and fears, which bypass the intelligence. Director Nicolas Roeg plugs us back into our earliest and therefore most shared selves.

The most remarkable aspect of *Walkabout*'s simplicity is this: It does not contain enough information to understand it. Unless you come to it with some outside education, you cannot hope to make full sense of what you see. The title, for example, refers to an initiation ritual which every aborigine boy must undergo: three months alone in the rugged Australian outback, with no succor beyond his own wits and what primitive weapons he can fashion and carry. Only the smartest, hardiest boys pass through this arduous aboriginal bar mitzvah alive. So walkabout formalizes the adolescent's passage from childhood to adulthood at its literal extreme: If he remains a child, he cannot survive his walkabout; if he is not a man already, then he must become one or die. His fellow tribesmen need not know specifically of the trials he met and overcame. The mere fact of his return demonstrates his manhood. The protracted rite of passage affords the tribe a kind of enforced natural selection.

Now, I "understand" the word "walkabout"—can extrapolate its meanings in the film, as the title—because I found it explained in the screening invitation letter and again in the promotional notes distributed at the screening. Similarly, many moviegoers will get the gist of it from reviews, from friends who read reviews. Perhaps Twentieth Century-Fox will even decide to elucidate the title in their advertising. But within the film proper, no explanations can be found—not of the title nor of half a dozen other crucial developments. The explanations exist—*Walkabout* is scarcely intended as fantasy—but Roeg withholds them. That withholding constitutes a brilliant aesthetic decision. It makes all the difference. Inexplicably, then, an abo appears over the crest of a hill as a girl and her small brother are about to die of thirst and heat.

We saw them first, starched and uniformed, in school; glimpses of the city, Sydney; of their father, a businessman apparently; their mother at her housework. The father drove his children deep into the desert. The girl, fourteen, spread a blanket on the sand and laid out a picnic lunch. The boy, six, clambered behind some rocks firing at imaginary baddies with a toy pistol. The father, standing agitated by his Volkswagen, also had a gun, a real one. He drew a bead on his son and started shooting. The girl snatched her brother down behind the rocks and along a narrow ditch away from their father's shouts and bullets. The boy had no idea what was going on; the girl had just enough idea to appreciate the danger. Abandoning the direct murder of his children, but with the sure knowledge they could never find their way back to civilization alive, the father doused his car with gas, set it afire, and shot himself in the head. The girl shielded her brother from these events, but witnessed them herself. (They return to haunt the journey that follows.) Perfectly British, collected, controlled, she led her brother on a hopeless hike across vast desert.

After days, their meager food and drink used up, they came upon a tiny mudhole oasis. When that went dry overnight, neither had the strength to push on. So it is just then, all hope gone, that the young abo appears.

He has no way of divining how they came here. They have no way of divining how he came there. They need him, simply, and hitch up with him. He explains to them straight off about his walkabout, presumably, but he speaks only native dialect. No attempt is made, through subtitles or whatever, to render his meanings intelligible to us.

At first, the abo prepares to leave the brother and sister as casually as he happened upon them; she repeats to him their need for water, wa-ter, as though believing a slow and careful pronunciation of that easy word could not fail her. At last the small boy acts out drinking. Instantly, the abo catches his drift, grins, returns to the mudhole and sucks up drink through a reed. The girl never "understands" anything the abo says, nor can she get anything across to him directly. The abo never thinks to present an amiable face nor an engaged expression. The girl cannot relate to him.

From the start, the boy is the medium of communication between them. The two males make themselves understood to each other by means of mime and an implicit simpatico which allows them to chatter endlessly together, engrossed despite the fact that neither ever masters more than a word or two of the other's language.

There's a weather-research team in the desert and I feared for a bit that one of the international scientists would meet up with the three children and, chewing reflectively on his pipe, would start *explaining* everything for us: what walkabout consists in, why the aborigines stuff the father's corpse in a tree trunk, why the young abo paints and feathers himself and dances for the girl all night long and why, when she fails to respond, except with fear and embarrassment, he commits suicide. But the scientists never do encounter the children, and we are left to fathom such mysteries on our own, as best we can. Dimly, as the children themselves do. Their adventures remain as weird, at once as immediate and inaccessible, as the amazing reptiles of the outback. Reptiles, strange birds and insects frequently command the screen in gigantic close-ups, the better to remind us how unfamiliar with life we still are.

In childhood, one moves through the world without comprehending much. One asks about things, certainly, but mostly one simply takes in, without asking, without "understanding," never able to articulate what's happening. *Walkabout* lulls us back into this state, where so much is not comprehended one cannot imagine where to begin one's questions. Where one feels at home with confusion. Tiny and isolated in our seats amid rows of seats, we gaze up at the huge figures on the screen and somewhere remember likewise gazing up at the then fabulous adults who inhabited our infant worlds.

Natural Mannerisms

STEFAN KANFER

Ever since Rousseau's *Social Contract*, the Noble Savage has been neither noble nor savage. Instead he has become a symbol, a stick with which "civilized" man beats himself. Has the city become a jungle? The Noble Savage's jungle is a city in the peaceable kingdom of man and nature. Does civilized man murder for sport? The native, like a lion, kills only what he needs. Is the intellect responsible for evil? The natural man does not think with his brain but with his glands—and by his actions exhibits a moral vigor.

This imaginary fraudulent creature has animated a great deal of escape fiction, from *Robinson Crusoe* to *Little Big Man*. Taken lightly, he is an object of literary curiosity. Written about seriously, he is preposterous. *Walkabout* makes the disastrous mistake of treating an aborigine not as a man but as a god.

An Australian father takes his two children for a picnic in the country. Minutes later he commits a lurid and unmotivated suicide. The teenage girl (Jenny Agutter) and her little brother (Lucien John) abruptly find themselves at the mercy of the outback, their only companion a sputtering portable radio. Ironies thereupon crowd the air like static: The instrument crackles with irrelevant news of the world while the two urbanized refugees fight elemental dread.

Meantime, a bushman (an authentic one named David Gumpilil) fearlessly traverses the country—the sky his ceiling, the air his blanket—boomeranging lizards and kangaroos in order to eat. Stumbling upon the lost souls, this natural man guides them through his Eden. *Walkabout* suddenly becomes a lyric travelogue, assaulting the harsh Flinders mountain ranges, trailing the little camels of the red desert near Alice Springs, mooning under the blooming quandong tree. Director Nicolas Roeg, who made his reputation as a cinematographer (*Fahrenheit 451, Far from the Madding Crowd, Petulia*), shows a precise and delicate Down Understanding. But give him anything human, and he seems as naïve as a third-former.

The camera cannot confront a grown Caucasian without making him a rapacious stock villain, nor can it present the savage as anything but an improbably heroic amalgam of Friday, Chingachgook and St. Francis. A pity. The cast are an attractive lot and, as some lyrically nude bathing scenes demonstrate, Miss Agutter possesses one of the lithest, blithest young bodies on public view. Were the eye the only judge, *Walkabout* might be considered a treat. But no, Roeg and his scenarist Edward Bond (*Blow-Up*) aim for the mind and miss wildly. Their preachy, anti-intellectual Natural Mannerisms are neither convincing nor new.

THE MUSIC LOVERS

False Notes

STEFAN KANFER

The Love That Dared Not Speak Its Name is allowed to shriek and bluster in *The Music Lovers*. The lovers are Muscovite aesthetes and neurasthenics; the music is supplied by Peter Ilyich Tchaikovsky, a doubly tragic figure. In nineteenth-century Russia, where homosexuality was punishable by imprisonment, the composer sought to "cure" himself by marriage. Instead, he became party to an unconsummated charade. But his encounters with other men left him with ineradicable self-disgust.

Seventy-seven years have passed since Tchaikovsky's death. In this epoch of emancipated morality, it would be reasonable to expect that his life would be reviewed with fresh empathy. But no; the same malignant attitudinizing that might have been applied decades ago is still at work.

Tchaikovsky (Richard Chamberlain) is first observed in the bed of his lover, Count Anton Chiluvsky. As played by Christopher Gable, the count is a vaudevillain complete with waxed mustache and leer. Tchaikovsky, fleeing from scandal, marries the nymphomaniacal Nina Ivanovna (Glenda Jackson). The outcome is nearly homicidal. (One night, wrote the tormented composer, "I was within a hair-breadth of succumbing to that blind, unreasoning, diseased loathing that ends in murder.") Tchaikovsky suffers a series of breakdowns. Nina ends her life in a sanitarium, hopelessly insane.

As the madwoman, Glenda Jackson does not damage her reputation so much as caricature it. In *Women in Love* she was the feminine soul brought beyond the melting point. Here again she writhes in agonies of longing, but her yowling and rug scratching are more reminiscent of feline heat than feminine misery. As for the composer, Chamberlain has the appearance and emotional range of an Aubrey Beardsley faun. After he gambols through the woods, one expects to find tiny cloven hoofprints.

But the cast has little significance in *The Music Lovers*. Its arch tableaux, its unstable amalgam of life and art, make it a director's picture. In *Women in Love*, Ken Russell turned D. H. Lawrence into tinted steam. In *The Music Lovers*, he makes Tchaikovsky step to the Dance of the Sugarplum Inverts. Women are thoughtless children or carnivores. Men are smirking androgynes or long-faced straight men like Modeste, Peter's brother. A classic exchange has Peter saying, "*Sixth Symphony, Opus 74*. It's too cold." Replies Modeste: "I'll give you a title—'The Pathetic.' "

Attempting to reveal psychology through music, Director Russell makes every character grotesque, every bar of music programmatic. Ballets are transformed into pastoral scenes, concertos into imaginary duels. In a crescendo of vulgarity, the *1812 Overture* becomes, in Tchaikovsky's beleaguered brain, an execution. Each cannon shot lops off the head of a tormentor: sister (Sabina Maydelle), patron, lover.

No matter how miserable his actual life, the classical composer tends to suffer in a new way on film. Cornel Wilde as Chopin in *A Song to Remember*; Stewart Granger as Paganini in *The Magic Bow*; Toralv Maurstad as Grieg in *Song of Norway*—all were grotesque travesties. Thus *The Music Lovers* is merely the latest entry in the continuing series Great Lives Trivialized.

THE DEVILS

Horror Show in a Convent

RICHARD SCHICKEL

Trade secret: reviewers sometimes make an emotional commitment to a director for reasons they cannot reasonably explain. There is just something in the man's style or sensibility that appeals to you and you find yourself defending, overpraising, when common sense dictates a strategic advance to the rear.

So it has been with me ever since I saw Ken Russell's *Song of Summer*, a television biography of the composer Delius, originally produced by the BBC and shown here—repeatedly—by NET. It

seemed to me the only great study of the process of creation and
the psychology of genius that we've ever had on film, palpable evidence that the man who made it was himself an extraordinary talent. This was a belief that flickered and sometimes flared brilliantly
as one studied the ambiguous success of *Women in Love*, the ambiguous failure of *The Music Lovers*. Conceding Russell's excesses,
I still couldn't get over the idea that we were in the presence of an
artist with a natural gift for his medium greater than that of any of
his contemporaries and a man with the courage to work very close
to the edge of madness—as his favorite subjects did. It was exhilarating, controversial and, more than once, stomach-churning.

Disgust was certainly one of the emotions Russell sought to in-
duce. But it was only one, and it appeared in a context that was
often ironic, sometimes pitiful and always balanced by scenes of
really heart-stopping beauty. In *The Devils*, his latest film, there is
nothing but disgust. He fills every frame with it, gives us no example of human decency or intelligence as a reference point. The
result is a film that is the *reductio ad absurdum* of the current
belief that the more revolting a work is the closer it comes to the
truth about the human condition, the closer it comes to being art
of a high order. In this scheme of values, the more middle-class
people who walk out before the end, the more the integrity of the
work is confirmed.

As you no doubt know, this "property" began life as a historical
footnote unearthed by Aldous Huxley and published in the 1950's
as *The Devils of Loudun*. In that admirably sober work he re-
counted, in almost case-study fashion, the story of a convent
peopled by sexually repressed women, none of whom apparently
had a true religious vocation, overtaken by mass hysteria and insisting that they were possessed by devils, whose agent was the local
priest, a libertine liberal named Urbain Grandier. Their temporary
insanity suited the purposes of Grandier's political and theological
enemies, and he was tortured and burned at the stake as a result.
At the time the work seemed, in addition to being an interesting
curiosity, a rough—though uninsistent—parable about McCarthy-
ism, which was fair enough.

But that was only its beginning as a palimpsest on which to impose the intellectual concerns of the moment. By the 1960's, when
John Whiting's stage version appeared, Grandier had been transformed into an existential hero of sorts. He was flawed in the fashionable modern manner—thus, to the impressionable at least, a

satisfactorily ambiguous hero—but a reasonable man standing up nobly in opposition to unreason: a sort of sexy man for all seasons. Pretty obvious, I thought, but still respectable.

But here we are in the Seventies; and though vestiges of Whiting's Grandier still cling to Oliver Reed's performance, the fact is that he and the ladies of the convent have become nothing but an excuse for a horror show. There's a plague, which gives Russell the opportunity to show us running sores—and the remedy of leeching —in close-up. There are orgies, there are attempts to purge the nuns of their devils by enemas, there are tortures and burnings and homosexual revels and just plain human faces, so ugly in their slavering venality that we want to turn away from them too. Then, finally, there is just emptiness, a sort of numb objectivity that is a last resort for those who don't vote on this movie with their feet. It is not a mood that encourages emotional involvement, a caring search for human or historical parallels.

All one can do is ask, with the sympathy born of past pleasure: why? Why this waste of talent? Why this perversion of a rare gift? Why this insistence that despair, which is proper to our time (or any time), must be pushed over into black hopelessness? It is becoming a middle-brow convention at least as boring as finding Joe McCarthy under Cardinal Richelieu's cassock and no more productive of moving, lasting art.

UNE FEMME DOUCE

The Ignored Bresson

PHILIP T. HARTUNG

The arrival of a Robert Bresson film new to this country is for many of us a cause for huzzahs. But for a larger number of moviegoers it is only a so-what occasion. I can think of few other film-makers of distinction whose works have been so bypassed even by thoughtful audiences for whom they were intended. So it is to be hoped that his current release *Une Femme Douce* (called in some English-speaking countries *A Gentle Creature*) and its maker will win the attention they deserve.

Right from the beginning, uncompromising Bresson proved a problem to his commercial distributors, although with his first two feature films well-known writers collaborated with director Bresson in writing his scripts. Jean Giraudoux wrote the dialogue for *Les Anges du Péché* (1943) and Father R. L. Bruckberger served as religious adviser on this story concerned with nuns and convent life. Jean Cocteau wrote the dialogue for *Les Dames du Bois de Boulogne* (1945), a complicated love story with a Paris social background. While these two films won some praise from critics, they were box-office failures. And it was five years before Bresson made his next picture.

The tremendous success of *Diary of a Country Priest* (1950) after Bresson's years of struggling along has always reminded me of Emily Dickinson's poem about the little gentian that tried to be a rose and failed, and all the summer laughed. "But just before the snows there came a purple creature that ravished all the hill; and summer hid her forehead and mockery was still." At the poem's end, the poet asks, "Creator, shall I bloom?"

With *Diary of a Country Priest* Bresson bloomed in a big way. He wrote the script himself (from the novel by Georges Bernanos) and never used collaborators again—although he sometimes based his plots on known works. In stunning black-and-white photography, *Diary* tells the sad story of an intensely sincere young priest who fails to win his parishioners; they prefer to adjust religion to their own modes of life instead of following any rules of conduct laid down by their strict pastor. The young curé becomes unpopular and then ill. When he dies, we realize his death is a form of escape from the mean-spirited people he tried to help.

Escape is often a theme for Bresson, and his next film, *A Condemned Man Escapes* (1956), is an intellectual thriller that concentrates on the planning and execution of a Frenchman's escape from his Gestapo captors. Interestingly, we hardly see the Germans at all, but we get to know the prisoner well—and we become him as *we* escape.

I found myself quite cool to Bresson's next movie, *Pickpocket* (1959), probably because the non-actor in the title role was so unconvincing that the story itself didn't seem very interesting. It is obvious in *Pickpocket* that Bresson's insistence on using nonprofessionals does not always work. The only other Bresson film I did not care for is *Au Hasard Balthazar* (1966), and this was because a donkey plays the main character and animal stories are just not my dish of tea. Even as a child I avoided *Black Beauty* and *Dog of Flanders*. *Balthazar*, which was highly praised by many critics, is no doubt meant to be an allegory about man's cruelty. I found it a bore. No doubt donkey-lovers loved it.

While some critics were cool to Bresson's 1962 *The Trial of Joan of Arc*, I was most enthusiastic and liked it even better than Carl Dreyer's *Passion of Joan of Arc*. Bresson wrote his script from the transcript of the trial itself, and we realize from it that Joan was not just an illiterate country lass. Bresson's Joan conducts herself well, and we feel as we watch the film: This is a woman, this is a saint—something we never feel from Dreyer's endless close-ups.

The heroine of Bresson's current picture, *Une Femme Douce*, is also a real woman, but no saint. The film opens with her suicide; and flashbacks show us what led up to it. It is a touching and bitter story, first showing the penniless young woman pawning a few last treasures, winning the attention of the pawnbroker, and, after a brief (almost no) courtship, marrying him. The marriage is a disaster; and their middle-class lives together become dull and uninspired. Bresson's austere direction portrays their lack of companionship perfectly.

As usual, Bresson uses non-professional actors, and the portraits by the two leads are excellent: Dominique Sanda as the pretty young wife who dreams of better things; Guy Fragin as the stuffy husband who doesn't understand his wife at all. Even as the camera departs from the flashbacks from time to time and returns to the present with the dead wife on the bed and the husband standing or kneeling beside her, we realize that the husband still does not understand what happened or how he failed his wife.

Une Femme Douce is Bresson's first film in color, and he uses it beautifully. This one, like most of Bresson's pictures, does not make it easy for audiences. But we are well rewarded for attending and paying close attention.

DRIVE, HE SAID

Petrified Pretensions
JAY COCKS

Drive, He Said is a bush-league disaster that might have passed unnoticed, and perhaps unmade, but for the participation of Jack Nicholson. His much touted performance in *Easy Rider* won him the chance to make a movie almost literally all his own: he collaborated on the scenario for *Drive, He Said*, then directed and co-produced it. While other fledgling directors would be allowed to fail in comparative privacy, Nicholson's reputation makes his failure agonizingly public.

Nominally about the spiritual agonies of a basketball star at a large university, the movie makes several elaborate feints at symbolism, then quickly collapses under the weight of its petrified pretensions. Nicholson seems to be after a kind of existential melodrama: The basketball player frozen by his own spiritual malaise, with his roommate, the campus radical who goes mad in the last reel, representing the inevitable result of purposeful action in an insane world. But the film is too incoherent to sustain such interpretations. The action sways sloppily between the ballplayer and the radical, straddling an unwieldy subplot concerning the ballplayer's romance with a bitchy, nymphy faculty wife.

Nicholson manages a few nice touches. A scene of attempted rape late in the film conveys just the right feeling of psychotic tension. There is also a funny, if by now familiar, freak-out at the draft board and a shrewd performance by Bruce Dern as the basketball coach. Nicholson is not so fortunate with the other actors. Michael Margotta is scruffy and strident as the radical, William Tepper adenoidal in the role of the basketball player. Karen Black, playing the faculty wife, offers only a dreary variation on her basic *Five Easy Pieces* performance. It should be pointed out that the title of Nicholson's movie, and the Jeremy Larner novel before it, is derived from a fine short poem by Robert Creeley, which ends "drive, he sd, for/christ's sake, look/out where yr going." It is a pointed, challenging caution that Nicholson badly needs to heed.

JACOB BRACKMAN

The characters in *Drive, He Said,* Jack Nicholson's first film as a director, seem intensely real, although in an entirely non-documentary way. Another dimension of realness exists at the outer limits of recognizable personality types: a realness of distilled essence. Occasionally, you encounter pure "types" in real life, people who seem to embody a terse definition absolutely, in every extenuating detail. Such people are what they are so unambiguously that if an actor were assigned to portray, say, a ruthless-executive-on-the-make, or a sensitive-poet-locked-inside-his-shell, or whatever, you could say to the actor, "Go hang around so-and-so for a few days, study his moves, get him down to his last mannerism, his last inflection, and that's all you'll need. You'll be perfect."

It's no secret that the run of movies nowadays which trade in these "essential types" are bad movies. *Drive* is likely to be mistaken for a bad movie by those who mistake its archetypes for "stock" types, or "stereotypes," like the people in *Joe.* A "type" comes into play most often because he's as close as the film-maker can come to creating a believable person. Many film-makers just aren't clever enough to distinguish a character, to particularize him, not even simple-mindedly, by writing an odd malapropism into his vocabulary, or by casting an actor with a speech impediment or a blotchy purple birthmark over half his face. Particularizations may be intended to camouflage a character's type-hood; to set him off by easy complexities, to warn us, disingenuously, against presuming too quickly to understand him. Conversely, as in *Drive,* they may be intended to *underscore* a character's type-hood, not to deviate from an essence but to manifest it in perfect miniature.

Any one character from *Drive* could appear unchanged in a naturalistic film—he would be the most *extreme* personality there represented, doubtless, but he would be sufficiently detailed and true to himself—to his own extremity, if you will—to fit in anyhow. Just as an archetype or two can fit in at an actual party. What gives *Drive* its fantastical quality is that *all* its characters are "real" in this archetypical dimension. It seems that Nicholson chose the Campus Turmoil genre—a genre which proved itself bankrupt before producing a single illuminating film—precisely in order to assemble these divergent types, inspired cartoons, and allow their polarized essences to collide abrasively. He was after the resultant sparks, evidently, and sparks do fly.

Michael Margotta (who looks like an East Village version of Nicholson himself) plays Gabriel, the compleat psychedelic radical. His righteous Yippie riffs grow madder as Speed and fatigue build together inside him. A bearded professor of guerrilla theater, determined to outbizarre his students, tells Gabriel to flunk his Army physical by non-stop farting. But Gabriel reasons that the draft net has tightened since the professor's day. He's not even willing to risk *acting* crazy. He sees his survival at stake; only *being* crazy will guarantee him survival. And before long his amphetamine popping and marathon sleeplessness (on top of rough times with police and the military) do produce some classic paranoid symptomatology.

In between following Gabriel's escalating outfreakage, we get to know his roommate Hector (William Tepper), an All-American basketball star fumbling with some quieter crises of his own. One of the earliest shots in the film shows Gabriel watching a basketball game on TV, surrounded by other hippie guerrillas, his face nearly lost in hair, rapping. But as soon as we see the roommates alone together, we realize that their polarization—longhair versus athlete —is nowhere near so clear-cut as the opening images implied. They *both* have long hair. To Gabriel, the revolutionary prophet, playing basketball is an idiotic cop-out—"staying after school in your underwear." To Hector, it's not all that defensible, either— nothing remotely gung-ho, sis-boom-bah. Hector just likes to play basketball, that's all. He's good at it and it makes him feel good. In his own ambling, droopy-lidded style he connects to the System no better than Gabriel. No visions of apocalypse inflame his imagination, to be sure; his disaffection has not yet reached that advanced stage. Perhaps it never will. But neither does he believe in what he's been taught about how the Game Is Supposed to Be Played.

Probably Hector will turn pro. He cannot think of a decent alternative. But he's losing heart. He can no longer get himself up for the old college try. He has nothing but contempt for the shucks of organized sports: the inane post-game TV interviews; the slick hustlers in the front office; the inedible, overpriced hot dogs at the stadium. But what else can he do with himself? He's a Greek major. When he mentions that, he laughs.

Meanwhile, Hector's life has been complicated by several further relationships. He's entangled in a maddening affair with a professor's bored wife, Olive (Karen Black), the sort who lies moping abed, takes ballet, toys with a young man's affections for a bit of added distraction. He's her puppet on a string. Olive's professor husband is the perfect impotent intellectual, baffled by his wife's caprice, invariably paralyzed by the pros and cons of any issue which cries out to be resolved straightway from the heart. Hector's basketball coach (Bruce Dern) seems possessed by a desire to win so keen as to border on the pathological. Dern brilliantly fleshes out those actual coaches one sees pacing the sidelines during televised college basketball games—twitching with agitation inside his Ivy coat and tie, shouting corny exhortations onto the court, conferring, decreeing substitutions with a tense slap on a bench warmer's fanny. As much as Hector is detached, the coach is fully concentrated, fully into basketball—not the poetry of the game but the contest itself. He devotes himself to the clichés of sport—giving a piece of yourself, caring, fighting, never saying die—with every ounce of his being.

Since each of these extreme characters is always himself—his "type"—to the nth degree, Nicholson can achieve one exquisitely dramatic confrontation after another by bringing them on screen in various combinations. Each character in *Drive* is on a trip all his own. Any casual meeting among them is potentially melodramatic, conflagratory. Each has adopted a distinctive, highly defined posture toward the disorder of modern American life. So each scene sets off its own little fireworks display.

TWO-LANE BLACKTOP

Three for the Road

PAUL D. ZIMMERMAN

Even before its current release, *Two-Lane Blacktop* had been the object of extraordinary pressures. *Esquire* magazine boomed it as the film of the year and printed its screenplay in toto.

For months, movie people in and out of Universal studios have been heralding this latest road film as the ultimate new movie and Monte Hellman as the great underground director only now getting the chance he should have merited on the basis of two Western quickies he made in 1965 which were seen in the U.S. only on television.

The movie itself, however, is a modest effort—with much to be modest about. It is the ultimate *now* picture, a celluloid summary of every trend in current cinema—the well-traveled metaphor of the car race as a search for the self; the wandering hero cut loose from mainstream society; the concentration on the super-cool codes of the youth culture; the rock hero as movie star—in this case soft rocker James Taylor and Dennis Wilson of the Beach Boys; and the all too common critique of dominant American values like winning and striving.

Director Hellman plays against his material, which saves his film from crushing its audience with all its contemporary paraphernalia. At no point does the movie insist on its messages or indulge its interests. Instead, Hellman turns the voltage so low that one is tempted to take the film's pulse to see whether the projector is still rolling.

Taylor, looking like Prince Valiant with a woman's eyes, and Wilson, as his mechanic and buddy, cruise the country seeking out drag races at which their souped-up Chevy can bring home enough bacon to fuel them for a few more miles. On the way they pick up a young button-nosed drifter, Laurie Bird. They are a strange race, these three in the car, the cool new breed of young people who signal instead of talking—a back rub means a night in bed, a simple shake of the head cancels a life together, a shrug and a few steps lead to a change of partners.

Hellman does not ask much from any of his amateurs. He is showing young people whose silence sequesters their feelings from the possibilities of pain, so Taylor, Wilson and Bird don't have to act, only emote a sense of stifled self. Warren Oates, as the half-mad loner who seeks a sense of purpose by challenging Taylor to a race from the Southwest to Washington, D.C., thrives in this amateur company. He steals what there is of the picture almost by default—croaking and chattering amiably to the music of his car stereo, spouting fresh fantasies for each new hitchhiker, grinning popeyed at his own sass.

Out of Hellman's vision of life as a rite of passage measured in motels and hamburgers, symbols tentatively take shape. The cross-country competition turns into a cooperative effort at survival. Laurie Bird becomes increasingly the winner's prize—and, when she takes flight with a stranger, the sense of the competition collapses. Winning is nothing without caring, the story implies ever so gently.

But neither are stories worth much without caring—and this is where *Two-Lane* finally fails. Hellman's heroes remain insulated from us by their own failures to feel. We are part of the world they pass through invisibly—and so they remain as foreign and opaque as ever.

EL TOPO

Is El Topo *a Con?*

VINCENT CANBY

One of the most successful films now playing in New York hasn't even opened here yet. That is, officially. It's a Mexican film called *El Topo* (The Mole), and it's a two-hour-plus, surreal fantasy, which, since New Year's, has been playing midnight shows (1 A.M. on Fridays and Saturdays) at the Elgin Theater, on Eighth Avenue near 19th Street. With a handful of reviews in the underground press and none to speak of in the straight press, the film has been attracting capacity audiences, many of whose members are apparently repeaters who come back to turn on and to be turned on.

The film's local sponsor, Douglas Films, and the management of the Elgin have done practically no formal advertising. When they are extravagant, they add to the regular Elgin ads the tagline: "*El Topo* at midnight." Even so, there has become attached to *El Topo* the sort of multi-leveled chic that makes it a required experience for the experience-collecting young, and that has, on a couple of occasions, I'm told, practically emptied Elaine's at that point in the evening when the more aged merrymakers face the alternatives of either going home or getting into fights at the bar.

Clearly, all of this is the result of extraordinary word-of-mouth, that mysterious phenomenon that once turned *Abie's Irish Rose* into one of the greatest hits the American theater has ever known and that, more recently, transformed *Airport* into the biggest money-making movie of 1970. *El Topo* is by way of being this year's underground *Airport*, the sort of film that appears to render film criticism superfluous—which always sounds like a swell idea until I see the film that is supposed to score this cultural breakthrough. *El Topo* is no exception, and when I saw it early one recent Saturday morning, I was about equally torn between my wonder at the uncritical reverence with which the Elgin audience received the film and my impulse to say something loud and rude.

I must admit at this point that I approached the movie with mixed emotions. After all, I had just read the review by Steven Fuller in *Changes*, in which he said, among other things, that: "*El Topo* is a masterpiece as much as it is a testament to one man's genius in this decaying world. Director [Alexandro] Jodorowsky has implanted deliberately almost every conceivable symbol system known to intellectual man. . . . Each man reads what he wants to into the film. A. J. Weberman reads Dylan and revolutionary politics into it, as he does into everything. The reviewer from *Rolling Stone* reads his own ineptitude into the film by his inability to use his eyes. . . ."

I certainly didn't want to read my own ineptitude in the movie, nor was I exactly keen on seeing some kind of reflection of my mind's weaknesses, Glenn O'Brien, in *The Village Voice*, had said: "[Jodorowsky's] art is too violent for the most violent nation in history. The hero is too proud, too self-conscious, and asks too many questions. But it is this very repulsion that *El Topo* elicits, this confusion that it reveals in weak minds, which makes it a work of cinematic cruelty, a weapon of spiritual revolution. . . ."

Has *El Topo* really rendered film criticism superfluous, or is it spawning a kind of fascistic film criticism that hopes to strong-arm the opposition with suggestions of reflected ineptitude and confused minds?

I'd hazard the guess that a certain amount of the pro-criticism and of the pro-audience reaction generally is itself the result of calculated intellectual intimidation within the film itself, which has four acts subtitled "Genesis," "Prophets," "Psalms" and "Apocalypse." Now no movie that has the surface sheen of one of Sergio Leone's superior, made-in-Almeira Westerns (and at least three times as much simulated blood and cruelty) can easily be described as meaningless when its first act is Genesis. That, at least, seems to be the name of this game. It is not enough, however, to say that because every man can read into a movie what he wants, the movie is an artistic meta-experience. One might just as well isolate Nathan's, on the corner of Broadway and 43rd Street, and invite the rest of us to take a trip on our various, totally subjective responses to the sights of spilt clam chowder and coagulating mustard and the smells of hot dogs coming down to room temperature.

At this point, I suppose, I should backtrack to describe *El Topo*, which was written, directed and co-produced by Jodorowsky, who also plays its title role. El Topo is a mythic gunman who looks very much like Clint Eastwood's Man with No Name but whose barrenly beautiful desert landscape seems to have been borrowed from Fellini and stocked with images—such as the one of a bandit sucking on the toe of a lady's slipper—used earlier and better by Buñuel. Jodorowsky is, I'm told, a Chilean, in his early forties, who has had considerable success as a stage director in Mexico City and whose first film, *Fando and Lis*, an adaptation of the Arrabal play, was released here last year. I somehow missed *Fando and Lis*, but the last paragraph of Roger Greenspun's review of that film could also apply to Jodorowsky's latest effort: "For all of its invocations of theater of cruelty, *Fando and Lis* hardly ever scares up anything stronger than unpleasant whimsy."

It isn't that *El Topo* is not about anything, but rather that it's about too much. Inventorying it is like sorting out the contents of a turkey buzzard's stomach: There is very little that's not there, but nothing much has been digested. To start with we are told—by a title card—that the mole spends its life burrowing tunnels upward toward the sun, and that, when he sees the sun, he is often blinded. As moles are blinded, so once were Icarus's wings melted —and we are off into the sort of movie that is so full of symbology that we appreciate occasional, fleeting views of plain old landscapes with nothing in them. There is, after a while, only so much that nothing can mean.

In "Genesis," El Topo rides a black stallion across the desert with his small naked son hanging on behind him. They come upon a village whose citizens have been massacred by bandits, and El Topo sets out to take revenge on the gang, which is led by a colonel who is probably God. God is eventually castrated by El Topo, His Son. In "Prophets," El Topo, who has abandoned his son to the monks, and is now accompanied by Woman more evil than Eve, undergoes a series of epic trials in his quest for knowledge, physical perfection and spiritual salvation. He succeeds in each through deception and murder, then he dies (is it in "Psalms"?), only to be resurrected in "Apocalypse," for another series of adventures that lead back to the beginning of the film.

God, original sin, Catholicism, Zen, Lao-tse, Christ, the conventions of movie Westerns, Ulysses and his Odyssey, aphorisms ("My butterfly net is stronger than your gun." "Perfection is to get lost")—they're all there, in a movie that is all guts (quite literally) but that has no body to give the guts particular shape or function. The movie has no life of its own. Jodorowsky is not interesting or inventive enough as a film-maker to restructure reality, as, say, Buñuel does in his surreal classic, *L'Age d'Or*. He simply enumerates, catalogues, and I can believe Fuller's rather awed statement in his review in *Changes* that Jodorowsky's library "contains thousands of volumes covering every imaginable subject and literary period." He could be the William Randolph Hearst of the movie intellect and *El Topo* his rather grotesque, ego-salving San Simeon.

Much has been made of Jodorowsky's excessive cruelties, as if the depiction of a world soaked in crimson paint, and in which faces disintegrate before our eyes in all sorts of fancy photographic effects, had some sort of cleansing effect ("a spiritual revolution," O'Brien calls it). The fundamental effect, however, is one of elaborate, expensive movie mechanics. How does he do it!

A number of underground critics have compared *El Topo* to *Satyricon*, which is natural enough, I guess, since Jodorowsky outdoes Fellini in his fondness for freaks—pinheads, amputees, humpbacks, and the like—but because the movie is without fundamental order it never succeeds in becoming anything more than a high-class sideshow. Instead of the theater of cruelty, we have an amateur theatrical of the absurd. It is also, for all of its violence, rather prim and passionless, which is partially obscured by the director's fancy camerawork. However, it's his use of things like zooms and stately pans, and his fondness for Busby Berkeley-like overhead shots, that deny Jodorowsky's real interest in "almost every conceivable symbol system known to intellectual man." It's as if he didn't trust the austerity of his vision (as Buñuel does) and felt compelled to hoke it up.

The movie isn't all bad. There are a few genuinely funny and terrifying moments, such as one sequence in which four bandits set out to rape four not exactly pure monks. Then, also, the Mexican Government apparently would like to disown the film on the grounds that it's anti-Catholic. It was invited to compete at the Cannes Festival, now in progress, but the Mexican authorities reportedly refused to sanction its official showing, as a result of which it is being exhibited at the festival unofficially.

I have the feeling that the Mexican authorities are a little like the members of the Elgin audience with whom I saw the film. I was amazed when, at the end of the screening, there was so little audience response. I would have assumed that a film with this much underground reputation would have prompted cheers. There was some desultory applause, but most of the people around me seemed to want to be told whether it was good or bad, if not what it really meant. It's difficult, especially at three o'clock in the morning, to admit that you've been conned. Instead, like all those people who were taken in by the Duke and the Dauphin and their Royal Nonesuch, the audiences march out of the Elgin and urge their friends to go. It would be a terrible mistake, I suspect, to show the movie at an earlier hour.

THE LAST MOVIE

Hollis Alpert

If cooler heads had prevailed in our film industry, the financial and, to a degree, the artistic success of *Easy Rider* would have been regarded as a fortuitous happenstance, perhaps as *The Sound of Music* of the head set. Instead, the boys involved with the making of the picture, notably Dennis Hopper, Peter Fonda, and Jack Nicholson, were at once raised to prophetic status and handed the wherewithal to steer our films of the Seventies on the true and righteous path. All three have now turned in their pictures, and what, then, has been begotten? Jack Nicholson directed *Drive, He Said*, an ugly, meandering ode to a discontented basketball star. Fonda gave us a mystical little Western, starring himself, called *The Hired Hand*. And presently we have Dennis Hopper's

The Last Movie, which is claimed to be an allegory "concerning the destruction of innocence."

Just what or whose innocence is being destroyed in this sorry cinematic mélange is impossible to determine; my own guess is that the reference is to whoever allocated the million or more dollars required to mount what we might loosely call the production. Presumably there was a script, for credit is given to Stewart Stern for its writing, and presumably there was also a story to begin with, since credit for that is allocated to Mr. Stern and Mr. Hopper. What appears on the screen, however, all but defies linear description, and here I am deliberately playing into Hopper's hands, or maybe head, for clearly his intent is to be non-linear, to evoke a multileveled film experience having to do with the making of a stock Western in Peru and its effects on the natives and on one film cowboy (Hopper). But I find myself trying to straighten the film out, to clarify it, when what happens on the screen leaves mainly a residue of bewilderment.

At any rate, the time is presumably the past, present, and future, and there are flashbacks, dreams, flashforwards, and all the tricky stuff so beloved by the "new" movie-makers. Bits and pieces do now and then connect with the viewer, but whenever order is about to emerge from disorder, Hopper interrupts and flashes on the screen a title: SCENE MISSING. More appropriate would have been: SENSE MISSING.

THE HIRED HAND

STANLEY KAUFFMANN

The Hired Hand is seriously flawed but serious, and well worth seeing. It opens with a blurred-focus, slow-motion shot of a stream with one man fishing and another swimming naked. When a film opens with a "lyrical" shot, your heart has a right to sink. But the subject (two men) and the visual tenor turn out to be very much a part of this film. The camera "arias" are integrated most of the time with what the work is after.

Peter Fonda is one of a trio of footloose wanderers in the old West. One of them is murdered for his horse. Fonda and the other pal, Warren Oates, take some revenge, then head back to Fonda's long-abandoned wife and child on a farm—something Fonda had been planning to do anyway, since he's tired of drifting.

On the farm, through the sacraments of hard work, Fonda and his wife are reunited. Oates leaves, is captured by the murdering horse thief, and Fonda goes to rescue him. The rest is a kind of rite, in which a cycle of continuity is enacted.

Fonda directed, and it's a creditable debut, but the cinematic qualities of the film must be called a three-way job: done by him and Vilmos Zsigmond, the cinematographer, and Frank Mazzola, the editor. Zsigmond has tried to unite earth and sky and things and people as co-inhabitors of space and time. Mazzola has used almost the whole contemporary editing vocabulary: very slow dissolves (*so* slow that they're not old-fashioned), occasional sequences with alternate frames removed (so that, briefly, the characters move like the astronauts in those early TV shots from the moon), occasional freeze-frames. And he has used the last device a bit differently: a sequence ends with a freeze-frame, which is then followed by another freeze-frame of the very same shot; a sequence begins with a freeze-frame, which is then very gently urged into motion.

The object of all these techniques is, apparently, to refract realism into its essences; and through this visual enlargement, to let a large theme—larger than the story—speak. Trying for this, the film-makers have not completely avoided some preciousness. A lantern shines conveniently through Fonda's beard to frame him in gold; sunsets are *always* gorgeous; and there is some of that detestable focus-racking. (Changing focus in mid-shot. If the foreground is fuzzy and background clear—or vice versa—the foreground becomes clear and the background fuzzy—or vice versa.) But the richness of the pictures is not just a lot of loose syrup that flows off the screen and into your lap. It's contained by a purpose. Which I'll come to.

As actor, Fonda is earnest and intent, but he lacks substance. He is only quiet, not quietly forceful. He does nothing really wrong; he simply *isn't* enough. It's cruel, perhaps, but true to say that what his role needs is his father, at the son's present age. Oates is pleasing as the taciturn-trusty friend. Verna Bloom, who was the young Appalachian widow in *Medium Cool,* has a good deal of the grim earthy passion needed for the wife. The reticent score by Bruce Langhorne touches the film perfectly from time to time. The clothes by Lawrence G. Paull give homespun veracity.

(But why don't directors and designers watch actors' hands? Don't they know what farmers' hands look like? Not like Fonda's and Bloom's, I can tell them. Make-up and *acting* would help.)

The script by Alan Sharp is mostly straightforward and easy. Because it's so unconcerned with plot, two plotty elements stick out. How does the horse thief's messenger find Fonda? Why does Fonda ride into that town to face three men openly in a suicidal shootout? Both moments are meant to be ritual matters, I suppose: the messenger of fate and the union with that fate; but the mode of the film asks for more plausibility.

And the theme under it all? Nothing less than (let's call it) the Masculine Principle in a time of transition. That principle is the base of the myth of the frontier, the quintessence of the idea of new lands. It's always concerned with men, as bearers of the myth, as adventurers and companions. The greatest American novel, *Moby Dick* (a kind of frontier epic), has an all-male cast. The generic American myth, the Western, is all-male. Women are only ornaments and rewards, never dynamic characters, in the classic Western; and marriage is usually where the story ends. Underneath the Western form is the idea of Natural Men, adventuring together, unbound by women and the society they represent. The wife in *The Hired Hand* tells the husband that his friend, with whom he has wandered for seven years, has had more of him than she has had. When the husband is shot, he whispers to his friend, "Hold me, Arch."

I'm not talking about latent homosexuality—at least not in any libidinous sense. This film is concerned with a theme that literary critics have often discerned in our novels: life as adventure versus life as service, self-love (either the Loner or the man with a human mirror) versus other-love. Essentially, the film is about the crossing, if not the passing, of a frontier. (Note: the wife lives on a farm, not a ranch.) One of the reasons we have all loved good Westerns, as John Ford understood, is their gesture of freedom, from place and possessions: not alone the much-mooted triumph of plain Good over plain Evil but the idea that all your possessions are on your saddle and you can *go*—into great space—and make your way with or against men in much the same situation.

(Women have loved Westerns, too, of course, which may indicate an old, deep-seated envy more valid than one of penises.)

But *The Hired Hand* is not about cribbing and confinement but about maturing (Fonda *wants* to return); not about dimming and decline but about civilization, which, if it still means anything, means increase through loss. In its small, imperfect, moving way, that's what this film celebrates.

VIVA LA MUERTE

HAROLD CLURMAN

In *The Nation* of November 29, 1971, speaking of Fernando Arrabal's play *And They Put Handcuffs on Flowers,* I said that "I wished to compare the relative effectiveness of theatre and film in the depiction of brutality and horror." I was unable to do so at the time because I had not yet seen *Viva La Muerte* (Hurrah for Death), which caused a sensation at the Cannes Film Festival last May. I have now seen the film, directed by Arrabal himself.

The film packs a terrific wallop. It does so in its least "realistic" images—to be more precise, in those scenes of fantasy which are part of the imaginings of Fando, a twelve-year-old boy, who is the · film's central figure. There are analogous scenes in *And They Put Handcuffs on Flowers,* but when done by live actors in front of us they do not exert the same force. The immediate fleshed reality makes what we see more of a "show," artificial!

Viva La Muerte takes place during the last days of the Spanish Civil War of 1936–39. We first see Fando (Arrabal was such a boy at the time) as several army jeeps carrying Franco's men ride through the hills proclaiming their imminent victory and shouting their determination to wipe out their enemies, even if it means killing half the country's population. Their battle cry is "*Viva La Muerte!*"

Whether this is factual or not I cannot say, but it sets the tone of the film in a historical sense. The plot itself shows Fando, whose father has been arrested and is supposed dead, learning that his mother, fanatically religious, has denounced her husband as an atheist and a "Red." Fando, devoted to his father, tells his mother that when he grows up he too will be an atheist and a "Red." What follows are chiefly the ghastly fantasies of his father's execution and attendant circumstances.

The film, as well as Arrabal's other work (novels, plays, poems), reveals the searing effect of his childhood experiences. There is in it a ferocity without parallel in any other modern dramatist except Genet. Though Arrabal writes in French (which is the language of the film) and lives in Paris, his work is profoundly Spanish. He employs peculiarly Hispanic religious symbols, even in his venomous rejection of the Church. Cruelty, horrendous obscenity, tortured sexuality are all part of his artistic vocabulary. The unconscious in all its polluted flow pours through the spectacle of his imagination. There is no visual metaphor, howsoever repellent, that he spares us. We come away from the film shattered not only by the horrors of the conflict in Spain but by the content of a life warped by everything which preceded that conflict and its psychological after-effects.

I doubt that all the violence which festers in Fando's mind could dwell in a twelve-year-old boy's subconscious, but it is certainly in Arrabal's consciousness as an adult. No matter, in *Viva La Muerte* we recognize everything Arrabal hates in the old Spain: the sooty bigotry, the repulsive superstition, the repression of sexual impulse, the backward schooling, the stupid torture in the disciplining of children. The odor of blood and human contamination pervades everything.

The film is divided into photographed scenes showing Fando, his grandfather, mother, aunt, playmates as they exist in reality— some of these have moments of wry humor and charm—including some which explore the quasi-innocent perversions of adolescence; and other scenes, photographed or projected in drawings, in which the facts and fumes of actuality are visualized as the havoc in his soul. The latter compose the most telling parts of the film. The drawings, especially, are conceived in the vein of certain examples of surrealist graphic art in which thoughts are converted into abominably sadistic and scatological visions.

Most surprising and ironical is a little Danish nonsense song that frames the film and in which a child's voice gives vent to confused notions involving shadows and echoes. It is a winningly gay song which suggests that, beside and beyond all the hideous wretchedness we have beheld, there still remains something else and better in life. Anger and hate alone rarely produce anything more than sick or distorted art. *Viva La Muerte* is a picture I am not likely to forget.

VLADIMIR AND ROSA

Godard Proceeding

PENELOPE GILLIATT

Jean-Luc Godard won hatred for *See You at Mao* and *Pravda*. He had rejected his own past films: he called his own *Breathless* bourgeois; he set up the Dziga-Vertov film-making group to produce movies in which conventionally antagonistic people would work together and the legend of the director as *auteur* might be quashed. Now he has made *Vladimir and Rosa*, for which he is likely to be hissed. We always take it out of our poets when they change gauge, and Godard remains a poet, although he truly means now to be only a didacticist and an inquirer; it is the case of Brecht, whose wit, amplitude, and courtesy of observation confound his angry theory all the time.

Godard begins here with photographs of Lenin, and with a discussion addressed to himself about the meaning of theory and practice, about the economics of making a new revolutionary film with the loot and guile acquired from the one before, and about how to show a political fact politically. He is honestly troubled for the young. Education, work, the draft and the Army, cops and prison: the struggle is worst in four areas, says the commentary, doing its best to be infuriatingly trite and not quite making it. Godard tries to be unseductive, dogmatic, and documentary, but what he chooses to show is constantly beautiful, hesitant, and raised into the fictional. He is making a film about many things. On the surface, it is about the Chicago trial. Judge Hoffman is enacted by a dowager-faced man with his hair parted in the middle. He has a magazine of nude girls in front of him, and he doodles on it when he seems to be taking legal notes. Yet Godard can't quite manage to make his idea of the man a travesty; it isn't within his powers. The shots of Hoffman are stylized, intercut with beautiful Victorian compositions of jurors whose dulled interest may suddenly be caught so that their heads are pulled toward an unseen speaker on one string, like something in an understaffed puppet theater. The judge is often shown to be fascinated and intelligent. His arms twice jerk upward across his eyes in a marvelously theatrical gesture of a settled man's feud with the new. Godard uses Brechtian parable-stagings of cops and riot handling. He himself appears, looking stern, having fun. He puts as much distance as a film director can ever have put between actor and character, between lesson and playing, between identification and distant, untearful scrutiny. And yet his film's nature is sometimes greatly moving in its simple devotedness. He knows, for instance, how people live together. There is a Women's Lib girl and her love in the film: we know in two seconds that they are crazy about each other and are struggling to cope on new ground. The girl keeps on relentlessly printing revolutionary posters on the floor, as if nothing else were on her mind. The man flails. He tries to understand. So do we all. In one marvelous shot, when she seems furious and when Godard doesn't press on us that they greatly like each other, she simply gets him to stand behind her, in a close-up, with his hands just showing round her head, and to speak from behind her in echo: "Try to think with my voice." The rage and ache of the shot are so clear, the point graphically so beautiful, that Women's Lib explains itself for good. It is not about man-hating or about wages, this; it is the question of fiction, the question of comment, and also the question of living with somebody—the question of imagining what it is like to be someone else.

Godard's film has the tone of notes to himself: "It is more important to link conclusions to experience than to other conclusions." It experiments with images of an empty red chair, standing for Bobby Seale's absence from the Chicago trial. Godard scrutinizes himself fiercely about everything. It all comes into question. The black frames he has used since 1968? They hid a vacuity, he implies. They were nothing but cryptic. A bladeless knife without even a handle. "They weren't black," he says. "They were colored, just as in any James Bond movie." He is too harsh with himself here, of course. He couldn't be crass if he tried, though he has often tried hard. His sensibility is as delicate and intractable as usual in these new films-of-revolution: His political thought can't hope to equal the poetry of his style or the stab of his questions. He also has a glorious dry sense of humor. This film has a recurring sequence of an interviewed radical and a man with a mike affably tripping up and down beside each other alongside a tennis net in the middle of a doubles game; the conflicting absorption is terribly funny, and so is our own worry about whether the ball is going to hit the interviewer, and so is our greater fascination with the game than with what is being said—a game that pulls our heads as the testimony in the Chicago trial pulls the jurors'.

Godard has taught us a lot. His nervous films make us realize that living is to read a text that we can't decipher except in fragments. He knows when lovers' eyes meet and when they look away. He shows us halfway people giving away their bodies but preserving their spirits. Like TV newsreels, he has taught us to take in stray leads on behavior very fast. He expresses a modern sort of anger with himself for inventing offhand romantics who so celebrate a life without afterthoughts, action without foreseen results, for that is exactly the opposite of what he dialectically thinks. *Breathless* precisely contradicts the effort of *Vladimir and Rosa*. But, being who he is, Godard in this new, anti-romantically intended film still makes us see his central girl's wish to be understood by a particular loved man prevailing over her demagogic anger.

His is always a cinema of literacy. When he thought he was making a Bogart movie, he was making *Alice in Wonderland*. *Le Petit Soldat* is full of nostalgia for the Spanish Civil War as well as loathing for the situation in Algeria. His contempt for functionaries is as much an artist's as a revolutionary's. When he makes films disconnectedly—with jump cuts, or with this particular movie's music-hall-sketch shape—he gives you the feeling that he is finding separate things at the bottom of a mine which have to be brought to the light even if we are pit ponies and now blinded. He has taught us to look at faces. It wasn't Coutard's famous photography that originated these inescapable studies of intransigent heads in close-up against walls, standing for the generation without parents and without backgrounds, for people who are the authors of themselves. (The cameraman isn't credited, on Godard's new principle of film-making, but he isn't Coutard.) It shows us Godard's idea of the way it is to be alive. On your own, face front, back against the wall. The faces are often silent for a long time. Then, after seeming to be icons, they speak, and you look with the freshness of listening to the first talkies, when well-known faces suddenly acquired voices. It is like the hallucination—it must be common—that a baby being fed with a bottle can suddenly seem to push the bottle away and speak a full-grown sentence.

Godard shows the inside of things by staying outside, and he remains light. If you look at someone long, he says, it is like looking at the sun. You will stop seeing at all. His films' frail existence can become eloquent and upsetting in itself. It is like the lives of his people: sometimes they can manage, sometimes they can't. This is what makes his pictures moving in their person. They have glimpses of a grace that they achieve only now and then.

4

THINGS TO COME

A CLOCKWORK ORANGE

Kubrick's Brilliant Vision
PAUL D. ZIMMERMAN

From the beginning, he has struggled to control both his work and his world, as if the uncertainties of the human condition would rip him to pieces if he relinquished his hold for even so much as a second. But it is precisely this inexhaustible drive to orchestrate even the smallest details of his life and his art that has made Stanley Kubrick the most provocative and brilliant of today's American directors.

At forty-three, the creator of *Paths of Glory, Lolita, Dr. Strangelove* and the visionary *2001: A Space Odyssey* has earned his place beside Bergman, Buñuel, Truffaut, Fellini and a handful of others. Now Kubrick has a new movie called *A Clockwork Orange*, taken from the brilliant and shocking novel by British writer Anthony Burgess. The film is not without its small failings, for a man who makes as many daring artistic leaps as Kubrick is bound to slip from time to time, just as he is insured against ever boring us. *A Clockwork Orange* is also a characteristically frosty piece of filmmaking, shorn completely of sentiment, working through brilliant ironies and dazzling dramatic ideas that please us, provoke our laughter, galvanize our intellects, win our admiration—but never touch our hearts.

But then, no director has it all—tenderness and crystal detachment, a sure feel for sentiment and Olympian brilliance. It is enough that *A Clockwork Orange* works on its own terms, as the kind of tour de force of the intellect and imagination that marks Kubrick as a true genius of the cinema.

The film moves on many levels at once—social, psychological, moral and mythical. It is set in a London of the near future in which roving gangs of Teddy boys rule the night, venting the frustrations and boredom of their lives in acts of rape, robbery and wanton beatings. Alex, the hero, is a prince of this adolescent underworld, leading his three "droogs," as pals are called in the special slang the teenagers talk, in endless acts of mayhem—mugging drunks for sport, grabbing girls for what Alex (who narrates the film) calls "the quick in-out, in-out," breaking into houses on "surprise visits" to rape, maim, kill and steal.

Like Shakespeare's Richard III, Alex is despicable in what he does, but graced with a wit, energy and demonic imagination that make him superior to any other figure in his world and make him a perversely winning character. Kubrick is careful to protect our reluctant allegiance to Alex—by stylizing the acts of brutality he commits, by making his victims unpleasant, by distancing the audience from what would otherwise be an intolerable level of violence through an inventive use of music.

Kubrick turns a savage, hard-crunching battle between Alex's droogs and a repulsive rival gang into a ballet by Jerome Robbins gone mad. In another episode, Alex breaks into the house of a writer and brutally rapes his wife—all the time singing and soft-shoeing an insouciant version of "Singin' in the Rain." On another surprise visit, which leads to Alex's capture by the police, there is a battle of the sexes in which he clubs a tough health-club lady to death with her own outsized phallic sculpture—all choreographed to the antic strains of Rossini's "Thieving Magpie" overture. Kubrick scores a super-speeded-up orgy between Alex and two nymphets with the feverish strains of the "William Tell" overture, turning an already clever characterization of casual teenage sex into a brilliant comic ballet. His use of the satanic second movement of Beethoven's Ninth Symphony captures in its angry humor, its demonic energy, its bitter but affirmative spirit, the essence of Alex's character.

As a hero, Alex has a great deal more than music going for him in gaining the loyalties of an audience. As Kubrick points out, "the most interesting and often engaging characters in any film are the villains." More important, Malcolm McDowell imbues Alex with his own winning arrogance and charm in a performance of extraordinary vitality and intelligence. And as a fantasy figure Alex appeals to something dark and primal in all of us. He acts out our desire for instant sexual gratification, for the release of our angers and repressed instincts for revenge, our need for adventure and excitement.

The elegance that accompanies Alex's penchant for what he dubs "ultra-violence" is the pivotal paradox of the film. Its shocking content has earned it an X rating, but Dr. Aaron Stern, the film industry's code administrator, believes there should be special ratings for X films of such exceptional quality. "Violence itself isn't necessarily abhorrent," says Kubrick. "From his own point of view, Alex is having a wonderful time, and I wanted his life to appear to us as it did to him, not restricted by the conventional pieties. You can't compare what Alex is doing to any kind of day-to-day reality. Watching a movie is like having a daydream. You can safely explore areas that are closed off to you in your daily life. There are dreams in which you do all the terrible things your conscious mind prevents you from doing."

Violence is a common denominator in all Kubrick's films. In every one of his movies, someone is murdered. "Although a certain amount of hypocrisy exists about it," he says, "everyone is fascinated by violence. After all, man is the most remorseless killer who ever stalked the earth. Our interest in violence in part reflects the fact that on the subconscious level we are very little different from our primitive ancestors."

Alex is finally caught, ironically done in by his one bit of humanity, a love for Beethoven that sets his gang against him. In a scene characteristic of the film's clarity and economy, we watch Alex as he enters the penitentiary systematically stripped of his clothes, his effects, his name, his swagger—his self. All that remains of his freedom is his fantasy life, which he puts to good use. He studies the Bible to score points with the prison chaplain—all the while imagining he is whipping Christ on the way to Calvary, killing Romans, basking in a bevy of naked handmaidens.

But soon even his fantasy life is confiscated. He is transferred to a reconditioning center where he is injected with a nausea-inducing drug and forced, with his eyelids clamped open, to watch films of violence and sex until the very thought of his old diversions makes him gag and retch. The government, proud of this new solution to crime in the streets, makes a display of Alex as the star guinea pig of this new therapeutic behaviorism. In a "scientific" demonstration Alex is pushed around by an actor and teased by a nude girl—and his only reaction is to lick the actor's shoe and grovel retchingly at the girl's feet. The close-up of tongue on leather, like the frames of Slim Pickens riding the suicidal H-bomb in *Dr. Strangelove*, shows Kubrick's genius for fixing an aspect of the human condition in a single image, here Subjugation itself.

Alex is returned to the world, where he meets all those whom he has abused and is mercilessly beaten for his transgressions. We accept these coincidences, for Kubrick's stylization of the story has clearly cast it in mythical terms. "Telling a story 'realistically' is such a slowpoke and ponderous way to proceed," says Kubrick, "and it doesn't fulfill the psychic needs that people have. We sense that there's more to life and to the universe than realism can possibly deal with."

In *A Clockwork Orange* this mythic realism has produced an icily brilliant vision of an imminent future in which Western society has become a mod slum, super-technologized and squalid at the same time. Culture has collapsed into a pervasive pop-art bad taste: Alex's prole parents are caricatures, Dad with his big lapels, Mum with her violet hair and micro-skirts. Politics too has been reduced to caricature—there is no middle ground, only warfare between advocates of anarchy and of total control. Alex and his droogs hang out at the "milk-plus" bar, swigging doped milk at tables formed of erotic sculpture. They speak a lingo that reflects a vicious decay of feeling: ubiquitous television has turned "see" into "viddy"; the adjective of approval is "horrorshow"; money is "deng," with its excremental connotations.

But at its most profound level, *A Clockwork Orange* is an odyssey of the human personality, a statement on what it is to be fully human. Alex's adventures are, in one sense, the adventures of the id itself. Alex embodies all of man's anarchic impulses. Shorn of his individuality in the penitentiary and of his fantasy life in the conditioning program, he ceases to be a human being in any real sense. His resurrection at the end, as he regains his ability to act out his lusts and aggressions, represents an ironic triumph of the human psyche over the forces that seek to control or diminish it.

Stanley Strangelove
Pauline Kael

Literal-minded in its sex and brutality, Teutonic in its humor, Stanley Kubrick's A Clockwork Orange might be the work of a strict and exacting German professor who set out to make a pornoviolent sci-fi comedy. Is there anything sadder—and ultimately more repellent—than a clean-minded pornographer? The numerous rapes and beatings have no ferocity and no sensuality; they're frigidly, pedantically calculated, and because there is no motivating emotion, the viewer may experience them as an indignity and wish to leave. The movie follows the Anthony Burgess novel so closely that the book might have served as the script, yet that thick-skulled German professor may be Dr. Strangelove himself, because the meanings are turned around.

Burgess's 1962 novel is set in a vaguely Socialist future (roughly, the late Seventies or early Eighties)—a dreary, routinized England that roving gangs of teenage thugs terrorize at night. In perceiving the amoral destructive potential of youth gangs, Burgess's ironic fable differs from Orwell's 1984 in a way that already seems prophetically accurate. The novel is narrated by the leader of one of these gangs—Alex, a conscienceless schoolboy sadist—and, in a witty, extraordinarily sustained literary conceit, narrated in his own slang (Nadsat, the teenagers' special dialect). The book is a fast read; Burgess, a composer turned novelist, has an ebullient, musical sense of language, and you pick up the meanings of the strange words as the prose rhythms speed you along. Alex enjoys stealing, stomping, raping, and destroying until he kills a woman and is sent to prison for fourteen years. After serving two, he arranges to get out by submitting to an experiment in conditioning, and he is turned into a moral robot who becomes nauseated at thoughts of sex and violence. Released when he is harmless, he falls prey to his former victims, who beat him and torment him until he attempts suicide. This leads to criticism of the government that robotized him—turned him into a clockwork orange—and he is deconditioned, becoming once again a thug, and now at loose and triumphant. The ironies are protean, but Burgess is clearly a humanist; his point of view is that of a Christian horrified by the possibilities of a society turned clockwork orange, in which life is so mechanized that men lose their capacity for moral choice. There seems to be no way in this boring, dehumanizing society for the boys to release their energies except in vandalism and crime; they do what they do as a matter of course. Alex the sadist is as mechanized a creature as Alex the good.

Stanley Kubrick's Alex (Malcolm McDowell) is not so much an expression of how this society has lost its soul as he is a force pitted against the society, and by making the victims of the thugs more repulsive and contemptible than the thugs Kubrick has learned to love the punk sadist. The end is no longer the ironic triumph of a mechanized punk but a real triumph. Alex is the only likable person we see—his cynical bravado suggests a broad-nosed, working-class Olivier—and the movie puts us on his side. Alex, who gets kicks out of violence, is more alive than anybody else in the movie, and younger and more attractive, and McDowell plays him exuberantly, with the power and slyness of a young Cagney. Despite what Alex does at the beginning, McDowell makes you root for his foxiness, for his crookedness. For most of the movie, we see him tortured and beaten and humiliated, so when his bold, aggressive punk's nature is restored to him it seems not a joke on all of us but, rather, a victory in which we share, and Kubrick takes an exultant tone. The look in Alex's eyes at the end tells us that he isn't just a mechanized, choiceless sadist but prefers sadism and knows he can get by with it. Far from being a little parable about the dangers of soullessness and the horrors of force, whether employed by individuals against each other or by society in "conditioning," the movie becomes a vindication of Alex, saying that the punk was a free human being and only the good Alex was a robot.

The trick of making the attacked less human than their attackers, so you feel no sympathy for them, is, I think, symptomatic of a new attitude in movies. This attitude says there's no moral difference. Stanley Kubrick has assumed the deformed, self-righteous perspective of a vicious young punk who says, "Everything's rotten. Why shouldn't I do what I want? They're worse than I am." In the new mood (perhaps movies in their cumulative effect are partly responsible for it), people want to believe the hyperbolic worst, want to believe in the degradation of the victims—that they are dupes and phonies and weaklings. I can't accept that Kubrick is merely reflecting this post-assassinations, post-Manson mood; I think he's catering to it. I think he wants to dig it.

This picture plays with violence in an intellectually seductive way. And though it has no depth, it's done in such a slow, heavy style that those prepared to like it can treat its puzzling aspects as oracular. It can easily be construed as an ambiguous mystery play, a visionary warning against "the Establishment." There are a million ways to justify identifying with Alex: Alex is fighting repression; he's alone against the system. What he does isn't nearly as bad as what the government does (both in the movie and in the United States now). Why shouldn't he be violent? That's all the Establishment has ever taught him (and us) to be. The point of the book was that we must be as men, that we must be able to take responsibility for what we are. The point of the movie is much more *au courant*. Kubrick has removed many of the obstacles to our identifying with Alex; the Alex of the book has had his personal habits cleaned up a bit—his fondness for squishing small animals under his tires, his taste for ten-year-old girls, his beating up of other prisoners, and so on. And Kubrick aids the identification with Alex by small directorial choices throughout. The writer whom Alex cripples (Patrick Magee) and the woman he kills are cartoon nasties with upper-class accents a mile wide. (Magee has been encouraged to act like a bathetic madman; he seems to be preparing for a career in horror movies.) Burgess gave us society through Alex's eyes, and so the vision was deformed, and Kubrick, carrying over from *Dr. Strangelove* his joky adolescent view of hypocritical, sexually dirty authority figures and extending it to all adults, has added an extra layer of deformity. The "straight" people are far more twisted than Alex; they seem inhuman and incapable of suffering. He alone suffers. And how he suffers! He's a male Little Nell—screaming in a straitjacket during the brainwashing; sweet and helpless when rejected by his parents; alone, weeping, on a bridge; beaten, bleeding, lost in a rainstorm; pounding his head on a floor and crying for death. Kubrick pours on the hearts and flowers; what is done to Alex is far worse than what Alex has done, so society itself can be felt to justify Alex's hoodlumism.

The movie's confusing—and, finally, corrupt—morality is not, however, what makes it such an abhorrent viewing experience. It is offensive long before one perceives where it is heading, because it has no shadings. Kubrick, a director with an arctic spirit, is determined to be pornographic, and he has no talent for it. In *Los Olvidados*, Buñuel showed teenagers committing horrible brutalities, and even though you had no illusions about their victims— one, in particular, was a foul old lecher—you were appalled. Buñuel makes you understand the pornography of brutality: The pornography is in what human beings are capable of doing to other human beings. Kubrick has always been one of the least sensual and least erotic of directors, and his attempts here at phallic humor are like a professor's lead balloons. He tries to work up kicky violent scenes, carefully estranging you from the victims so that you can *enjoy* the rapes and beatings. But I think one is more likely to feel cold antipathy toward the movie than horror at the violence—or enjoyment of it, either.

Kubrick's martinet control is obvious in the terrible performances he gets from everybody but McDowell, and in the inexorable pacing. The film has a distinctive style of estrangement: gloating close-ups, bright, hard-edge, third-degree lighting, and abnormally loud voices. It's a style, all right—the movie doesn't look like other movies, or sound like them—but it's a leering, portentous style. After the balletic brawling of the teenage gangs, with bodies flying as in a Western saloon fight, and after the gang-bang of the writer's wife and an orgy in speeded-up motion, you're primed for more action, but you're left stranded in the prison sections, trying to find some humor in tired schoolboy jokes about a Hitlerian guard. The movie retains a little of the slangy Nadsat but none of the fast rhythms of Burgess's prose, and so the dialect seems much more arch than it does in the book. Many of the dialogue sequences go on and on, into a stupor of inactivity. Kubrick seems infatuated with the hypnotic possibilities of static setups; at times you feel as if you were trapped in front of the frames of a comic strip for a numbing ten minutes per frame. When Alex's correctional officer visits his home and he and Alex sit on a bed, the camera sits on the two of them. When Alex comes home from prison, his parents and the lodger who has displaced him are in the living room; Alex appeals to his seated, unloving parents for an inert eternity. Long after we've got the point, the composition is still telling us to appreciate its cleverness. This ponderous technique is hardly leavened by the structural use of classical music to characterize the sequences; each sequence is scored to Purcell (synthesized on a Moog), Rossini, or Beethoven, while Elgar and others are used for brief satiric effects. In the book, the doctor who has devised the conditioning treatment explains why the horror images used in it are set to music: "It's a useful emotional heightener." But the whole damned movie is heightened this way; yes, the music is effective, but the effect is self-important.

When I pass a newsstand and see the saintly, bearded, intellectual Kubrick on the cover of *Saturday Review,* I wonder: Do people notice things like the way Kubrick cuts to the rival teenage gang before Alex and his hoods arrive to fight them, just so we can have the pleasure of watching that gang strip the struggling girl they mean to rape? Alex's voice is on the track announcing his arrival, but Kubrick can't wait for Alex to arrive, because then he couldn't show us as much. That girl is stripped for our benefit; it's the purest exploitation. Yet this film lusts for greatness, and I'm not sure that Kubrick knows how to make simple movies anymore, or that he cares to, either. I don't know how consciously he has thrown this film to youth; maybe he's more of a showman than he lets on—a lucky showman with opportunism built into the cells of his body. The film can work at a pop-fantasy level for a young audience already prepared to accept Alex's view of the society, ready to believe that that's how it is.

At the movies, we are gradually being conditioned to accept violence as a sensual pleasure. The directors used to say they were showing us its real face and how ugly it was in order to sensitize us to its horrors. You don't have to be very keen to see that they are now in fact desensitizing us. They are saying that everyone is brutal, and the heroes must be as brutal as the villains or they turn into fools. There seems to be an assumption that if you're offended by movie brutality, you are somehow playing into the hands of the people who want censorship. But this would deny those of us who don't believe in censorship the use of the only counterbalance: the freedom of the press to say that there's anything conceivably damaging in these films—the freedom to analyze their implications. If we don't use this critical freedom, we are implicitly saying that no brutality is too much for us—that only squares and people who believe in censorship are concerned with brutality. Actually, those who believe in censorship are primarily concerned with sex, and they generally worry about violence only when it's eroticized. This means that practically no one raises the issue of the possible cumulative effects of movie brutality. Yet surely, when night after night atrocities are served up to us as entertainment, it's worth some anxiety. We become clockwork oranges if we accept all this pop culture without asking what's in it. How can people go on talking about the dazzling brilliance of movies and not notice that the directors are sucking up to the thugs in the audience?

THE ANDROMEDA STRAIN and THX-1138

Two Glimpses of a Bad New World

RICHARD SCHICKEL

The typical creator of science fiction, whether he works in print or on film, differs from the creator of other kinds of fiction in that he is usually not primarily interested in giving us a unique set of characters. His concerns are those of the social commentator making projective speculations about what might happen if some technology or social problem should develop dangerously, unchecked by humane concerns or imaginative planning. It is sufficient that characters speak coherently about the issues at hand. And there is always the plot, suspenseful and melodramatic, to keep our attention from wandering.

In this sense Michael Crichton's best-selling novel *The Andromeda Strain* was a conventional work of SF, perhaps even skimpier than most in its characterizations, but compensating for that lack by a punchy basic plot: the effort of a scientific team to identify and find a cure for a killer bacterium brought to earth by a space probe. Director Robert Wise's film is faithful to the novel. Its one significant departure—turning one of the investigators into a woman (chubby, grumpy Kate Reid) is a distinct improvement. The film, like the novel, effectively draws on the history of previous scientific crises (*i.e.*, the news that the Nazis were developing an atom bomb, the Russian launching of Sputnik) to show us how we might attempt to meet our first biological crisis. Also like the book, but less fortunately, it has a certain monotony of tone, a sense that all the rich implications of such a crisis are not fully developed. For instance, there is a hint that the government may have been deliberately grubbing around out there in space, looking for a doomsday bug to hold against an enemy. But it remains only a hint. *The Andromeda Strain*, despite the care that has been lavished on its production, remains a conventional genre piece, by no means lacking in entertainment value, yet rather more ponderous than those quick, lively, occasionally eccentric B pictures that used to treat of similar subjects.

By contrast, George Lucas' *THX-1138*, a first feature that is the outgrowth of a prize-winning short subject he made in college, is a much more intriguing adventure. He has dispensed with complexities of plot as well as character simply to show us a man (his name is the film's title) trying to escape a world he never made (but which we may be in the process of making) some five centuries hence. Lucas seeks to sustain our interest merely by presenting his plight through a series of striking visual images, absolutely pure movie stuff that owes nothing to conventions borrowed from literature, and he comes amazingly close to bringing it off.

It's a white-on-white world, this underground city where his automatons exist, their lives planned and controlled by computers. Sex is forbidden, procreation is by test tube only. THX gets into trouble when his roommate deprives him of his daily dose of sex repressant. This makes him too nervous to work successfully at his job, inconsolable by the God (actually a recorded announcement) whom you can dial on the phone, undistractable by the wall-sized TV which offers, among other amenities, a fix of violence whenever you need it—without your having to sit through a boring plot to get to the good part.

Lucas has a million such grabby ideas. Children are educated by having knowledge dripped into their veins. The cops are robots, judges computers, jail a white void. Lucas' tone toward his macabre material is one of controlled irony; the result is the most exciting directorial debut in a long time. If *THX-1138* never quite makes us really care about these people who were rendered subhuman long before the movie began, it still is an intelligent, deftly made visual trip—the best thing of its kind since *2001* and, in its basic pessimism perhaps a more devastating portent of things to come.

LITTLE MURDERS

Subcutaneous Cinema

ARTHUR KNIGHT

George S. Kaufman's old line "Satire is what closes on Saturday night" proved almost prophetic for the original Broadway production of Jules Feiffer's *Little Murders*. It opened on a Tuesday in April 1967 and ended its run four nights later, as if on cue from Kaufman. Miraculously, however, the play survived. A London production a few weeks later won the Best Foreign Play award from the British critics; a 1969 off-Broadway revival, directed by Alan Arkin, developed into a substantial hit—substantial enough, at least, to warrant its purchase by Twentieth Century-Fox for movie purposes. Both Arkin and Feiffer were included in the package, and, ironically, its coproducer and star is Elliott Gould, who had played Feiffer's apathetic protagonist in the short-lived first production.

The timing for this latest incarnation of Feiffer's black comedy could hardly be better. What seemed merely eccentric behavior in 1967 has become a recognizable part of the paranoia of the Seventies. The random assassinations, bombings, and mass riots, rendered offstage in 1967, have since entered our homes almost every evening via television. The lack of commitment, the unwillingness of people to become involved, that shocked all of us so much in the Genovese case has since hardened into an accepted, acceptable public posture. Violence stalks our streets—violence, it might be noted, that even Feiffer had not envisaged when he wrote his play. In the few years since *Little Murders* first appeared, much of our citizenry has learned to live with this fact, erecting its own puny defenses against that ugly world outside.

What the film does, and with dire intensity, is to demonstrate not merely how puny those defenses are and how callous we have become to the daily outrages in our cities but how easily, through the slight hyperbole familiar to Feiffer fans, our entire society might be sucked into the vortex of overreaction. Perhaps the most terrifying aspect of *Little Murders* is that today it seems neither grotesque nor absurd but rather an only mildly distorted mirror of our times. To be sure, the film is black enough, but the comedy is no longer funny because we happen to be living with its tag lines.

It is to the credit of the new production company of Jack Brodsky and Gould that, despite this shift of emphasis, they proceeded to open up the play in ways calculated to augment the shock rather than the laughs. On the stage, the perils of New York crept in through the interstices of barricaded windows and cautiously opened doors. In the film, they are omnipresent. Lights fail in the Newquist apartment, and conversation goes on as if nothing had happened. Gould and his girl friend walk down a street where buildings burn and corpses are carried out on stretchers, and no one seems to notice. There are muggings, bombings, riots, but it is all part of the daily routine. Even when Gould, with bloodied shirt and bloodstained face, rides the New York subway, no one looks up. Today, it is more than apathy; naked fear is making our cities unlivable, and this fear haunts every frame of *Little Murders*.

And yet, for all the seriousness of its underlying purpose, the film is funny. Just as Feiffer's cartoons generate a mordant chuckle of recognition, there is laughter at the parody of an all-American family following the all-American conventions through what has to be the world's most dreadful dinner party ever tendered a prospective son-in-law. The Feiffer wit is also evident in the protracted monologue of Lou Jacobi explaining why he, as a judge, will not perform the marriage ceremonies without reference to God—and no less so in the equally protracted, and provocative, sermon by Donald Sutherland, minister of the First Existentialist Church, explaining why he will. ("Jesus died for our sins," he says. "Dare we make His martyrdom meaningless by not committing them?")

Arkin, in his maiden venture as a feature-film director, has a tendency to let his performers become a bit shrill (including his own performance as a paranoid police lieutenant). And Feiffer, in his maiden venture as a feature film writer, relies far too heavily on his incredible ear for today's language, far too little on his no less discerning eye. But the cast, recruited in the main from Arkin's off-Broadway production, is almost beyond reproach, and the film is relevant, risible—and profoundly disturbing.

An Overdrawn Feiffer Cartoon

RICHARD SCHICKEL

Little Murders asks us to imagine something that is by no means unimaginable—namely, a near future in which the violence, inconvenience and general breakdown of civilized human and institutional arrangements that we are now experiencing in the cities escalates to a lunatic level where we actually exchange shots with our fellow paranoids. And try to protect ourselves by barricading ourselves behind bulletproof shelters. And manifest, through all manner of lesser physical and verbal assaults, all those bad vibes we've thus far managed to keep, if not under control, then within limits.

The conceit is not without possibilities. And Jules Feiffer, who adapted his own play for the screen, has created any number of good scenes that might have worked as revue sketches or, indeed, as the basis for Feiffer cartoons. One thinks of Elliott Gould meeting his fiancée's parents for the first time. Or trying to talk to his own parents over a gap of too many years. Or being the captive audience of a relentlessly autobiographical judge. Or being married by a minister far gone in the moral relativism of mod theology. Even more familiar material works pretty well under Alan Arkin's bump-and-run direction: gags about utilities that don't work, Catskill resorts that plasticize their inmates, oedipal relationships between fathers and daughters, and American moms who cling to the raft of etiquette while heavy existential seas threaten to drown them. Indeed, Arkin himself, as a cop alternately trying to wheedle and bully some law and order into the world, contributes a grotesque cameo that vies with Elizabeth Wilson's Mom as the best bit in a film crammed with strong and highly professional comic acting.

Still, the afterlife of the piece—the residue it leaves in one's mind after the laughter in the theater dies down—is, to borrow another familiar gag, "nasty, brutish and short." Feiffer is, commendably enough, trying to transcend the natural limits of his gift but, this time at least, he fails. There is no plot—just Gould meeting and marrying this girl (played by Marcia Rodd) who insists on transforming him from near catatonia into the man of her bourgeois dreams; and him making it, ironically, after she has been gunned down. There is no organic relationship between these neurotic foreground characters and the background of (unexplained) psychotic violence against which we see them.

Feiffer's humor, as we've come to know it in his cartoons, is a thing of neurotic moments and slightly askew surfaces. We laugh at it, I think, as we laugh at overheards in lobbies and on buses. But that does not mean we really want to spend much time with his people, any more than we want to get to know a lot more about those strangers we enjoy eavesdropping on. On the evidence of *Little Murders* they turn out, just as we feared, to be rather dumb and depressing. Feiffer can give them a semblance of life only by jerking them around, tormenting them, really. But he cannot imagine them with a depth and dimensionality that would allow them to grow and change naturally and thus engage us as human beings.

Finally, one remembers that his cartoons usually ended with a shrug or sigh of resignation, as so many situations did in the Fifties, when he so well caught our mood. But the radicalization of his middle-brow audience has proceeded apace and he seems to fear— probably correctly—that such conclusions, however true they may be, will not satisfy them. They lust after apocalypse, and here he tries to give it to them while at the same time withholding his own full commitment to its inevitability. In any event, in his confusion he has clearly mislaid the compassion that always used to be present in his work and for which radical-chic attitudes are no substitute. The result is a forced and faltering movie, full of good bits, but without true feeling for its people or for the world they inhabit, and with no strong sense of its own place in, or point of view about, that world.

5
LONELY AMERICANS

DESPERATE CHARACTERS

STANLEY KAUFFMANN

Any white person who owns anything is under siege. Particularly if he's not young. A mansion or a one-room apartment, a Mercedes or a secondhand compact, if he owns anything, he is hated. The class war seems to be coming to the knife-edge, but as Marx didn't quite foresee, it's not only a war between haves and have-nots, it's also a war between generations and races. The white poor hate the white nonpoor. (How many city people have had their country places broken into lately? Friends of mine, with a small house on a remote mountain road, have arrived three times in the last six months to discover thefts.) The young rob the nonyoung, and justify this "ripping off" on moral, almost evangelist grounds. And as for races, the brute fact—in New York, at least—is that every white person is an animal in a game preserve whom nonwhites can hunt at their pleasure.

I'm *not* forgetting historical reasons for all these matters. I *have* read *Soledad Brother.* I *have* read Proudhon on property. (And I know that many nonwhite people, too, are robbed daily.) But I'm not talking about causes and guilts, just about the facts of living day to day in this country as the white nonyoung owner of *anything.* You are a target. That's not Minuteman scare-talk. I don't think that anyone who lives in (say) New York today can honestly deny these conditions, no matter what his social-political beliefs.

This is the climate of *Desperate Characters*, the feeling that grips a couple in their late thirties—people who have a house in Brooklyn and another in the country, well-disposed people of the now-despised liberal persuasion, who feel they are living in a state

178

of siege. But this state of physical siege is simply the locus for a state of moral and spiritual siege. What they feel within and be-tween themselves is derived, fundamentally, from the same causes as what they see around them. Their physical unease—setting the burglar alarm before they go out for the evening, watching the new slovenly neighbors corrupt the community—is ultimately tied to the causes of their deepest unhappiness.

He is a lawyer whose partner, a lifelong friend, has just left for a more socially responsive practice, and the split is a tacit agony. She is a translator of French when she works, childless ("I've got a uterus like a pinball machine"), who has had one love affair and may have more. Brightness has fallen from their air. Hope is a question that has to be thought about.

The chief metaphor of the story is a cat bite. The wife feeds a stray cat outside the door, and it bites her. There is some question as to whether the cat is rabid. It must be caught, and presumably killed, for examination. The wife is bitten on a Friday night and won't know till Monday whether she's been infected. (It all takes place on one weekend.) At the end, on Sunday night, the question is still open. The symbolism is a trifle heavy because it's so clear: the stranger outside repays help with viciousness, may have poi-soned the life inside just because he was outside and had to accept help, and may be killed in order to protect the life inside. Still it's used without verbal underscoring, except for one moment near the end.

Paula Fox's novel *Desperate Characters* (1970) fixed all this with comprehension and incisiveness. Now Frank D. Gilroy has made the book into a film. That's really the gist of the matter: He's made a good novel into a good *film*—has written, directed and produced it himself.

This is the same Gilroy who wrote *The Subject Was Roses*, a Pulitzer Prize play that did nothing to raise the status of that prize and was later a film that did less. He has written other plays and films, with spots of interest in them, but even the best in his best work did not prepare me for the quiet authority, the *accepted* real-ism (unflaunted), the subtlety of performance, and the visual vital-ity of this picture. In making a film about the doubtfulness of hope, Gilroy himself has shown why it still springs.

He has adapted the novel with a sure sense of the filmable, the expandable, the contractable. For instance, the whole account of the wife's affair, instead of a substantial flashback as in the book, is handled in one long slow pan in the lover's office while an unanswered telephone rings and rings. He enriches the essences of the book: He has put in a scene in a subway car, in which we hear a man conversing amiably; the camera moves over the wife's face and other silent faces till it reaches the chatting man who is talking to himself, while everyone else in the car sits silently, not even looking at him. As he continues to talk and they continue to ignore him, the scene cuts off. And Gilroy has given us a party scene that, for once, doesn't try to be the epitome of the Rotten and Superficial, it's just a party. (Out of which two young hips stride disgustedly.)

The dialogue is acute and self-conscious—the *characters'* self-consciousness: people who, like so many today, do not merely live their lives, they see themselves as characters in novels or films. Much of this dialogue is from Fox, but a good deal has been tempered by Gilroy or is new.

The director's theater experience is apparent and valuable. What he does with his actors within the confines of any one scene, any one take, contributes tremendously to the integrity of the whole. Timing is precise, never hurried, never limp; inflections are sharp; voices and eyes work in relation to other voices and eyes.

In a rather daring move Gilroy has cast Kenneth Mars as the husband. My only previous knowledge of Mars is as the comic Nazi playwright in *The Producers*, not a memory I treasure. But Gilroy obviously knew something that nobody else knew, because Mars produces exactly the right performance, an intelligent man turning sour, which frightens him even as he masochistically enjoys it, a man fighting for a chance to remain decently, creatively cynical. All through the role Mars touches it with tiny sparks of imagination. For instance, he and his wife are discussing a friend called Tanya. Mars says thoughtfully, "I hate Tanya," then clears his throat—*after* he makes the remark! This tiny inversion—another actor might have cleared his throat just before the line—turns comic cliché into comic truth.

Shirley MacLaine is the wife, and this is one time when "accrued" persona works against a star. I've never thought much of her abilities and have never thought her very attractive (outside of her first appearance in *The Trouble with Harry*). Even now she doesn't exactly suggest that she's a repository of profound secrets, and her face is not precisely the modern tragic mask, but this is easily the best performance of hers that I've seen. Gilroy has at least put her in touch with reality.

In his one long sequence Gerald O'Loughlin is excellent as the soberly drunken ex-partner who calls at midnight and takes Mac-Laine out for coffee. As an aging divorcée, Sada Thompson is brittle and barbed and piteous. Jack Somack, her friendly ex-husband, is the one actor who contends with his role a bit; it isn't quite digested.

Gilroy has done a good job of *seeing* his story. His very first shot, under the titles, pulls back from a Brooklyn street to the backs of some houses, then down to the back of our couple's house—one long slow arc. Then we see them, but don't hear them, conversing behind a window. (Only street noises through this opening. There are music credits, but I can't remember a note of music.) This first sight of them through the glass, as we are outside watching and not hearing, sets the right opening mood. Sometimes Gilroy strains: There are too many overhead shots. But he's looked at Hopper paintings and knows how to tell us something about Brooklyn dawn; he's looked at Bergman films and knows how to suspend two people in an agar-agar jelly of deadened love. And he's seen, too, how to make his film reinforce itself, as when he uses a duplicate composition for irony. The first time we see the couple's pleasant country house, it's on the right side of the screen and, after a moment, they drive in from the left. When we first see their care-taker's dowdy house, it, too, is on the right side of the screen and, again after a moment, the couple drive in from the left. The repetition, with a different, cheaper subject, is a shrewd comment.

The end of the story leaves us where we started, outside their Brooklyn home. A lot of pain has been seen and implied, and is by no means cured, but now it's quiet again. End of the picture, but only an intermission in the drama of the bourgeois.

This is a film of authenticity, of delicately realized intangibles: small-scale about large issues, truthful without settling for honest-to-God TV fact. All the more credit to Gilroy—and to MacLaine, without whom it would probably not have been made—because there was small reason to expect this work from them. I submit, too, that the year that sees two such first films as this and Barbara Loden's *Wanda*, not to mention Fonda's somewhat lesser *The Hired Hand*, is not the year to be despondent about the future of film in this country.

Lives of Noisy Desperation
MOLLY HASKELL

The worst thing about the random violence of New York, from the ranting of crazies to the ransacking of robbers, is how little in the way of edification or marketable life experience can be gained from it. Apart from a few dinner-party anecdotes (dwindling in originality and variety as the number of incidents increases), or an anthology piece in *The Voice* if you have acquired a sufficient backlog, there is no mileage, social or moral, to be derived from getting mugged or having your Sony stolen or being propositioned on the telephone. So great is their number and similarity that such incidents, horrifying as they may be to the victim, are nothing more than theatrical routines, clichés which have to be gimmicked up in the retelling with reversals and twists and compound elements (as in *Little Murders*) if they are to have any life at all. *The Out-of-Towners*, a compendium of stock episodes, fell so flat that no amount of obscenities could heavy-breathe any life into it.

In *Desperate Characters*, adapted and directed by Frank Gilroy, incidents of such gratuitous violence are interspersed with outbursts of personal frustration and hostility, in the attempt to create the effect of an epidemic. But they remain different orders of experience, and the two main characters, a husband and wife played by Shirley MacLaine and Kenneth Mars, are divided between being victims of a disease called New York and the subjects of their own lives for which, either by mismanagement or by default, they are responsible. And this, the moral dimension and most interesting aspect, is the one about which Gilroy tells us least.

Before seeing *Desperate Characters*, and without having read the novel by Paula Fox on which it is based, I had the impression it was about a lower-income family stranded in a state of physical siege by the forces of poverty around them. Not at all. They are an upper-middle-class couple (he is a lawyer) living in a Brooklyn brownstone which they have renovated, and their desperation is as much metaphysical as physical. Underlying the surface anxiety, the fact that they are growing old and farther away from any chance of sustained ecstasy, weighs more heavily than the cat bite which may

—but probably won't—lead to rabies and which forms the unifying thesis of the film.

In waiting out the weekend, the couple undergo a variety of experiences which amount to a crash course in shock—encounter therapy: Otto has a falling out with his best friend and partner, in which the partnership is dissolved; Sophie befriends and is bitten by a stray cat; they go to a party where Sophie sees her ex-lover; a rock is thrown through a bedroom window; there is a threatening phone call; Otto is conned out of money by a black; Sophie calls on friend Sada Thompson, whose discussion of her relationship with her ex-husband so depresses Sophie that she flees; Sophie has a heart-to-heart talk with Otto's ex-partner, a confrontation with ex-partner's wife; and so on, culminating in the looting of Sophie and Otto's country house, apparently by the caretaker.

You will have noticed there are a lot of "ex-"s, and maybe that's what the film is about: ex-lives. But one never gets a backward glimmer of unrealized potential, or any knowledge of the hopes on which the disappointment is based. We know only that Sophie and Otto live in the worst of all possible worlds: a world of maximum violence and minimum passion. But beyond this, their trials are of such a different order and some, like the lovely confession by Sada Thompson in which she suggests that happiness comes in half-notes, do not seem trials at all.

And there are different kinds of desperation. The quiet kind, of which Thoreau wrote and to which the title refers, is the *modus vivendi* of people who are trapped (and probably strapped), whose lives are so impacted in routine as to give them no room for maneuver, and who have only necessity to keep them going. By contrast, Sophie and Otto, with the luxury of choice, and the choice of luxuries, have everything but necessity. They can have country houses or not, have children or not, have affairs or not, or live in New York or not! And if asked, they would probably say, "New York is terrible, New York is this, but we would rather live here than anywhere else." Because if New York is their despair, it is also their hope, their religion, the only spiritual value in their lives. It is the place where they can have affairs, sexy drinks, or soulful lunches; can live in (praise be!) nuclear families, and evade relatives; can participate or disappear. By not suggesting this, the film is an extension of the masochistic half truth of "we the victims," and deprives Sophie and Otto of the uniqueness which would have made them truly universal.

That we never become involved in their fate is through no fault of the performers—Shirley MacLaine and Kenneth Mars are quite good, managing to seem both edgy and numb at the same time. They are kept remote and representative by Gilroy's highly theatrical scenario and *mise-en-scène*. The dialogue is stylized—short, quasi-incomplete sentences creating a staccato effect, interlocking monologues—an effect which works well for the secondary characters, particularly the Sada Thompson scene with its antiphonal rhythms and echo-chamber staging. But the stylization is more difficult to sustain with the two main characters. We are given abstract people in a concrete setting, and we keep wanting their feelings to break through the artifice of counterpointed dialogue.

MINNIE AND MOSKOWITZ and *MADE FOR EACH OTHER*

ANDREW SARRIS

Minnie and Moskowitz and *Made for Each Other* exemplify a curious tendency of recent movies to pair up by trying to be different in the same way. Such pairings not only embarrass the claimants to originality; they can be commercially fatal in this era of comparison shopping at the movie marts. In 1970 *M*A*S*H* stole an absurdist war-is-a-howl march on *Catch-22,* and the year before both Julie Andrews and Barbra Streisand did almost identical roller-skate numbers in *Star!* and *Funny Girl* respectively. In 1971 *The Last Picture Show* ran roughshod over *The Last Movie. Sunday, Bloody Sunday* took out much of the topical steam from *Desperate Characters,* so much so, in fact, that Penelope Gilliatt very gallantly supplied a rave review for *Desperate Characters.* Both *Punishment Park* and *Billy Jack* recited an apocryphal "law and order" speech by one Adolf Hitler to bolster their teenage paranoia. Then there were all the dope operas—*Born to Win, Panic in Needle Park, Jennifer on My Mind, Believe in Me, Dusty and Sweets McGee,* and *Skezag.* Medical malfeasance popped up on parallel tracks in *Such Good Friends* and *The Hospital*. That *Macbeth* followed hard upon *King Lear* we could discount as mere coincidence.

The lesson was clear nonetheless. Even during the decline and demoralization of the alleged movie factories, thematic repetition has persisted, though perhaps not so much by conscious plagiarism as by an unconscious absorption of thematic particles in the social atmosphere. What this means for the future is simply that many joyously futuristic journalists will discover that more artistic individualism in the cinema does not in itself guarantee greater variety, either topically or stylistically. After all, how much difference is there between one artist's navel and another's?

What *Minnie and Moskowitz* and *Made for Each Other* have most vividly in common is the trouble their protagonists take to appear self-consciously, even ostentatiously unglamorous. That is to say unglamorous, not unattractive. Gena Rowlands and Seymour Cassell, the eponymous lovers of *M & M*, and Renée Taylor and Joseph Bologna, the playwrighting player-writers of *Made for Each Other*, are all enormously attractive in a scruffy urban way. Still, they are all losers by the cruel standards of movie mythology, and not only losers but loners. The men's jobs are either unspeakable (Cassell's Moskowitz virtually dropping out as a parking-lot attendant), or unmentionable (Bologna's Giggy Pinimba involved very vaguely in personnel work). The women are so shell-shocked by a series of disastrous relationships that they have gone into hiding, Gena Rowlands' Minnie behind dark glasses and Renée Taylor's Pandora Gold behind a performer's patter. Hence, the process that unites the two couples is not so much chemistry as therapy. In each instance, two emotional cripples limp into each other's bruised arms after having screamed at each other through most of the movie.

Where the two movies diverge is in the formal structuring of the relationships. *M & M* is genuinely open-ended in a bizarre sort of way, whereas *Made for Each Other* is improvised within a predetermined pattern. The very thin line between illusion and reality, fiction and gossip, persona and performer, is hopelessly blurred in both movies. John Cassavetes directs not only his wife (Gena Rowlands as Minnie), her mother (Lady Rowlands as Minnie's mother), her brother (David Rowlands as the bumbling minister), his own mother (Katherine Cassavetes as Mrs. Moskowitz), his three children (Nicky, Xana, and Zoe), Seymour Cassell's lovely

wife (Elizabeth Deering), Cassell's mother (Elsie Ames) and two
children (Matthew and Dylyn), but even himself in an unbilled
appearance as Minnie's bad-scene married-man affair. A home
movie? Not exactly. The incestuousness of the casting never gets in
the way of the movie. Indeed, the recognition factor emphasizes
the stylization factor.

Cassavetes has always been more formal and stylized than he
seemed at first glance. When many critics were hailing his first
film, *Shadows*, for its "realism" and "sociological penetration,"
Parker Tyler intruded with his insights into an elaborate camera
style built around the actor as character constructor. *Too Late
Blues* and *A Child Is Waiting* marked a development of this style
with more conventional material, and then *Faces* and *Husbands*
signaled the explosion of the Cassavetes style into baroque histri-
onics. On the whole, I prefer *M & M* to *Husbands* but not to
Faces. Gena Rowlands is especially dazzling in her warmly womanly patience with the hilariously roosterish outbursts of Cassell's
Moskowitz and Val Avery's Zelmo Swift, the latter the funniest
and most monstrous characterization of the year by far. Cassavetes
gets his laughs not through the supper-club calculation of Taylor
and Bologna but rather through a genuinely unpredictable reaction
to the problems of characterization and storytelling. Too often he
strikes false notes, as when Cassell stops off at 42nd Street to see
The Maltese Falcon. Movies like *The Maltese Falcon* never play
42nd Street anymore, and, anyway, a disturbingly disoriented cat
like Moskowitz wouldn't be grooving on Bogie at this time. Cassavetes and Cassell are another matter, but the plot is not about
them but about a character they've made up between them, and I
can't follow this character through to the idyllic romance and marriage with Minnie. I enjoy Gena Rowlands and I enjoy Seymour
Cassell and I enjoy the interplay between the two performers, their
congeniality so to speak, but I simply cannot buy the compatibility
of the two characters. The problem for me is that as much as Cassavetes has entertained me and amused me and even exhilarated
me, he has not led me finally into the magical realms of myth,
fable, and sociological observation. Hence, I still don't believe that
Minnie and Moskowitz ever got married.

The difficulty with Renée Taylor and Joseph Bologna is of a
different order. I do believe that they got married because the gossip columns say that they are married in real life. Also, I suspect
that a great deal of their improvisational material, especially in the

lovely and idiosyncratic sex scenes, is the kind of precious stuff that is distilled in the laboratory of real life. What I don't believe is much of the background they invent for characters that are beneath them on the social and cultural scale. Renée Taylor's most delicious bit as a performer within a performer comes when she announces to a cheesy night-club audience in Brooklyn that she will do a Dietrich number from *Der Blau Engel!* A beautiful moment, but its thrust is satirical rather than confessional, and the whole encounter context of the Taylor–Bologna relationship is similarly muddled by the conflict between the confessional insights of the players and the satirical outbursts of the characters. It is only in the very last moment of the film, the moment that is frozen with Renée Taylor's ineffable forever and forever smile at Bologna's forever and forever sadness that I am convinced of the union of this couple. Unfortunately, too much of what leads up to this final moment is taken up with unimaginative obstacle-building, the dreariest of all methods of making up a plot. But do see *Minnie and Moskowitz* and *Made for Each Other* for the wealth of behavioral talent.

WANDA

STANLEY KAUFFMANN

Probably the most difficult subject to make interesting in art these days is the prole. For at least twenty years our aesthetic attention has centered on such matters as alienation, communication, and identity crisis, problems that are the prerogatives of those who don't have to worry about tomorrow's grub. When a film or play or novel deals with blue-collar folk, we get an anticipatory feeling of *déjà vu*, as if the subject has already been well dealt with in art and there is little to add. In certain senses this is true: Snobbish as it sounds, the range of interest in the truck driver tends to be less than in the advertising executive (even). Most proletarian art deals chiefly with injustice, and most of what changes from one proletarian work to another is the data.

Just because I believe this, *Wanda* is all the more welcome. It's about a working-class girl, and it goes past mere authenticity to some depth, therefore to aspects of universality. At least equally impressive, it marks the writing and directing debut of Barbara Loden, who also plays Wanda and who distinguishes herself in all three fields. Miss Loden is well known as a theater actress. Her performance of the Marilyn Monroe role is about all I remember favorably from the first production of Miller's *After the Fall.* Still I—and most others, I think—would not have expected her to be able to write and direct a film as good as this. Her performance, too, has surprising qualities.

Wanda, I guess, is meant as a homonym for wander. She's a Polish-American girl, from the Pennsylvania coal fields, who drifts away from her husband and two small children simply because she lacks the power to feel for them; drifts with no more luggage than her pocketbook into a motel with a traveling salesman, then drifts into a liaison with a nearly psychopathic criminal. Somehow his fits of fury bind her to him; she is unable to leave the comfort of that fury even when she knows she is coasting with him into crime. We sense that his outbursts are the strongest show of true feeling that anyone has ever offered her and since she has no great depths of feeling to offer anyone else, she clings to the strongest feeling that comes her way.

The man's bank-robbing plan fails, and he is killed; through her persistent stupidity (she gets to the bank too late to play her part), she escapes. Then, after resisting a sexual assault from still another pickup and after bursting into tears for the first time, she seems launched on a career as a barroom hustler.

This is most distinctly not a crime story, not a low-budget *Bonnie and Clyde.* It concentrates on Wanda, on the accidents of her strictured life, which happen to include an encounter with a criminal. It's a modest account of a pilgrimage, even if unknowing and squalid, from beginnings that had numbed her powers of response or protest, through various kinds of disregard and abuse, with almost complete acceptance. The film succeeds in large measure because it's quietly made, taciturn in its fierce concentration on this nearly dumb creature, and because it almost never asks for pathos. Every effort is at succinct chronicle, so gradually Wanda acquires, in her vulnerability and her humiliations, some aspects of an agonist. I know nothing of Miss Loden's religious beliefs, but this strikes me as essentially a Catholic film.

Michael Higgins plays the robber with excellent egocentric madness, yet telling us that this man is the product of his life, living it out as defensively as he can. Miss Loden is very careful not to play Wanda as a victim; she makes her a victim by playing her as a girl who is struggling every moment of her life. The struggle is weak and handicapped, the results are misfortunes and defeats, but she never pities herself, until the very end. The last shot is a freeze-frame—one of the few really apt recent uses of that device—in which Wanda sees that the rest of her life is going to be a steep slide, and not a long one. Wanda looks like an easy part, but it would be easy only for an inferior actress. Miss Loden succeeds beautifully because, inside the cage of inadequacy, we sense the bafflement and fruitless fight. Her performance is sure to be widely underrated because it's not the least bit showy; but it's a work of understanding, imagination, and talent.

Her direction and writing are not much less talented. The film was shot in 16mm, now blown up to 35mm, so the texture is grainy and the color mediocre, but—*ex post facto* rationale, perhaps—the look of it fits the subject. Some shots, like Wanda in white walking through the coal fields, are a little arty. But note, for instance, a sequence near the end: Wanda stands in front of a tavern window; a girl comes out of the bar, passes her, goes up an outside stairway, appears at a window on the other side, comes down again and comes around to Wanda—all shot from one position with a panning camera, the action designed so that one position could accommodate it and so that we get the feel of a web being woven around Wanda.

The virtues (considerable) and faults (few) of the writing can be shown in one passage. During her first night in bed with the robber, Wanda says to his back, "Mr. Dennis, don't you want to know *my* name?" A life is in that line. Without turning, he replies, "No." A touch too heavy. If he had just grunted or said nothing, had just let her line hang there, the point would have been unhammered.

In the last three or four years, a number of attempts have been made, of varying worth, to deal with American life as it is. Almost all of them have dealt with the young or near young, exemplifying aspects of complicated social or political crisis, with at least some attributes of intellection. But, as Robert Coles and others keep reminding us, most of the country, like most of the people on earth, do not live at that level; Hobbes' state of nature—with life nasty, brutish, and short—hasn't changed much for them in three centuries. Wanda came out of a society that had ravaged her afferent powers and her adaptive intelligence long before she was on her own. Miss Loden's triumph is that she has realized this truth without stopping at case history; her writing, direction, and acting make *Wanda* a small, good work of art, and make Miss Loden a very welcome addition to the film scene.

6

DOCUMENTS

THE SORROW AND THE PITY*

Harold Clurman

While in Paris last June I saw *Le Chagrin et La Pitié,* a long documentary film which was recently shown at the New York Film Festival under the title *The Sorrow and the Pity.* I did not know at the time that I was going to review it and didn't take note of its manifold details. But the film impressed me strongly; I hope it will gain general distribution.

The director, Marcel Ophuls, and his assistants who composed the film set out to illuminate the historical past—the time of the Nazi occupation of France—by viewing it from the vantage point of the present. They interviewed a large number of people— French and German—political and military figures, lawyers, shopkeepers, peasants, collaborators and resistants who were in one way or another involved in the dreadful events. The film's inquiry is focused on the activities of the Nazi occupants and the native citizenry in the industrial city of Clermont-Ferrand. The film-makers achieved cinematic unity by placing the intellectually towering person of Mendès-France, who for a while was a prisoner of the Vichy government, in the film's central position.

After the picture was exhibited (almost clandestinely), Mendès-France asked someone, "How am I as a picture star?" My answer is "very good." His directness, quiet humor, dignity, unemphatic

---

* This film did not actually play in the United States until 1972. It did appear at the New York Film Festival in October 1971 and on the basis of that showing, won a special award from the National Society of Film Critics. Additional discussion of *The Sorrow and the Pity* will appear in next year's Society anthology.—EDITOR

forcefulness and clarity in speaking of his "adventures" and views endow the film with poise and weight.

The Sorrow and the Pity offers insight not only into the specific character of one moment in French and European history but into history in general. This film persuades one—as do few books, novels, plays or eyewitness reportage—of the truth of Karl Marx's aphorism. "History walks on two feet"—in other words, that it is enacted by ordinary as well as extraordinary men and women.

Very little history is purely "ideological." When a peasant is asked why he joined the resistance, his answer is "I saw that the German soldiers were eating well, and we had almost nothing." The Gentile lawyer who defended Mendès-France, accused of desertion, tells the interviewer that the chief judge instructed the court that questions of religion (Mendès-France is a Jew) were to be excluded from consideration, but that anti-Semitism was very much in evidence anyway. A prominent personage and former collaborator, now regretful of his role, is asked whether, just before the outbreak of the war, he would have felt insulted at being designated a fascist. He answers in the negative. Women, now employed or in business for themselves, who suffered the degradation of having their heads shaved because they had "fraternized" with the Germans, answer the investigators in tough self-defense.

A now retired German officer is questioned at his daughter's wedding (with all guests present) about his duties as commander of the occupying forces in Clermont-Ferrand. He wears all the decorations awarded him by the Nazi government. "Are you embarrassed to be displaying all these medals now?" "No," he answers, "only those who didn't win them are embarrassed." When further interrogated as to whether he would act once again as he had during the occupation he answers with complacent assurance, "Yes, I would."

Mendès-France, found guilty and therefore in danger of death or long imprisonment, undertook to escape. He was about to lower himself by a rope from the window of his cell when he noticed a young man on the street below having difficulty coaxing a girl to yield her favors to him. Mendès-France confesses that he was rather impatient with the procrastinating girl. However, she finally consented, and Mendès-France was able to effect his escape. He fought as an aviator for the liberation of France.

I am an admirer of French culture, so I was unhappy to learn on my return to Paris in 1947 that not all of France had been resistant. How naïve! I heard a woman, sitting in the Tuileries Gardens, whisper furtively, "We were better fed under the Germans"; she looked up at me apprehensively as I passed. At the opening night of Sartre's *Death Without Burial*, about the struggle between the militant collaborators and the resistants, the audience split according to their former political stance and engaged in fierce vituperation against one another, causing total pandemonium. Arthur Miller's *Incident at Vichy* (1964) could not be produced in Paris lest it arouse ancient animosities (it is only now about to open there).

Watching *The Sorrow and the Pity*, I think of France, one nation among many. I understand not simply "this is how and what happened" but this, almost anywhere in the world, is what can happen again. The history of mankind is not a pretty tale. Still we live!

CALCUTTA

DAVID DENBY

"Please do not understand me too quickly," André Gide once implored. Is there any reason why one civilization shouldn't expect a similar courtesy in its dealings with another? *Calcutta*, the extraordinary documentary by Louis Malle, is gallantly restrained in its interpretations of an alien culture, and it comes as a great relief after years of officious, know-it-all documentaries and travel films which did little more than reflect the preconceptions of the filmmakers.

Confronted with the unprecedented misery of this huge Indian city and the general incomprehensibility of Indian life for the Westerner, the director has scaled down his ambitions and his presumptions. To bear witness to an extreme human situation and to delineate a great mystery without explaining it all away—these are the director's obvious intentions. We learn a great deal and want to learn more; we are hurt by the suffering that we see and also hurt that we can't understand more about it. How many films leave us with feelings like these?

Malle is an extremely sophisticated man, a New Wave film-maker of exhilarating cleverness and grace; his intelligence is every-where evident in *Calcutta*, but not his high spirits—for that quality you should rush to see *Murmur of the Heart* while it is still in town. *Calcutta* was made during a break in Malle's career, when he was temporarily disenchanted with fiction films. He went to India early in 1968 with a crew of only two men—cameraman Etienne Becker and soundman Jean-Claude Laureux; they returned with forty hours of film that was subsequently edited into eight separate programs on India for the BBC. The series, of which *Calcutta* is a two-hour portion, vexed the Indian government so much that it closed down the BBC office in New Delhi.

In view of the fact that the film was shot almost four years ago, one can't help wondering how much worse the city has become since the refugees started pouring into Calcutta from East Pakis-tan. What we see is certainly bad enough. Fortunately, we are al-lowed to do a lot of looking and listening and wondering on our own; the narrator, that loathsome presence in documentary films, doesn't show up until well into the movie, and in this case he is only the director quietly telling us, in fluent English, some simple, terrible facts about the immense city.

The movie opens with a series of individual shots of Calcuttans performing their ablutions in the Hooghly River, the city's filthy and sacred waterway. One man rubs his chest and back with fero-cious concentration; another jumps up and down in the water, as if exercising on a trampoline; a third brushes his teeth. In the back-ground we see large freighters at anchor and bits of floating gar-bage. Then the film moves to the streets (where it will stay, almost to the end): innumerable people and vehicles fight for the right of way in the middle of the road; men cling precariously to the out-side of buses or trains or ride on top; small herds of goats or buffa-loes make their way through the streets, and at times men and cows squat equably beside one another on the sidewalks. At other times, we see a man lying dead on the sidewalk or out in the road—the cars steer cautiously around him.

This frenetic intermixture of man, beast, and machine prepares us somewhat for a scene near the end that was shot in one of the city's worst slums. In this place physical matter seems to have lost its distinctive function and station in life: hogs, infants, offal, roosters, rubble, dead rats, water, cows—everything is mixed together. Civilization may not have emerged from such a conglomerate ooze, but it will certainly recede into something like it.

How can an American react to scenes like these? When our own documentaries draw attention to a social problem, they almost always insist or imply that the problem is an anomaly in our society which could be eradicated if people were a little less complacent. The viewer may even join a process which starts with working up feelings of outrage and shame, and includes forming a public pressure group, placing ads in the Sunday *Times* and possibly celebrating the passage of legislation. The problem may remain, of course, but we still associate documentaries with reform, with action.

But what actions could begin to solve the problems of Calcutta, a city in which 40 per cent of the eight million inhabitants lived in subhuman conditions in 1968? "There *must* be a revolution in India" were the words that kept running through my head, but afterward I realized that Malle's film did not hold out any such prospect.

The people of Calcutta are as much surrounded by religion as we are by advertising. There is a moving scene in which a group of railway employees gather for an impromptu religious ceremony after working hours, and another in which a Sunday-afternoon crowd, strangers to one another, sit down in the park and pray together for hours. We can't help feeling that the very rituals and observances and taboos that make life bearable and give it meaning and shape may also form the bulwark against massive social change.

At one point a violent Maoist student demonstration comes to a complete halt to let a religious procession pass by. This is a wonderful moment—think of the tenderness and respect that is implied by such a gesture—but Malle leaves behind the clear implication that the Calcuttans are a people in need of political consciousness as a dustbowl is in need of rain. We see a group of dark-skinned Madrassi who have left their villages in search of work and who have quickly settled to the bottom of the social scale; Malle tells us that their lives have been completely disrupted, and as they press forward toward the camera and stare into the lens, he permits himself a rare subjective observation: "They are surprised that anyone would come to film them, or would pity them, or would be indignant."

Suffering and pain do not seem to have made these people less attractive; this movie, for all its horror, is filled with extraordinarily beautiful faces. Malle explains that many Indians believe that they will be reborn, that life is only a brief moment in a cosmic cycle. At one point he asks a beggar why he gave up everything at the age of twenty and took to the streets, and the man replies, "Because life is an illusion." The physical degradation of Calcutta dismays us; we know our reaction to it, even if we can't imagine what should be done about it. But the beauty and calm in these faces reflect some kind of super-earthly exaltation that is miles beyond our comprehension or capability.

THE CLOWNS

Pierrots and Augustes

STEFAN KANFER

Robert Benchley once divided the world into two kinds of people: those who divide the world into two kinds of people and those who do not. Director Federico Fellini (La Dolce Vita, Satyricon) is firmly in the first category. In his new film, The Clowns, Fellini separates mankind into two classic species of fool: Pierrot and Auguste. Pierrot is the familiar circus clown in floppy white and conical hat, elegant and haughty. The clown Auguste is an eternal tramp, crumpled, drunken and rebellious.

No man escapes. Picasso and Einstein, says Fellini in a published exegesis of the film, are Augustes. Middle-class parents are Pierrots; their children Augustes. Hitler: a white clown. Mussolini: an Auguste. Freud: a white clown. Jung: an Auguste.

Fellini's fourteenth film, like all of the maestro's visual operas, is a flamboyant search for self. This time he prowls the enchanted place of his youth, the circus, but the spectacle of childish memory is a specter to the mature man. The circus has changed or vanished, the clown acts are diminished beyond recognition.

But on a Fellini journey, reality is only a pebble in the shoe. He turns the world into his circus and, in a liberated, quasi-documentary style, resurrects some of history's great *pagliacci* with their cornucopia of practical jokes, smashed hats, pulled chairs, popping balloons and squirting flowers. Fellini's pretense is to restore the icons of his youth for the pleasure of today's children, but beyond the easy delights is a philosophy clearly aimed at adults.

From time to time the camera breaks away from the center ring to inspect clowns in senescence, brittle little men who recall Falstaff's lament: "How ill white hairs become a fool." In the midst of unabashed gaiety, Fellini ushers in bitterness: an Italian lion tamer who trains his beasts in German because "it is the only human language that they understand." The film's zenith is a funeral staged *con brio*—the spectacular obsequies of a clown, his hearse drawn by men in horse suits, his widow a clown with pendulous breasts, the orator a grotesque who maligns the deceased (suffocated by an ostrich egg at the tender age of two hundred) as vile and worthless.

Here Fellini insists on the last laugh. If the human condition is a melancholy joke, he implies, then death is its punch line and hilarity the only proper response. The film-maker pretends to have no "message" in *The Clowns*; when an actor asks him the meaning of his film, a bucket drops over the director's head in mid-reply. But absurdity itself is a commentary. It is also the perpetual delight of this indelible, grieving comedy in which the viewers, Pierrots and Augustes all, are the stars.

ROBERT HATCH

In his prologue to *The Clowns*, Federico Fellini tells us that, as a small boy in an Italian provincial town, he was captivated and terrified by the clowns of a circus that pitched its tent just below his bedroom window. Subsequently, he began to see the eccentrics and grotesques of his neighborhood (the neighborhood seemed to have its full share of them) as tanbark zanies. Now he offers a nostalgic tribute to that comic tradition.

Fellini's responsiveness to clowns and clowning has been apparent in his previous work, particularly in those pictures—*La Strada*, *Nights of Cabiria*, *Juliet of the Spirits*—that were built around his wife, Giulietta Masina—herself an instinctive and most appealing clown—but also in such others as *I Vitelloni* and 8½. It demonstrates a faith in the indestructibility of the utterly vulnerable, a kind of idealism of human survival against the odds. There are seeds of sentimentality and excess in the notion, and Fellini has never particularly shied from either; but there is also rigor in it: The clown is never extinguished, true enough, but he is ever on the brink of extinction. What a destiny!

So now Fellini brings a brilliant, historic company of clowns into the ring and focuses the resources of his research and sympathy upon them. He is a wonderfully evocative film-maker and it should be a magic film. It repeatedly promises to become so, but in the end it has not. Somehow, when Fellini confronts the clowns directly, they evade him. Of course, they are on hand in great numbers and presented in the most intense and appreciative detail; but the exhilaration, the feeling of identity, the miracle of a past really recaptured—these promises are not fulfilled. The picture keeps losing momentum, letting you escape.

I think part of the trouble may be that "clown" has become a metaphor, something that happens to a concept only when its actuality is beyond recall. We all know, or think we know, what the clown quality is in human behavior, but the reconstruction of clowning itself seems much less than what we have in mind. Masina, it is obvious, has a clown's heart; it makes us love her and fear for her. But these veritable clowns—forever banging one another on the head with huge, weightless mallets, dueling one another with jets of water, snatching stools from under one another's bottoms, falling in every conceivable attitude of inconsequential agony—are they what the word means to us? Are they amusing; can one extract any instruction from their antics without becoming patronizing and pretentious? Like witches and centaurs, Trojans and the Borgia family, clowns are part of our heritage; I doubt that they can any longer be part of our direct experience.

And further, it seems to me that Fellini erred by making his film in the form of a documentary on the process of film-making. This device, which inevitably involves a pretense of spontaneity, a false intimacy, always puts me on guard. I suppose that Fellini used it here to proclaim his very personal involvement in the subject matter. Also, he needed an integrating narrative, and the material and personages he could bring together were sadly fragmentary. But the effect, too often, was to upstage the very people he was bent on celebrating. When he goes to visit old clowns, surrounded by the clippings and posters of their fame, still game to sketch the outlines of their once witty dexterity, attention flows toward the director, his camera and production crew, crowding the scene. Particularly with clowns, it was a dubious idea. They are fragile; Fellini is dominating. They are finished; he is in his prime. Fellini making a picture about clowns is something quite different from a Fellini picture about clowns. I doubt that—so late—he could have made the latter; I am not glad that he went ahead with the former. There are instants of flashing and cheeky good humor in the film, but overall, it has a vaultlike chill.

THE HELLSTROM CHRONICLE

Quick, Henry, the Flit!

ARTHUR KNIGHT

If, as is eloquently argued in *The Hellstrom Chronicle*, "life's only purpose is life itself," then—as this unique film also affirms—the insect world is obviously far better equipped for survival than we humans. The insects are far more adaptable. They can build an immunity to DDT, for example, in a single generation, or change shape, form, and color quickly to conform to environmental differences. More important, unlike mankind, the insects are instinctively dedicated to preserving the species. Within the structure of an ant colony or a beehive, each member performs its own simple function, to which every moment of its brief life is totally dedicated. And all of this frantic activity is for one purpose only—a continuation of life. Man and the insects alone continue to be fruitful and multiply, according to the film's fictitious Dr. Hellstrom, and in the ultimate showdown the insects are bound to win.

Some interesting philosophic questions are raised here, and I am inclined to believe that part of the purpose of this fascinating David Wolper production is to stimulate such reflection. If the price of survival is losing one's identity in a faceless society where the value of each life is subordinated to the greater good of the species, are we then in the end not less than human? Indeed, is there any point at all to survival in a mindless, depersonalized, devaluated world directed to nothing beyond mere survival? Perhaps it is unfortunate that man, having a brain, has not used it to bring forth a more equitable, more peaceable kingdom, but can we as humans possibly settle for the strictly functional life of the bee or the ant?

There are few enough films that can generate such disturbing yet fundamental questions, and fewer still that do it by means of fresh, even unprecedented, scientific footage that presents the many aspects of insect life in magnificent color and alarming close-ups. There are shots—such as the shimmering death dance of the May flies—that are beautiful beyond belief, and others—such as the relentless march of the driver ants—that are as frightening as an avalanche. Best of all, David Seltzer, the writer of *The Hellstrom Chronicle*, has devised a means of setting all of this forth in an original and constantly arresting manner. Its narrator, Dr. Hellstrom, appears to be a gratingly cocksure young man with a mission. He talks, he irritates, and his very manner demands our grudging attention. It is not so much a letdown as it is a relief to discover in the end that he is in fact an actor, Lawrence Pressman, and that we can preserve our image of the detached man of science. But by that time the damage has been done. We have *listened* as well as looked. I can only add that since I saw the film, no insect can cross my path with impunity. If it's kill or be killed, I'm starting my side of the fight right now.

DERBY

Track with a Brass Ring
JAY COCKS

It seems at first far too facile and fragile an idea for a full-length movie: the roller derby as a metaphor for America's competition, violence, degradation. Scenes of derby competition worked well in films like *Petulia* and *Medium Cool* because they were used as secondary symbols, episodes that were part of a more complex whole. But an entire feature devoted to the derby, its stars and its life styles? Director-Cameraman Robert Kaylor confounds all expectations in *Derby*. He does it by treating the competition not as a symbol but as a sorry fact of life.

His film is about one real skater who has made it big (Charlie O'Connell, captain of the San Francisco Bay Bombers), and another who wants desperately to follow him around the same successful turn. Mike Snell works in the Firestone Tire plant in Dayton, Ohio, and dreams of making it in big-time derby competition. Kaylor intercuts footage of O'Connell and Snell: the derby hero bashing his rivals, leading his team, conducting a tour of a moneyed man's San Francisco, and Hero Worshiper Snell going through the day-to-day hassles of making a tentative kind of life for himself and his family. Kaylor captures scenes and feelings—factories, roadhouses, dance halls, motorcycles—that make similar attempts in *Joe* look like musty melodrama.

Kaylor uses a kind of modified neo-realist technique in which real people re-enact real situations. The results are often stunning. There is a pervasive tone of desperation in *Derby*, a sense of ironic, backhanded success about O'Connell and a pitiful aimlessness in Snell. As the documentary ends, he gets on a motorcycle and rides out to roller-derby school in San Francisco. Snell says he wants to "better" himself, but *Derby* has made it clear that success will mean no more than living a hollow dream.

BLUE WATER, WHITE DEATH and *DERBY*

Why Does Derby *Die and* White Death *Live?*

VINCENT CANBY

Anyone still laboring under the impression that critics can make or break movies might investigate the highly dissimilar fates of two recent documentaries, Robert Kaylor's *Derby* and the Peter Gimbel–James Lipscomb *Blue Water, White Death*, both of which opened to rave reviews and one of which died after only five weeks. Because movies do not often vanish, or dissolve, or get cut up and sold for scrap after a poor first run, *Derby* will, I assume, be again available in subsequent-run theaters in the not too distant future.

I would hope that it will then find an audience, but I'm not too optimistic. The lack of interest in the film expressed by New Yorkers has not been a regional failing. In spite of good reviews almost every place it's opened, the *Derby* box office has been disappointing in a uniform way—the first several days of business are pretty good, and then the receipts begin to dwindle, which industry statisticians interpret as meaning that most of those few people who do go to see it don't like it and lose no time in telling their friends.

All of which baffles me, as I'm sure it must baffle its distributor (Cinerama) and especially Mr. Kaylor, the man who directed and photographed it and whose first theatrical feature it is. After all, hasn't Mr. Kaylor been brought up to believe that no matter how outrageous or dim or unpublicized a first film is, if it receives the support of the critics, it will probably be a hit? Next to why I like a film or not, I'm most interested in learning why certain films become hits and flops, with and without critical support. However, it's as open-ended an endeavor as the pursuit of happiness, and nobody ever really knows for sure, not even with hindsight.

Like Barbara Loden's *Wanda*, another critical hit that failed to cause any excitement at the box office earlier this year, *Derby* takes as its universe the lower-middle-class American milieu that has, perhaps, more to do with the way things are in this country than does the middle-middle-class milieu of the silent majority, of television sitcoms and soaps. Although Miss Loden's *Wanda*, after a brief moment of glory, drifts towards disaster, and Mr. Kaylor's real-life hero, Mike Snell, is headed toward a triumph as a roller-derby star, both characters have a good deal in common. They evoke a sense of rootlessness and waste that a lot of people, including those moviegoers who never bother to wonder why we must have new models of air-conditioners and automobiles every year, find profoundly depressing.

The real soft underbelly of American life that most Americans don't want to know about is not, I suspect, the ghetto existence whose horrors are of such extreme degree they inspire a kind of romantic compassion and revolutionary resolve. Rather, it's the world of the Wandas and Mike Snells, of characters whose dreams (when and if they have them) are small, who live lives of notably poor visibility, who have access to just about all the material pleasures ever known to man—through television sets, toasters, washing machines, *Playboy*—and yet who have no special causes or identities. I say that with the awareness that, within *Derby*, Mike Snell does have a cause and an identity, which give a cheerful, optimistic shape to a film that otherwise makes no attempt to romanticize a very bleak environment, an environment that most of us would prefer to ignore.

It's somewhat easier to rationalize the popularity of *Blue Water, White Death*, which includes some of the most smashing man-against-beast footage ever filmed by anyone anywhere at any time.

The film is the record of Mr. Gimbel's search, financed by Cinema Center Films, for the great white shark, first off South Africa, then off Ceylon, Mozambique and, finally, off southern Australia. Peter Matthiessen's *Blue Meridian*, published by Random House, is the prose record of the same search, and can best be read in conjunction with the film. Nothing in Mr. Matthiessen's prose comes close to conveying the extraordinary beauty and sense of participation contained in the film's underwater sequences, but then the film never suggests that its players—Mr. Gimbel, the rich boy who made good, and his principal associates, Stan Waterman of New England and Ron and Valerie Taylor of Australia—are anything more (or less) than good-natured chubbers off on a happy lark.

It's apparent that Mr. Matthiessen has both respect and affection for the people he is writing about, to such an extent, in fact, that his prose sometimes takes on its own hearty, chubberlike tone, not evident in his *The Cloud Forest* and other works of reportage. Mr. Matthiessen persuades Mr. Gimbel and the others to talk about their feelings in courting disaster in such spectacular ways, but it may be that the mystery, at least, as it concerns one man, is explained in a passage that, at first, seems irrelevant.

At one point, Mr. Matthiessen asked Mr. Gimbel if he felt he had gotten to know Ron Taylor, the superb and almost inhumanly unflappable skindiver and underwater photographer. "The question," writes Mr. Matthiessen, "made [Gimbel] uncomfortable, and he thought awhile before he answered it. 'Ron's a very dedicated guy,' he said, 'and all he thinks about is his profession—for example, he only reads technical material, and can't understand why the rest of us bother with fiction.' He paused again. 'You know, I like Ron very much. I really do, but sometimes talking to him is like talking to that diving suit'—here he pointed to the suit hanging on his cabin door—'There's nobody there.'"

It's not, I think, that there's nobody there exactly, but that Ron Taylor exists in a dimension different from you and me, as do, maybe to a lesser extent, the other members of the expedition.

Mr. Matthiessen writes intelligently and amusingly about some of the tacky attempts to give the film human interest, particularly some sequences that had Valerie Taylor "marveling at flightless rails, thumping tortoises and wandering breathless through the magic wood." He adds: "It seemed to me that the surface footage depended too heavily on Valerie's lovely face and professional acting ability in a film where acting has no place, and that these winsome excursions all over the shores of the Indian Ocean would slacken the tension of the film, and rot it with cuteness in the bargain."

The finished film is not without its moments of cuteness, but they hardly matter since the rest of the film is superbly realized. Not since I was about six, and suffered the exquisite pains and pleasures of Frank Buck's *Bring 'Em Back Alive*, have I been so pleasantly exhausted by an armchair adventure. The world has become small and comparatively tame, but, in the great white shark, *Blue Water, White Death* has found a beast so physically awesome, and still so little known, that it restores some sense of respect (and terror) to our conception of the natural order of things.

7
THE THIRD WORLD

THE HOUR OF THE FURNACES

Stanley Kauffmann

The Hour of the Furnaces is a film phenomenon and a phenomenal film. This Argentine documentary runs four hours and twenty minutes, plus two intermissions, and is a clear, unambiguous call for revolutionary violence. It was directed by Fernando Solanas, thirty-five, who wrote the script with Octavio Getino, thirty-six. (Solanas also photographed, Getino did the sound.) Both of them have been making short films in the past decade. Their work here is sometimes crude, sometimes suspect, and is certainly not unfailingly gripping, but they have made an impressive and vehement film of immense energy.

It has three main sections, "Neo-colonialism and Violence," "Act for Liberation," "Violence and Liberation," and there are numerous subsections. To criticize the argument of the film calls for a knowledge of Argentina—and a copy of the script!—to which I won't pretend. The thesis, varied and repeated, supported with news clips, commentaries, quotations, statistics, and interviews, can be stated fairly simply: Argentina began as a Spanish colony and, after independence (1816), continued as an economic and cultural colony of Great Britain. The U.S. developed great interests there, and through this century U.S. power has supplanted British power, though the British still have a strong cultural hold. (See the dress and amusements of the upper class.)

The first really Argentine politics in Argentina was Peronism. Perón was maligned abroad, principally by the U.S., because his economic developments and social welfare programs, his payment of the foreign debt, all interfered with foreign investments and control. The U.S. conspired in the overthrow of Perón, nominally as a pro-democratic move, actually to install a regime more friendly to its influence. Post-Perón governments, like earlier ones, have been oligarchic, plutocratic, militaristic, and brutally repressive, and have depended heavily on outside cultural and economic resources. The largest political party in Argentina is still the Peronist one; it can be the spearhead of a people's revolution which is what is needed in all Latin America. "Two, three, more Vietnams," as Che said.

All the above is subject to some question, even on the basis of superficial knowledge like mine. But the size of the Peronist bloc (30 to 40 percent of the population) and the possible alliance between Peronism and the far left were reported in *The New York Times*, by Malcolm W. Browne, on October 3, 1970. Anti-Americanism is a great unifying force among political factions in Latin America. If it be argued that there are Latin American countries much worse off than Argentina, there is also a country—Uruguay—that has always been much better off; and see the recent history of their Tupamaros.

Besides the questions that may nevertheless be asked of the film's facts, there are also questions about their presentation. What's the point of the gory slaughterhouse scenes? Argentina lives by beef production and will do so presumably under the most popular government. We are told ominously—twice—that four people die a minute in Latin America. By my figures, this is also the rate in the U.S. We are told that true culture depends on the complete liberation of man—in which case we will never have true culture. (I would have thought that one reason for art is that man is *not* completely liberated, and will not be.) We are shown a man being beaten by a group of men in mufti, then being dragged face down through the mud. How do we know that he wasn't a CIA agent who tried to get into a Peronist meeting? There are many instances of beating and gassing where sympathy is asked immediately for the victims, with no fixing of facts.

But, keeping one's guard up as well as possible, one still is overcome by a sense of selfish, cruel, exploitative power in the hands of a few. As usual in all tyrannical situations, East or West, black or white or brown, there is no slightest reason to believe that the oppressed are the moral superiors of their oppressors and will behave better if and when they triumph; but that's hardly a reason for the oppressed to accept things as they are, particularly if they are the majority.

So we come to the nub of the matter: the advocacy of violence. In politics, I don't see how a view on violence can be held as a universal absolute, which is why many of us who object to the Vietnam war still do not call ourselves pacifists. The Argentine peasant, who has inherited generations of wretchedness, who has seen women and children machine-gunned by police, is in a very different emotional and, I think, moral position, in regard to violence, from the American university student who is (rightly) protesting the campus presence of Dow Chemical. Although it is chilling to see this film come *three times* to a climactic call for violent revolution, I think that to deplore it in terms of the nonviolent campaigns which one advocates in the U.S. is almost to verge on the smug. It's a bit like people on a diet telling the underfed that they're better off thin. If violence is immoral, as it objectively is, we still have to recognize that there are situations where objectivity is impossible; that there are situations where violence may have to be used to drive out even greater immoralities.

In terms of cinema technique and imagination, Solanas has done everything he could to make his work a *film*—to break out of the old booby trap of propaganda: which is that propaganda films rarely change anyone's mind; they only heat up the previously convinced or the susceptible. True, he says halfway through Part Two that his film is not for mere spectators, but I think that by then he hopes to have hooked those—Latin Americans, anyway—who started as mere spectators. He has worked to make his picture *visually* interesting. He used to work on advertising films, and one can see it in his use of varying optical techniques for the many words on screen. The editing is sharp, often with staccato intercutting of action and verbal message. The sounds and songs are effective. (I should probably specify that it's all in Spanish with subtitles.)

And sometimes the film is genuinely beautiful. There's a well-composed, deep-focus scene in which an old Patagonian peasant sits before his shack, speaking with simple stateliness of the horrible past and his undimmed socialist enthusiasm. There's a scene in which the camera travels past an odd assortment of silent men waiting in a cellar, then passes a curtain on the other side of which a young whore is seated on the edge of her bed, taking her lunch break. There's a slow 360-degree pan over the Buenos Aires roof-tops, while a voice speaks of its condition and history, and the excellent photography itself underscores what is being said.

In a further effort to break the film forward *off* the screen, to keep it from being something to watch, Solanas has arranged moments where the film can be stopped and discussed. And he has left it all open-ended, so that further testimonies and interviews can be added.

The Hour of the Furnaces has been shown only clandestinely in Argentina but openly in some other Latin American countries and in Europe. The gifted Italian director Marco Bellocchio has said, "It's not a film, it's a gun." But (as he knows) it would not be a gun unless it were a film. I hope the reality of that gun will be seen in this country, and I hope against hope that it may influence our policy abroad. Time runs out.

Solanas has made a message picture with more than one message. In its force and commitment and stature, it's the best film—of any kind—that I've seen from Latin America.

RAMPARTS OF CLAY

ARTHUR SCHLESINGER, JR.

Having long been turned off by quasi-documentary films about primitive peoples, I went to see *Ramparts of Clay* with foreboding. It has always seemed that the invasion of a tradition-bound culture by sophisticated movie people wielding sophisticated equipment must lead to falsification; the very presence of so elaborate an intrusion cannot but make the locals behave differently. Only the supreme artists, Robert Flaherty or F. W. Murnau, have escaped the risk of manipulation and the flavor of condescension. The visit to our brothers in the hills becomes a contemporary version of a pastoral, comforting the urban audience with its illusion of understanding and relationship.

Nor was I reassured by the epigraph from Frantz Fanon, the approved voice of the Third World: "The bourgeois phase in the history of underdeveloped countries is a completely useless phase. When this caste has vanished . . . it will be seen . . . that everything must be started again from scratch." This proposition is, at best, exceedingly doubtful. Even Marx believed that underdeveloped countries had to go through the bourgeois phase to qualify for Communism. Engels called the French conquest of Algeria "an important and fortunate fact for the progress of civilization." The Fanon touch seemed to portend a counter-pastoral designed to gratify the anti-bourgeois proclivities of a bourgeois audience.

But I was wrong. The film opens with a girl straining at a well rope. Behind stretches a bleak village in a sullen brown landscape. The sound track catches the creaking of the rope, the cackle of chickens, the noises of the village. Suddenly one realizes that there will be no musical background at all—and is inordinately grateful. The cadence of the film seems to embody the cadence of the village life. But one is not bored; the austerity of the conception is oddly compelling.

In time the traces of a plot emerge. The men of the village go on strike when their wages as stonecutters are reduced. The militia arrive and sequester them for three days; then go away. A village girl, the girl at the well in the opening, is disturbed by the premonitions of a larger world outside. In a remarkable sequence, terrifying in its violation of personality, the older women, perceiving her restlessness, surround her and spatter blood on her face. In the end, she flees into the wasteland, heading—who knows?—to the city or to death.

The young director Jean-Louis Bertucelli has achieved a sense of total visual and aural authenticity. He understands, as he has written, that *cinéma vérité* is a myth, "for, from the moment the camera focuses on an event, it ceases to be objective. . . . Truth lies in the dramatic approach, not in the technique." His characters and images are not recorded from the outside, as in a travelogue; they have instead a rigorous fidelity to the inner truth of the village life. His passionate and economical artistry produces a work of singular strength and beauty.

The film's history has points of interest. The Tunisian government insisted on controlling the script and direction; so Bertucelli shot the film in Algeria. The film, however, has been shown in neither Tunisia nor Algeria. It is almost as if these countries were concerned to prove Fanon right. But Algeria, at least, claims to have passed beyond the bourgeois phase; and Fanon, had he lived, might have come to understand that the enemy often may be less economic than political authority. A better epigraph would have come from Yeats: "Hurrah for revolution and cannon come again!/The beggars have changed places, but the lash goes on."

HOA-BINH

Robert Hatch

To make a gentle picture about South Vietnam today is an extraordinary ambition; *Hoa-Binh* is an extraordinary picture. It is about a little boy named Hung (Phi Lan) and his baby sister who, against all probability, survive alone in the city and suburbs of Saigon at war. The children's father, a pedicab driver, has slipped off to the Vietcong; their mother dies of a carcinoma in the American infirmary. A wicked aunt scorns them and slaps them and pockets the money she has been given to feed them. With his sister on his hip, young Hung (I would guess he is ten) sets off for the docks and streets of the city to earn a living for them both by unloading junks, shining shoes, hawking papers and begging along the café tables.

Since we all know what befalls abandoned children in a land at war, the Damocles suspense of *Hoa-Binh* becomes almost unendurable. But the sword never falls, and in the last scene Hung breaks into a run from far down the street and flings himself into his father's arms. Just above, I mentioned a wicked aunt; that is the clue: *Hoa-Binh* is a fairy story. By telling it so, the French director Raoul Coutard (his wife is Vietnamese) accomplishes two purposes: He reminds us that, while the purpose of war is to kill, the purpose of art is to celebrate life; and by extending to his young protagonist a compassion that is as arbitrary as a magic wand, he makes us guiltily aware of the extremes to which art must go if it would celebrate life in contemporary Vietnam. A bomb explodes in a neighborhood theater, and the audience vomits out to die in the street. Hung is crouching in the midst of the carnage, protecting his sister with his body. Suddenly he leaps to his feet and, unscathed, dashes away with her. This is an insult to our expectations and an occasion for acknowledging what our expectations have become.

Hoa-Binh begins with a child's voice asking, in French, "what is peace?"; in the course of the film men on both sides are heard to say that the war must go on—if need be for twenty, thirty years—until right prevails. Who will then answer the child's question? The opening ten minutes of the picture make the nature of helicopter war vivid beyond anything I have hitherto seen. American soldiers are everywhere, but the children through whom one absorbs the littered, exhausted fabric of Saigon are very small, and for the most part the very large intruders are evident as heavy shoes and muscular calves. Coutard is not "for" the Americans or "against" them; indeed, when they move into the action they are benign or neutral. Hung pays them little heed, since it is through his own people that he must hope to survive. They are good or bad, as people tend to be; the Americans are a neutral force, impersonal. At one point, Hung hears rumbling in the sky and asks his mother whether a storm is approaching; the look on her face is not easily forgotten.

Like the great Italian directors after World War II, Coutard has found his cast in the populace. A few of them are stiff with amateur sense of the occasion, but he has been triumphant with the principals. The father and mother speak almost entirely with their eyes and what they say is simply what life has been like for them these past ten years and more. I suspect that Coutard, who must be a director of surpassing tact, has told them no more than to show what they remember.

The boy Phi Lan is the miracle of the film. He is a perfectly real Vietnamese child, straight-limbed, quick as a lizard, with a face that responds like clear water to hopes and rebuffs. And at the same time he is Jack the Giant Killer, the youngest of the princely brothers who performs the impossible task and saves the lives of them all. He wears his father's hat; it makes him invulnerable. In his presence, it is impossible not to believe, at least a little, in fairy tales. We have not yet sunk to the point where we can endure the alternative.

GARY ARNOLD

One's curiosity about Raoul Coutard's *Hoa-Binh* begins to wither away before the opening reel is half played out. You enter with the vague hope of finally seeing a neo-realist movie emerge out of the folly and desolation of the war in Indochina, of experiencing a film as immediate and ardent as *The Children Are Watching Us, Open City* and *Shoeshine*. It's an idle hope. This belongs to that forlorn class of movies that gets high marks for sincerity and none for emotional impact or illumination; it's just feeble and mawkish, a cut below even the most routine and reticent television journalism.

It's not much fun to say any of this. Raoul Coutard is one of the world's greatest cinematographers, and he's not an opportunistic newcomer to this subject—he was a combat photographer in Indochina in the early Fifties, and his wife is Vietnamese.

One is predisposed to greet his first attempt at directing kindly, particularly in view of the subject matter, but *Hoa-Binh* doesn't sustain the impulse. If anything, it's a constant reminder that the talents of a director and a director of photography are not one and the same. *Hoa-Binh* needs to be firmed up structurally, to be performed less stolidly (the ability to use children and non-professionals expressively is exceedingly rare, and it doesn't appear to be an ability that Coutard will soon have within his grasp), to get a dramatic handle on its own material and release some of the compassion an audience is more than willing to offer it.

For example, one's own imaginative sense of what the basic story idea would involve in real life and should encompass on screen is never matched by the director. We're given the situation of a little boy, his father missing and his mother dead, who must find shelter and sustenance for himself and his baby sister in the slums of Saigon. Somehow, by dawdling and maundering along, Coutard manages to take all the sting and suspense and fear out of this terrifying, appalling situation.

Everything we learn about this simple, unsophisticated child tends to make us doubt his chances of surviving from one dawn to the next. He appears utterly lost and helpless. Incredibly, the film doesn't explore this condition and deepen a viewer's natural responsiveness to it (and the politics that brought it about). Instead, the film veers off its already wobbly track and restores the long-lost father (a Vietcong recruit, we discover) to his children, becoming a family reunion story as an afterthought.

One sits there baffled. This movie doesn't seem aware of its own potential with audiences, of how enormous the subject and the audience's feeling for this subject really are. There have been no fictional movies and few documentaries about Vietnam to speak of, especially if one chooses to speak of movies concentrating on the civilian population. So what does one make of *Hoa-Binh*, apparently well-meaning but essentially bland and dim-witted? For being beside the point, Coutard's film is almost in a class by itself.

8
THRILLERS

THE FRENCH CONNECTION

Urban Gothic

Pauline Kael

When Mayor Lindsay began his efforts to attract the movie-production business, it probably didn't occur to him or his associates that they were ushering in a new movie age of nightmare realism. The Los Angeles area was selected originally for the sunshine and so that the movie-business hustlers—patent-violators who were pirating inventions as well as anything else they could get hold of—could slip over the border fast. As it turned out, however, California had such varied vegetation that it could be used to stand in for most of the world, and there was space to build whatever couldn't be found. But New York City is always New York City; it can't be anything else, and, with practically no studios for fakery, the movie companies use what's really here, so the New York-made movies have been set in Horror City. Although recent conflicts between the producers and the New York unions seem to have ended this Urban Gothic period, the New York-made movies have provided a permanent record of the city in breakdown. I doubt if at any other time in American movie history there has been such a close relationship between the life on the screen and the life of a portion of the audience. Los Angeles-made movies were not *about* Los Angeles; often they were not about any recognizable world. But these recent movies are about New York, and the old sentimentalities are almost impossible here—physically impossible, because the city gives them the lie. (I'm thinking of such movies as *Klute, Little Murders, The Anderson Tapes, Greetings, The Land-*

214

lord, Where's Poppa?, Midnight Cowboy, Harry Kellerman, Diary of a Mad Housewife, No Way to Treat a Lady, Shaft, Cotton Comes to Harlem, The Steagle, Cry Uncle, The Owl and the Pussycat, The Panic in Needle Park, Bananas, and the forthcoming *Born to Win.*) The city of New York has helped American movies grow up; it has also given movies a new spirit of nervous, anxious hopelessness, which is the true spirit of New York. It is literally true that when you live in New York you no longer believe that the garbage will ever be gone from the streets or that life will ever be sane and orderly.

The movies have captured the soul of this city in a way that goes beyond simple notions of realism. The panhandler in the movie who jostles the hero looks just like the one who jostles you as you leave the movie theater; the police sirens in the movie are screaming outside; the hookers and junkies in the freak show on the screen are indistinguishable from the ones in the freak show on the streets. Famous New York put-on artists and well-known street people are incorporated in the movies; sometimes they are in the movie theater, dressed as they are in the movie, and sometimes you leave the theater and see them a few blocks away, just where they were photographed. There's a sense of carnival about this urban-crisis city; everyone seems to be dressed for a mad ball. Screams in the theater at Halloween movies used to be a joke, signals for laughter and applause, because nobody believed in the terror on the screen. The midnight showings of horror films now go on all year round, and the screams are no longer pranks. Horror stories and brutal melodramas concocted for profit are apparently felt on a deeper level than might have been supposed. People don't laugh or applaud when there's a scream; they try to ignore the sound. It is assumed that the person yelling is stoned and out of control, or crazy and not to be trifled with—he may want an excuse to blow off steam, he may have a knife or a gun. It is not uncommon now for fights and semi-psychotic episodes to take place in the theaters, especially when the movies being played are shockers. Audiences for these movies in the Times Square area and in the Village are highly volatile. Probably the unstable, often dazed members of the audiences are particularly susceptible to the violence and tension on the screen; maybe crowds now include a certain number of people who simply can't stay calm for two hours. But whether the movies bring it out in the audience or whether the particular audiences that are attracted bring it into the theater, it's *there* in the theater, particularly at late shows, and you feel that the violence on the screen may at any moment touch off violence in the theater. The audience is explosively *live*. It's like being at a prizefight or a miniature Altamont.

Horror is very popular in Horror City—old horror films and new ones. The critics were turned off by the madness of *The Devils*; the audiences were turned on by it. They wanted the benefits of the sexual pathology of religious hysteria: bloody tortures, burning flesh, nuns violated on altars, lewd nuns stripping and orgying, and so on. Almost all the major movie companies are now, like the smaller ones, marginal businesses. The losses of the American film industry since 1968 are calculated at about five hundred and twenty-five million dollars. Besides Disney, the only company that shows profits is A.I.P.—the producers of ghouls-on-wheels schlock pictures, who are now also turning out movies based on Gothic "classics." I don't believe that people are going to shock and horror films because of a need to exorcise their fears; that's probably a fable. I think they're going for entertainment, and I don't see how one can ignore the fact that the kind of entertainment that attracts them now is often irrational and horrifyingly brutal. A few years ago *The Dirty Dozen* turned the audience on so high that there was yelling in the theater and kicking at the seats. And now an extraordinarily well made new thriller gets the audience sky-high and keeps it up there—*The French Connection*, directed by William Friedkin, which is one of the most "New York" of all the recent New York movies. It's also probably the best-made example of what trade reporters sometimes refer to as "the cinema du zap."

How's this for openers? A peaceful day in Marseille. A *flic* strolls into a *boulangerie*, comes out carrying a long French bread, and strolls home. As he walks into his own entranceway, a waiting figure in a leather coat sticks out an arm with a .45 and shoots him in the face and then in the torso. The assassin picks up the bread, breaks off a piece to munch, and tosses the remainder back onto the corpse. That's the first minute of *The French Connection*. The film then jumps to New York and proceeds through chases, pistol-whippings, slashings, beatings, murders, snipings, and more chases for close to two hours. The script, by Ernest Tidyman (who wrote *Shaft*), is based on the factual account by Robin Moore (of *The Green Berets*) of the largest narcotics haul in New York police history until the recent Jaguar case. The producer, Philip D'Antoni, also produced *Bullitt*, and the executive producer was

G. David Schine, of Cohn and Schine. That's not a creative team, it's a consortium. The movie itself is pretty businesslike. There are no good guys in this harsh new variant of cops-and-robbers; *The French Connection* features the latest-model sadistic cop, Popeye (Gene Hackman). It's undeniably gripping, slam-bang, fast, charged with suspense, and so on—a mixture of *Razzia* and *Z*, and hyped up additionally with a television-thriller-style score that practically lays you out all by itself. At one point, just in case we might lose interest if we didn't have our minute-to-minute injections of excitement, the camera cuts from the street conversation of a few cops to show us the automobile smashup that brought them to the scene, and we are treated to two views of the bloody faces of fresh corpses. At first, we're confused as to who the victims are, and we stare at them thinking they must be characters in the movie. It takes a few seconds to realize that they bear no relation whatsoever to the plot.

It's no wonder that *The French Connection* is a hit, but what in hell is it? It uses eighty-six separate locations in New York City—so many that it has no time for carnival atmosphere: it crashes right through. I suppose the answer we're meant to give is that it's an image of the modern big city as Inferno, and that Popeye is an Existential hero, but the movie keeps zapping us. Though *The French Connection* achieves one effect through timing and humor (when the French Mr. Big, played by Fernando Rey, outwits Popeye in a subway station by using his silver-handled umbrella to open the train doors), most of its effects are of the *Psycho*-derived blast-in-the-face variety. Even the expert pacing is achieved by somewhat questionable means; the ominous music keeps tightening the screws and heating things up. The noise of New York already has us tense. The movie is like an aggravated case of New York: It raises this noise level to produce the kind of painful tension that is usually described as almost unbearable suspense. But it's the same kind of suspense you feel when someone outside your window keeps pushing down on the car horn and you think the blaring sound is going to drive you out of your skull. This horn routine is, in fact, what the cop does throughout the longest chase sequence. The movie's suspense is magnified by the sheer pounding abrasiveness of its means; you don't have to be an artist or be original or ingenious to work on the raw nerves of an audience this way—you just have to be smart and brutal. The high-pressure methods that one could possibly accept in *Z* because they were tools used to try to show the audience how a fascist conspiracy works are used as ends in themselves. Despite the dubious methods, the purpose of the brutality in Z was moral—it was to make you hate brutality. Here you love it, you wait for it—that's all there is. I know that there are many people—and very intelligent people, too—who love this kind of fast-action movie, who say that this is what movies do best and that this is what they really want when they go to a movie. Probably many of them would agree with everything I've said but will still love the movie. Well, it's not what I want, and the fact that Friedkin has done a sensational job of direction just makes that clearer. It's not what I want not because it fails (it doesn't fail) but because of what it is. It is, I think, what we once feared mass entertainment might become: jolts for jocks. There's nothing in the movie that you enjoy thinking over afterward—nothing especially clever except the timing of the subway-door-and-umbrella sequence. Every other effect in the movie— even the climactic car-versus-runaway-elevated-train chase—is achieved by noise, speed, and brutality.

On its own terms, the picture makes few mistakes, though there is one small but conspicuous one. A good comic contrast of drug dealers dining at their ease in a splendid restaurant while the freezing, hungry cops who are tailing them curse in a cold doorway and finally eat a hunk of pizza is spoiled because, for the sake of a composition with the two groups in the same shot, the police have been put where the diners could obviously see them. It is also a mistake, I think, that at the end the picture just stops instead of coming to a full period. The sloppy plotting, on the other hand, doesn't seem to matter; it's amazing how much implausibility speed and brutality can conceal. Hitchcock's thrillers were full of holes, but you were having too good a time to worry about them; *The French Connection* is full of holes, but mostly you're too stunned to notice them. There's no logic in having the Lincoln Continental that has been shipped from France with the heroin inside abandoned on a back street at night rather than parked snugly in the garage of its owner's hotel; it appears to be on the street just so the narcotics agents can spot it and grab it. There's an elaborate sequence of an auction at an automobile graveyard which serves no clear purpose. And if you ever think about it you'll realize that you have no idea who that poor devil was who got shot in the overture, or why. For all the movie tells you, it may have been for his French bread. But you really know what it's all in there for. It's the same reason you get those juicy pictures of the corpses: zaps.

Listen to Popeye's lines and you can learn the secrets of zap realism. A crude writer can give his crummy, cheap jokes to a crude character, and the jokes really pay off. The rotten jokes get laughs and also show how ugly the character's idea of humor is. Popeye risks his life repeatedly and performs fabulously dangerous actions, yet the movie debases him in every possible way. Hackman has turned himself into a modern Ted Healy type—porkpie hat, sneaky-piggy eyes, and a gut-first walk, like Robert Morley preceded by his belly coming toward us in those BOAC "Visit Britain" commercials. Popeye (the name is out of Faulkner, I assume) has a filthy mouth and a complete catalogue of race prejudices, plus some "cute" fetishes; e.g., he cases girls who wear boots. He is the anti-hero carried to a new *lumpenprole* low—the mean cop who used to figure on the fringes of melodrama (as in *Sweet Smell of Success*) moved to the center. Sam Spade might play dirty, but he had a code and he had personal style; even Bullitt, a character contrived to hold the chases and bloodshed together, was a super-cop with style and feelings. This movie turns old clichés into new clichés by depriving the central figure of *any* attractive qualities. Popeye is insanely callous, a shrewd bully who enjoys terrorizing black junkies, and the film includes raids on bars that are gratuitous to the story line just to show what a subhuman son of a bitch he is. The information is planted early that his methods have already cost the life of a police officer, and at the end this plant has its pat pay-off when he accidentally shoots an FBI agent, and the movie makes the point that he doesn't show the slightest remorse. The movie presents him as the most ruthlessly lawless of characters and yet—here is where the basic amorality comes through—shows that this is the kind of man it takes to get the job done. It's the vicious bastard who gets the results. Popeye, the lowlifer who makes Joe or Archie sound like Daniel Ellsberg, is a cop the way the movie Patton was a general. When Popeye walks into a bar and harasses blacks, part of the audience can say, "That's a real pig," and another part of the audience can say, "That's the only way to deal with those people. Waltz around with them and you get nowhere."

I imagine that the people who put this movie together just naturally think in this commercially convenient double way. This right-wing, left-wing, take-your-choice cynicism is total commercial opportunism passing itself off as an Existential view. And maybe that's why Popeye's determination to find the heroin is not treated unequivocally as socially useful but is made obsessive. Popeye's low character is used to make the cops-and-robbers melodrama superficially modern by making it *meaningless*; his brutality serves to demonstrate that the cops are no better than the crooks. In personal style and behavior, he is, in fact, deliberately shown as worse than the crooks, yet since he's the cop with the hunches that pay off, the only cop who gets results, the movie can be seen as a way of justifying police brutality. At the end, a Z-style series of titles comes on to inform us that the dealers who were caught got light sentences or none at all. The purpose of giving us this information is also probably double: to tell us to get tougher judges and to make tougher laws, and to provide an ironic coda showing that Popeye's efforts were really futile. A huge haul of heroin was destroyed, but the movie doesn't bother to show us that—to give a man points for anything is unfashionable. The series of titles is window-dressing anyway. The only thing that this movie believes in is giving the audience jolts, and you can feel the raw, primitive response in the theater. This picture says Popeye is a brutal son of a bitch who gets the dirty job done. So is the picture.

KLUTE

DAVID DENBY

Klute isn't art—anyone can see that—but it reminds us of the days when movies were made with a sense of responsibility to the audience's pleasure and understanding. It resolves whatever thematic material it chooses to introduce (an accomplishment that has become increasingly rare), and it has at its center a completely created character. The call girl embodied so faultlessly by Jane Fonda is as complex and attractive and intelligent as one of those upper-class tomboys that used to be Katharine Hepburn's specialty, and the audience responds to her spiritedness with gratitude and relief. For once, a character who is neither vicious, stupid, nor soft!

Klute has the information and detail of a superior piece of journalism; it allows us to comprehend a certain kind of life without forcing us to make an immediate judgment. Neither the scriptwriters (Dave and Andy Lewis) nor the director (Alan J. Pakula, whose first movie was *The Sterile Cuckoo*) are very good at the murder-melodrama stuff, but they have a very solid feeling for character and milieu. As Bree Daniel (Miss Fonda) and Klute (Donald Sutherland) search New York for missing friends, they descend into the sad and malevolent city of sleazy discothèques, whorehouses, junkie pads, and finally the East River, whose depths yield up a corpse—the final truth of Bree's world. It's a world that is saturated with violence, but the movie itself has very little brutality or sensation; the film-makers work through suggestion rather than shock. Essentially, they are interested in character; the milieu has been created so that we can see how Bree simultaneously resists and is drawn to its sordidness and disintegration, and how she finally escapes by clinging to a stolid and all-but-silent man who embodies the opposite qualities.

This story of regeneration—a Prostitute's Progress—completely engages our emotions while our reason tells us that tales like this shouldn't have happy endings. We ignore the improbability because Jane Fonda and Donald Sutherland make an amusing and satisfying couple: the sullen, neurotic, quick-witted city girl and the very silent, very straight small-town cop. His quietness is almost a form of aggression (in New York people are expected to talk a lot), and she responds belligerently and then seductively, trying to find a vulnerable point, a way of controlling him. But his steadiness gains her respect and, to her surprise, she finds herself attracted to him. *Klute* plays the old movie game of combining male and female opposites in a melodramatic crisis; it's one of the best combinations since Bogart and Hepburn in *The African Queen*.

SWEET SWEETBACK'S BAADASSSSS SONG

PENELOPE GILLIATT

Alas!—I mean, hurrah!—there exists a furiously tasteless picture called *Sweet Sweetback's Baadasssss Song.* It was made by a black man for blacks, and it is turning into a phenomenon of the industry. For the last three weeks it has been one of the top-grossing films in the *Variety* chart; for the first two of those weeks it was No. 1, outstripping *Love Story* by far. Even though there are many more white than black Americans, it seems that blacks at the moment are much hungrier for the cinema. Given the right film—and this is evidently the first feature film that has been anything like so right—the black audience can be the biggest moviegoing public in America. The cinema suddenly has as rich a market again as it had in the Depression. A movie theater is somewhere to go with a girl if your family lives eight to a room; a movie theater gets you away from the rats; a movie theater offers fables. *Sweetback* is a terrific fable. It is also a boot in the face for the wishes of moderates, black and white, who are likely to come away reeling. At three showings of the film at three times of day in two New York theaters, I saw hardly a white man and not one white woman.

Sweetback is presumably the first of a line of films. The next ones will get gentler, with luck, and better characterized, and signed with a clearer authorship than this, but they can never be anything like *Guess Who's Coming to Dinner?*, or lose the tongue they have found here, which is a shock in the cinema. It is a language of energy, stamina, cheek, fury, blue jokes, clan loyalty, swagger, and a murderous skepticism. The film's whole style of overstatement is grating, and meant to be. The film wasn't made for the approval of aesthetes. Europeans have always objected to the floridity of the five-hour color films produced in India, but India and Japan are famous for having a colossal movie output; when you think of what the Indians and the Japanese have in common with the public of this staggeringly appealing film, it may be no accident that their countries possess a style that has absorbed exaggeration, just as *Sweetback* is bent on going too far. That is the film's great sense of the popular, maybe. It is riling to the boss instinct in members of the old and the lucky nations, which warms to restraint in culture, as in strikers. But art and entertainment are natural guerrillas and troublemakers; a settled, well-off society will give them marks for taste and finesse when they control themselves and come to heel, but a place like black America will find an ally in a film that pushes its luck.

The picture was written, composed, produced, directed, edited, and starred in by Melvin Van Peebles, who showed a distinct glint of insurgence and of a witty, self-promoting, ambitious bad taste in his earlier film *Watermelon Man*. That was a comedy, with Godfrey Cambridge playing a bigot in whiteface who turns into a black overnight and so reluctantly has to loosen his grip on his most cherished character habits. He puts the change down to an overeffusive sunlamp. Van Peebles had relatively little say about the film, but he has made his new picture practically single-handed, with a back-to-the-wall belligerence that people in softer seats would find arrogant. He even put his own money into the picture—from *Watermelon Man*—and sponged from friends. Why pay bank charges? That was his basilisk-eyed question when he was talking to a white Hollywood friend about the financing. "If you believe in you, bet on you." The friend asked, "If you had five hundred thousand dollars, would you invest it all in the film?" Van Peebles reports the conversation in a paperback: " 'Of course I would.' And I meant it. 'I wouldn't,' [the friend] said, and he meant it. . . . It must be terrible to be white, I thought."

Against the usual opposition, but acting with more canniness than most, Van Peebles made the picture the way he wanted to by pretending it was a nude film. He wanted the aid of non-union people; he got it by affiliating with the lower depths of skin flicks, which are allowed by the élite cinema to operate outside union rules. The process of the film's survival was ruses and tactics, like the life of its hero, whose ethic is always to cheat the system. Van Peebles plays him. The man wears a brocade suit, a beautiful black hat at a debonair angle, and a mustache as dandyish as Clark Gable's. He looks stoic and peculiarly glamorous, although he lives at the bottom of the heap and spent his boyhood in a brothel. When he is handcuffed to a friend who gets beaten up by white cops, the cops undo the handcuff to get an ugly improvement of purchase, and after a bit Sweetback beats up the whites himself with the dangling handcuff, almost casually, and runs. No one gives him away—not a down-and-out, not a tart. The films of the Depression offered to unemployed, despairing people the idea of what it was like to be rich or to pluck an interlude of undiluted happiness out of the plodding calendar of welfare; this film holds out the image of a black frontier hero who survives every wound from whites and police, who holds enthralled any girl he likes, who makes peeping white cops nervous because a white woman wants him at an orgy, and who has more humor and self-command than anyone else around. The white authority figures in this film are a crumbling lot, amateurishly played, by a trick of casting that is certainly on purpose. The fable is a dream of weak cops and of power-driven white sensualists who have traveled beyond enjoyment. The blacks are funny, rude, unforgivable, with mouths forever closed against the other side, and equipped with blond wigs and drag wedding dresses that allow them to suggest a sarcastic hint of changing race or sex for the pleasure of a teased, yearning nobility. The glee in audiences when one of the enemy is killed closes the ranks against outsiders, but it isn't the rah-rah of *The Green Berets*, where straight murderousness was so encouraged that GIs were cheered for killing Vietnamese and the other way around without any obvious difference in glee and with a very obvious response to its brutish sort of *verismo*. *Sweetback* is another thing. It is fiercely on the side of a minority, and it takes the shape of a fable. The film sets a tone that is bound to be followed and that will later, to judge by the past, grow fonder of its characters. This angry start is impossible, haughty, not likable, but sometimes rather admirable in its context. What would it have been like if the French people had been free to make a film about themselves before the revolution? The English of the North Country before the Reform Bill? If the West's economy-in-little of Hollywood is to carry on working in some form—and it certainly is—what step does it take ideologically from this film, which doesn't *want* dishwashers or color TV, which has openly and derisively exploited Hollywood's anomalous system of blind-eye profit-making, but which in the midst of a bankrupt industry is making an enviable mint of loot out of the pockets of the rebellious underpaid?

GARY ARNOLD

Sweet Sweetback's Baadasssss Song is a stanchly unlyrical exploitation movie aimed at black urban audiences. In the order of their importance, commercially and otherwise, the exploited elements are sex and violence and jive and racial stereotypes and a bit of "revolutionary" pose-striking.

Artistically, *Sweetback* is a mess—and a minimally entertaining mess at that. Melvin Van Peebles, who directed and wrote and scored and edited and promoted the film and cast himself as the hero, a male headliner at a bordello specializing in sexual theatrics, is generally referred to, mistakenly but reverently, as "the first black American director." Of movies, that is. It would be more accurate to call him one of the first black directors to make a film (*The Watermelon Man*) for a major studio. What is less well known is that Van Peebles is a bad director.

The one-man-show aspect of *Sweetback* can be a little deceiving, since it doesn't indicate how thinly Van Peebles has spread his talents. To get *that* lowdown, one is more or less obliged to see the film and discover certain awful truths. For example: Van Peebles has miscast himself as the stud—he's so arch and snotty of demeanor that he would make more sense playing the role of a butler; there ain't no movie there—at least no movie with *dramatic* attributes, such as a protagonist with a reasonably human set of values at stake and a story that goes somewhere and suspense that's *sustained*; to top things off, the director-writer-star is also a tacky composer.

To put it mildly, Van Peebles is no Orson Welles, either behind or in front of the camera. The ego is more than willing, but the aptitude is weak. In fact, for adequate comparisons, one must scrounge around at the other end of the talent spectrum, among movie directors whose "touch" is unerringly unphotogenic or heavy-handed or disorganized. One thinks of Arthur Hiller or Richard Fleischer—or Elaine May in *A New Leaf*, a box-office hit as mystifying and disheveled as *Sweetback*.

In some ghastly, ludicrous way, it's conceivable that Van Peebles is furthering integration by proving that a crass or klutzy black director can make it as well as a crass or klutzy white director. At the movies it is rarely a case of "talent will out," and *Sweetback* seems to exemplify the more typical "hustle will out."

From all indications, *Sweetback* is certainly making it commercially, and this has aroused more interest than the film justifies on strictly cinematic merits. To judge by the box-office grosses quoted in *Variety*, the picture has hit its intended mark in just about every big city. For example, *Variety* reports a "sizzling" $94,000 week in Chicago, a "mighty" $58,000 in Philadelphia, a "smash" $20,000 at the Palace here in Washington (probably the largest take for this generally depressed downtown house since *Without a Stitch* played a year ago).

People who believe that all that smoke must indicate one hell of a fiery movie might be rather dismayed by the movie itself, especially if they've never patronized sexploitation films or if they're anticipating a conventional narrative movie. The only lively scenes in *Sweetback* are the sex scenes, particularly two rather elaborate, glossily photographed items—the bordello acts that introduce the hero to the audience and an encounter between the hero and a Hell's Angels Amazon.

The latter is a funny, lewd conception (photographically, it's also an ambitious double steal—*Scorpio Rising* crossed with the projection-room sequence from *Citizen Kane*) and indicates better possibilities than Van Peebles cares to develop. There might be a truly hilarious movie in the notion of a black Fanfan the Tulip, an adventurer-stud moving casually through a series of amorous, picaresque, satirical misadventures. However, it would require a couple of things that are sorely missing in *Sweetback*—a star (someone sexy or funny and preferably both) and a script.

Fundamentally, Van Peebles appears to be a flesh peddler: when there's no fornication on the screen, he doesn't know how to keep things interesting. A good three-quarters of the footage consists of shots of Van Peebles running over hill, dale and overpass. He gets the plot as far as having Sweetback kill two policemen. After that it's just one long, redundant runaround, with an occasional break for sex and ghetto vernacular. (Sweetback himself, by the way, is about the most inarticulate hero in talking movie history; I doubt if Van Peebles utters a dozen words in the course of the film.)

Van Peebles has one particularly significant weakness: he seems incapable of writing or staging dramatic exchanges between two or more characters. There was a similar problem in *The Watermelon*

Man and in his French picture, *The Story of a Three-Day Pass* (and since the latter was supposed to be a tender, bittersweet love story, the problem was critical in the extreme). If performers are at all effective in his movies, they're effective in isolation, breaking into comic monologues or angry tirades.

It is not an amiable weakness—and in a movie director it's slightly disastrous for practical purposes, since the conflicts are never humanized, objectified and clarified. One begins to feel that Van Peebles' egotism is not only monstrous but also artistically useless, since it's unable to accommodate other egos even for temporary dramatic effect. For instance, in *Story of a Three-Day Pass*, the exchanges between the shy black GI and his cynical Jiminy Cricket of a "conscience" were more interesting than the love scenes between man and woman. Van Peebles' conversations are invariably one-sided and self-centered.

It's possible that this peculiarly complacent and self-protective kind of egotism appeals to some young blacks in roughly the way the Jack Nicholson character in *Five Easy Pieces* appealed to some young whites. Viewed objectively, neither protagonist is worth a damn, but the movies always tend to feed and glamorize alienation rather than clarify it. In real life there is no shortage of black or white protagonists, with definite reasons for feeling alienated and definite social remedies in mind.

But at the movies one finds sentimental impostors where the heroes should be. There's Nicholson's Bobby Dupea, whom we're supposed to identify with because he's fashionably fed up with everything. Now there's Van Peebles as Sweetback, an inarticulate whore who suddenly finds a revolutionary heart of gold. That's about as far as "politics" goes in American popular entertainment, and Melvin Van Peebles is simply peddling some blatant flesh and fantasy on the black side of the street. The flesh is fairly picturesque, but the fantasy is probably too thin to sustain many people. It consists in pretending that Van Peebles has really told the whites where to get off, although it's achingly clear that as filmmaker and thinker, he hasn't begun to get it on.

GET CARTER

Arthur Knight

Mike Hodges, the writer and director of *Get Carter*, comes from television, and I suspect that the television syndrome is basically at fault here. In television series, such as *It Takes a Thief* and *Mod Squad*, the central characters are catapulted into a situation in the first, or "pilot," episode, but their motivations for continuing their activities are never examined again. They go through their routines, getting beaten up, shooting almost at random, making hairbreadth escapes in fast cars, and emerge victorious at the end of the program so that they can do it all over again the following week. The emphasis is on the action, not the people, and all sorts of weird coincidences enter into the scripting to make it possible for the stars to survive for at least another episode.

Get Carter, starring Michael Caine as Carter, departs from this formula only insofar as Carter does not survive. He is neatly plugged between the eyes at film's end. But in all other respects, this is television on the big screen—more sex, more violence, but no more attention to motivation or plot logic. At the outset, against the advice of his gang, Carter travels to Newcastle to avenge his brother's death. Hard guys block his path. In Newcastle, we learn that Carter's niece, who has appeared in pornographic films, just possibly is really his daughter. Is Carter out to avenge his brother's death or to punish the men who abused his daughter? Carter doesn't seem to care. As in television action shows, he kills indiscriminately—and the film positively revels in the killings. Caine, sounding startlingly like the Jimmy Cagney of the old Warner gangster movies, stalks through the picture with literally no change in expression. Playwright John Osborne is more effective as Carter's loyal opposition. But, then, villainous roles are always the more interesting ones in this sort of thing. *Get Carter* leaves one wanting more—or less.

9

COMEDY: DEAD OR ALIVE?

TAKING OFF

A *Fist, with the Hand Itself*
PENELOPE GILLIATT

Two very young girls dressed in the Stars and Stripes are piping away at a talent contest, slightly out of tune. Aged twelve, maybe. "Love, love, love, why don't people believe in it?" Plump faces, pacifying: flower children in the bud. The orange-juice-and-Vietnam generation, the only generation in history to grow up on war protest and vitamin tablets simultaneously. Their eyes slide off camera helplessly at the forthright end of the song, pining for approval from the audition panel. Then a hard-pressed suburban father (Larry Tyne, played by Buck Henry) is seen in a chair at a hypnotist's, trying to conquer smoking. Everyone has his own Everest. He concentrates on letting his hand float up, soberly. "Are you for living or are you not?" says the hypnotist, an inexpressive, kindly, somewhat bald man with a voice that lies there on the floor like a piece of very dead herring. He has a look that is an unholy mixture of priest and woman traffic warden. One has to respect the body, he says magisterially. "Slowly make a fist, with the hand itself." The characters in this film—*Taking Off*, by the Czech Miloš Forman, working in American for the first time, with a script by himself, John Guare, Jean-Claude Carrière, and John Klein—have been directed so that they speak most painstakingly, at the deliberate pace that is striking to elliptical Middle Europeans, with its long pauses for thought and its re-treadings and its exquisitely careful redundancies. "A fist, with the hand itself." No room for a mistake there. After a bit more of the same, the hypnotist switches on a record of himself, methodically using his patient's preoccupation in trance as an opportunity to give a rest to, er, the voice. Like most of the people in Forman's picture—like the tranquil girl who occasionally slips into the picture for a pleasant flash, stark naked and immersed in playing the cello—the hypnotist lives in sweet obliviousness of making an ass of himself. Teaching the patient how to roll his eyeballs upward in coma as the next part of the anti-smoking session, he explains that the exercise can be done anywhere by closing the eyes first, "so that the roll is private." The patient takes the earnest idiocy with due gratitude; he is a bashful man. A while later, a child of the generation gap—the patient's own daughter, secretly at the audition, about to run away from home but not really so unlike him—stands in front of the mike and can't get out a note. The number she has practiced gags in her throat like a candy swallowed by a small child running. "I'm sorry," she says. "Can I come back?"

Among other things, Forman's recklessly funny anecdote about the apocalyptic nation is about people's shyness, their shaggy-dog purposefulness, and their punishing stamina for more. Forman sees privileged human beings as having an instinct to continue that is fortunate for the life term of the species but ill-conceived for their own comfort, and he makes the observation in a style of charred comedy that is very Slavic. It is fine that he could work here with the same convincing and bitter funniness as in the Czechoslovakia where he made *Loves of a Blonde* and *The Firemen's Ball*. In *Taking Off*, he is much gentler toward his American characters than an American film-maker would be likely to be at the moment. They are engaged, to his mind, in idiosyncratic and testing concerns, and we are not reminded for a second of any of the other films that have washed over us about the nation's characteristics in crisis. Small endeavors of no necessity, answering the conventions of a society that Forman sees as if it were some instinctively Rabelaisian village gone out of kilter and hedged by tragedy, are embarked upon with solemnity and ardor. There is the obligation upon an American wife to enjoy sex, for instance. Two wives chat about husbands' animal impulses in an appalled *sotto voce*, and then throw themselves into splendidly affectionate and stilted spasms of Dionysian dance in their bedrooms for these animals' sakes. When Larry Tyne gets drunk about the disappearance of his daughter, because there is a matching ritual obligation on American middle-aged fathers to drown sorrow in drink, he begins to eat a hard-boiled egg to sop up the booze; you see him eying the egg beadily as it rolls off the counter onto the floor, correctly recognizing the impossibility of bending down to get it, salting another one with dignity, and then eating that without getting the shell off, clinging to insane proprieties about spitting it out. A vestigial politeness reigns in impossible, ludicrous, sometimes desperate circumstances. When four parents have been through a racking night of cheer—pot-smoking under tutelage to learn about their mystifying children, and then strip poker—the half-naked Larry, ill at ease about behaving with a kid's sort of abandon, still goes through the form of shaking hands at the door, though reeling and also struggling into a shirt cuff that has the button done up.

In *The Firemen's Ball*, Forman directed a celebrated wan scene of a beauty queens' contest. He has an eye for the damp way people try to sparkle at social functions. The parents in *Taking Off* have been programmed all their lives to dress up in black tie and sequins and to look as if they were enjoying themselves when a hundred of them are gathered together. So when the function happens to be a horribly unhappy meeting of parents whose children have run away—the Society for the Parents of Fugitive Children—the grief is hidden and the rules are served. There is a girl hippie at the dinner whom the orotund host in a dinner jacket introduces as if she were something on a TV jackpot show. She may have seen *your* lost child. Parting her long weeping-willow branches of hair hanging in front of her eyes, she bends down to look at each in turn of the photographs that are worn like cameos on the parents' spangled breasts. As the man at the microphone says, any one of the people in the queue may be the lucky one. The executive faces and the stiff hairdos affectingly express a generation and a class. The guests are made to seem no more ridiculous than any other prisoners of a period, and they are exonerated from complacency. Forman looks at the two sides of the age war and finds it a poignant conflict, with the parents faintly the more interesting because more formed, and more coerced by ineloquent conventions. The pop songs that the kids sing have a voice. There is one fine song that sets an unpublishable, metrically prim lyric to a madrigal warble, sung by a nice girl who looks as if she were majoring in ceramics; it will be agreeable if the record business has the humor to release it.

And meanwhile the parents in the film, crippled by politesse and fake office bonhomie and high heels, recover whatever rusting scraps of force and grown-up love they can from the wreck of their age group's self-esteem. They have old souls, but their world makes them behave like pre-1939 adolescents, giggling and dressing up, and having to grapple with a paralyzing secret diffidence. Lynn Carlin, the runaway's mother, is delicately hipped on modesty in the middle of the strip-poker romp; it is a sweet performance, longing for fun, prudish mostly for her husband's sake. The bereft parents have gone blissfully off the rails after a solemn indoctrination into dope at the SPFC meeting, where they have learned how to smoke pot from a bossy and rather mournful expert called in from the ranks of arcane youth. ("A joint has two ends. . . . Put the *closed* end into your *mouth*," says the pedagogue patiently, following it with a little lecture about not hanging on to the joint after a drag without passing it on to a neighbor. "That is very *rude*.") In the end it is the parents who are financially worsted, the parents who turn out to be the underdogs of the capitalist system that they are held to be running. But they have the last word. The runaway's song-writing boyfriend comes to a conciliatory dinner and the oldies do their best to make things work, the father faltering rather when he hears what the boy earns. He gracefully expected him to be on his uppers. "Two hundred and ninety thousand," says the lad. Larry splutters into the wine. (A pause would have been better, maybe.) "Before taxes," says the boy, equally graceful. After dinner he declines to play the piano himself, so Larry and his wife take over and finish with a terrific brave rendering of "Stranger in Paradise."

Perhaps it takes a foreigner to see New Yorkers not as the tense, mercurial, backchatting go-getters that native legend makes them but as Forman's lovingly cemented couples, moving slowly through their city with clogged tongues and admirably little ambition. Forman's film is another view of the land that most of its inhabitant film-makers now mechanically despair of; for instance, there is another new film this week, called *Making It* and indoctrinated in native self-deprecation, which deals in the usual machine-made way with a student and the generation gap and permissiveness. One might as well shut up about it, but one has to wonder if the American film industry knows how special it is in its obsession with the journalistically topical. Fiction usually assumes the freedom to move away. Shakespeare left his own time and place in nearly every play; Tolstoy went backward in *War and Peace*; Truffaut went backward in *Jules et Jim* and *L'Enfant Sauvage*; Kurosawa and

Wajda and Renoir and Visconti, too. But apart from *Bonnie and Clyde* and Westerns the American cinema at the moment is scared enough to keep newsworthiness and film financing as close together as foreign correspondents clustering in a bar who refuse to leave one another in the middle of an interesting strange country. It has fallen to a Czech visitor to take the curse off films about the generation gap. He really likes America. He could probably show us raw nerve ends in a drum-majorette rally.

Low-Altitude Flight
Jay Cocks

The comedies of Miloš Forman, notably *Loves of a Blonde* and *The Firemen's Ball*, have commonly been called humanistic, possibly because they refuse to be comfortably confined in any other genre. Their humor is neither primarily verbal nor visual; Forman's particular skill is ingenious observation, creating comedy from character and rigorously familiar situations. But his work also contains a trace of archness, a current of condescension. In none of his films has that tendency been more evident than in his latest, *Taking Off*.

Forman's subject for his first American film is, promisingly enough, the flight of adolescents, who each summer descend on Greenwich Village to get away from their parents and out on their own. The film opens with a massive audition for potential folk singers, then switches to the resolutely suburban home of Mr. and Mrs. Larry Tyne (Buck Henry and Lynn Carlin), who come to the tardy realization that their daughter has skipped. Tyne and his best friend (Tony Harvey) set out to track her down. They stumble into a local bar, get loaded and reel home, where they have a generous number of nightcaps with their spouses and generally make asses of themselves. Rather clumsily the less-than-novel point is made: parents are self-centered hypocrites who worry about their daughter's taking drugs while they numb themselves nightly with booze.

Forman never gets much farther; he just stands in the same place and keeps turning around. Father makes a second go at it, meets the mother of another fugitive girl and forgets his mission until a phone call from his wife interrupts a budding liaison. The parents join a fictitious society, SPFC (Society for Parents of Fugitive Children), experiment with marijuana and make even bigger asses of themselves. The daughter arrives home that night to see her parents, stoned on weed and booze, playing strip poker with another couple from the SPFC. So it goes, one uninspired variation after another.

Unsure of himself and perhaps of America, Forman has resorted to caricatures instead of characterizations, and drawn not on ingenuity but on bile. Even the device of the audition, which Forman has employed in two previous films, reinforces the general feeling of nastiness. He shoots the scene "live"—as far as most of the participants know, it is a real audition—and the fumblings and failings become the source of some crude, easy laughs. In partial compensation there are a couple of very funny performances by Vincent Schiavelli, playing a freak who tutors the SPFC in the art of blowing grass, and Buck Henry, whose acting shows shrewd restraint and a gratifying lack of the grandstand mugging that marred his appearance in *Catch-22*.

They help, but not enough to overcome Forman's simplistic misanthropy.

BANANAS

David Denby

Woody Allen is probably the best comic talent working in American movies today, but also about the most erratic. His new picture, *Bananas*, of which he is director, star, and writer (in collaboration with Mickey Rose), has some ideas that are so bad we may laugh simply because he's really going through with them; at other moments it seems he may yet become a popular satirist of genius.

Much of his humor is intentionally "stupid," intentionally sophomoric; like an irrepressible college humorist who somehow never graduated, he is always freshly enthralled by the world's absurdity, always eager to prove the power of far-out humor to take the measure of that absurdity. Occasionally his stupid jokes have a rather sneaky force if you're aware of the reality behind them. The film opens with a television show: It's *ABC's Wide World of Sports* bringing us live coverage of the assassination of the President of a small Latin American republic. The sequence features real sports announcers—Don Dunphy and ineffable Howard Cosell, looking like an inquisitive eel. Cosell interviews the participants: "Well, of course you're upset and that's understandable under the circumstances," he says to the dying President.

At his best Allen mocks the dead language of television, movies, and advertising by placing the clichés in an absurd context or by gleefully exaggerating them. (He has written his own blurbs for the newspaper ads: "Moving, rich, tense, taut, filligreed, and gossamer.") Most of his ideas, however, are closer to free-flying nonsense humor, exhilarating and undisciplined, but without the aggressive force of the film's opening. One has to speak of separate ideas rather than an over-all conception because Allen hasn't bothered to impose a unified style or theme on his material. Satire, burlesque, slapstick, and parody are all jumbled together. A courtroom sequence in which Allen is tried for subversive activities is simultaneously a halfhearted satire on the Chicago conspiracy trial and a parody of the Perry Mason show; a burlesque of revolutionary heroism and privation (Fidel Castro in the Sierra Maestre) is interrupted with parodies of contemporary movie clichés; and so on.

Allen is so impatient that he can't sustain or develop anything, and his movie keeps darting off in odd directions or pausing demurely for little interludes. Some of the gags are linked by a kind of comic free association, and the plot—Allen gets involved in a Latin American revolution to impress his ex-girlfriend—is so casual and intermittent that it seems to be there mainly to tease our assumption that a movie *needs* a plot. He unfortunately lacks the physical abilities of the great movie comics of the past—the athleticism and balletic grace that allowed them to recover from the most compromising mishaps with such brilliant panache that the recovery became the basis for the next gag. When Allen takes a pratfall he looks genuinely clumsy, and the sequence has to end. It is this failure to give his work any over-all comic line—both physically and intellectually—that holds his pictures down to the middling-good level.

Like those great men of the past, he is trying to create a consistent character for himself from movie to movie. The bank robber who couldn't write a legible hold-up note in *Take the Money and Run* is the same man who gets an invitation to dine with a military dictator in *Bananas* and arrives at the palace carrying a pastry assortment for his host. He is a man who would gladly ingratiate himself wherever possible if he could only overcome his truly radical incompetence. Terrifically inert by nature, he's so other-directed that he winds up performing heroic deeds just because people ask him. And when he acts, he's bound to run through the entire Yiddish lexicon for comic ineptitude: a *shlimazl* one minute, a *shmendrick* the next, a something-else the third. His contretemps with the talcum powder when he's preparing for his girl betrays the ingrained sloppiness of a man irrevocably removed from physical graciousness; the scene just falls short of being very ugly. Of course, he always manages to rob the bank, lead the revolution, and get the girl, so his clumsiness makes a rather feeble ironic point: If this fellow can succeed, then the world must be run by even greater idiots and worse incompetents.

As a satirist, Allen is not without the diffidence of his screen character. It's good that he's not protecting any of the conventional pieties (he's free, for instance to attack Castro *and* the CIA), and he has the originality to change an old emphasis or shift a familiar target (in a spoof of psychoanalysis he makes fun of the patient's revelations rather than the analyst's jargon). With the whole of American culture as his province he'll probably never run out of absurdities to work up into sharp little bits, but on the other hand, the lack of any moral or political position whatsoever prevents his work from having much bite. He has the sophistication for a truly cleansing American satire, but at present not the guts.

A NEW LEAF

VINCENT CANBY

When Henry Graham (Walter Matthau) learns that his fortune has finally run out, he is overwhelmed with quite reasonable self-pity. "All I am—or was—is rich. It's all I wanted to be." Henry's butler agrees: "You'll be poor in the only real sense—in that you'll have no money." The desperate problem demands a desperate solution: Henry decides to marry an heiress and then get rid of her with all possible dispatch.

A *New Leaf*, which was written and directed by Elaine May, who also co-stars in the film, is the story of Henry's reluctant character reformation through the love of a rich woman. It's also a beautifully and gently cockeyed movie that recalls at least two different traditions of American film comedy to which I've always been partial.

Not since the two-reelers of the 1930's in which Edgar Kennedy, the genius of the slow burn, made his accommodation with the idiocies of Florence Lake, his bird-brained wife, have there been displays of anger, frustration and greed as marvelous as those of Matthau in *A New Leaf*. Then, too, *A New Leaf* shares with the great screwball comedies of the Depression an almost childlike appreciation of money: It may not buy happiness, but having a lot of it helps.

Essentially, however, *A New Leaf* is a love story, since Henry Graham and Henrietta Lowell (Miss May) are eccentrics who could have been made for nobody but each other. He is a misanthropic, suspicious, hand-tailored, high-living playboy, whose preference is for Château Lafite '61, while she is a sweet, trusting, sloppy, nearsighted botanist, who drinks Mogen David Extra Heavy Malaga ("every year is good"), and who also happens to be loaded with money.

Although Miss May's approach to the writing and directing of film comedy is pretty consistently at the blackout-sketch level, reminiscent of her collaborations with Mike Nichols, the quality of the sketches in *A New Leaf* is so consistently high, and its cartoon characters are so human, that criticism of its form becomes academic. The entire project is touched by a fine and knowing madness.

I've always been aware of the fact that Matthau is an excellent actor, who is at his best in comedy, but until now I've only been able to suspect this of Miss May. Her Henrietta Lowell is a kind of spin-off of the gauche ladies who used to confront Nichols on television, but she's also as honestly appealing as she is funny. This has the effect of giving a surprising dimension to the kind of slapstick routine in which a lady manages to put on a Grecian-style nightgown by sticking her head and her left arm through the gown's only arm hole.

However, it doesn't do to describe too many details in such a comedy—they should be discovered. Everyone in the supporting cast is appropriately lunatic, especially James Coco, as Matthau's stingy uncle, who plans to leave his fortune to Radio Free Europe, but possibly excepting George Rose, as Matthau's philosophical butler, a role once played (more swishily but no better) by Eric Blore. Mostly, however, I admire Miss May's accurate appraisal of the weird world in which we live, in which peppermills are transistorized and sports cars are built to run faster than is possible on any highway.

A *New Leaf* opened under something of a cloud. Miss May sought, unsuccessfully, to enjoin the film's opening and to have her name removed from it on the grounds that Paramount, which financed the film, was releasing a version of which she disapproved.

Not having seen Miss May's version, I can only say that the film I saw should be a credit to almost any director, though, theoretically at least, Miss May is right. The only thing that gives me pause is the knowledge that its success will probably be used in the future as an argument to ignore the intentions of other directors—but with far less happy results.

GARY ARNOLD

More often than not seeing is disbelieving at the movies these days. The popular misconception is that nudity and profanity are spreading like wildfire and laying waste to the screen. However, one is much more likely to run into an "inoffensive" general audience release so haphazardly conceived and crafted that it seems to defy analysis.

One wonders how certain grossly miscalculated story ideas or bits of casting recommended themselves to experienced producers. Odder still, one wonders why the same mistakes or anomalies fail to upset a significant number of critics or viewers. Increasingly, our movies appear to suffer from a general sort of incompetence and demoralization. Never mind smut: The typical new picture is just mechanically imperfect, theatrically maladroit; it doesn't seem to function properly, in roughly the way that new cars or appliances or transit systems don't seem to function properly.

Take Elaine May's *A New Leaf*, a romantic comedy of almost fantastic ineptitude. Miss May portrays the heroine, an awkward botanist, and all too ironically the movie, which she also wrote and directed, appears to be the work of someone who is all thumbs. She hasn't been helped by the photographer, who gives everything that green-around-the-gills look one associates with low-budget horror vehicles. Still, the material and the casting and the direction, which seems to set the art of film-making back to the most primitive talkies, are outmoded and/or dumbfounding in their own right. This is the last sort of film comedy I would have anticipated from Elaine May.

The screenplay is evidently derived from a short story called "The Green Heart," and it suggests a mediocre English stage comedy insufficiently assimilated to American characters. One can imagine the story as a vehicle for Alastair Sim and Joyce Grenfell in, say, 1952. A suave, snobbish, impecunious playboy discovers that he's squandered his private fortune. To avoid debt and wage-earning, he's persuaded to look for a rich spinster; he finds her in the person of a wealthy, dowdy, absent-minded professor of botany.

Before partaking of his fiancée's fortune, the cad must eliminate some entrenched cads—the family lawyer and servants, who have been milking the heroine's fortune for years. Ideally, the story should probably end with the cad thoroughly reformed from mercenary into protector and triumphantly upstaging his rivals by making a clean breast of things to the lady.

The movie strings out the premise, delaying the inevitable change of heart or turning-over-of-a-new-leaf without really convincing one that a true feeling of affection or sense of honor has developed in the hero. Apparently, there was some thought of fabricating the material as a comedy of murder, with the cad attempting to knock off the botanist after their marriage; superfluous scenes indicating this possibility remain in the finished film.

But the principal confusion stems from the casting of the cad himself. For reasons that might as well be kept under the hats of everyone associated with the project, Walter Matthau has been asked to embody the sort of character that makes you think of maybe Alastair Sim or Dennis Price or William Powell or Clive Brook or David Niven or Cary Grant or Peter Sellers but never, in the depths of delirium, cried for Walter Matthau.

If a producer as cagy as Mike Frankovich can cast Goldie Hawn as a heartless trollop (in *There's a Girl in My Soup*) and a director as prestigious as David Lean can cast Robert Mitchum as a shy schoolmarm (in *Ryan's Daughter*) and comedians as talented and likable as Dick Van Dyke and Jack Lemmon can be misused time and time again, I suppose it's unfair to rap Elaine May, a novice director, for casting Matthau as a debonair cad. But it's a dilly.

Matthau is perfectly awful in this movie. He should emerge as either an amusing sneak or a real gentleman, but what we see is a comedian squirming to fit himself into a comic type that's absolutely wrong for his face, voice, physique and delivery. It's pointless trying to convince us that Matthau is anything within light-years of "an American of English extraction." He looks and acts physically uncomfortable, and it's painful listening to him take such pains with all the dreary epigrams; they're rendered drearier yet by his efforts to approximate "clipped" or "impeccable" English diction with a drawling, colloquial American diction that naturally resists such demands.

Matthau looks even more uncomfortable than he did in *Hello, Dolly!* Curiously, a similar thing happens: While the male lead appears to be in the throes of a slow burn, the female lead waltzes away with the picture. In this case, the theft is rather futile, because Elaine May's awkwardness as a director undermines her charm as a performer.

Most of the critics have been treating *A New Leaf* more deferentially than it deserves, probably because everyone likes Elaine May and wishes her well and wishes she'd been recruited for the movies a decade ago. The film's apparent success with audiences so far may stem from a similar feeling. I'd hate to believe people enjoyed the picture because they found Matthau's obvious discomfort funny, but Miss May's rather sweet ugly duckling may bring out in the audience the protective instincts Matthau is supposed to feel. Only two brief moments in the film amused me—Miss May's initial appearance in the far corner of the screen during a tea party and her attempt to get her head through the proper opening of her negligee —but I can imagine some audiences warming to her character's sheer *vulnerability*, and perhaps even to all the musty, creaky remnants of "classy" drawing-room comedy that make her film so antiquated.

It's a most peculiar movie debut, since the material and style seem to derive from conventions that comedians like Mike Nichols and Elaine May tried to parody or get away from altogether. Somehow, a great innovator has turned up with an unwieldy relic. It would be just as surprising if the late Lenny Bruce, after many years, got the chance to direct a film and decided *Mary Poppins* would be the ideal showcase for his talents.

PLAZA SUITE

Arthur Schlesinger, Jr.

Plaza Suite is no great shakes as a film. The director, Arthur Hiller, might just as well have abandoned pretense and photographed the Broadway play. Still, the film is exceedingly entertaining. The reason for this is partly the felicity of the performances, for which Hiller deserves some credit, but mostly the skill of Neil Simon, who wrote both the play and the screenplay. (The latter assignment must have taken him all of an hour.) Simon's art has rescued Broadway in the last decade; it is sustaining Hollywood in its time of decline; and it deserves a moment's consideration.

The world of Neil Simon is narrow: It is essentially the city, or specifically New York City, versus its inhabitants and visitors. He joins an astute observation of urban and suburban frustration with a sharp and evidently inexhaustible capacity for wisecracks. He began as a writer of farces; but recently his plays have steadily deepened, at least in their aspirations. His comic style clearly emerges from a vein of melancholy.

It is not easy to fuse farce and melancholy. *Plaza Suite* illustrates some of the difficulties. The first sequence describes a marriage in the last stage of exhaustion. Each partner, making a flickering effort to be kind to the other, is rebuffed. Neither can overcome long traditions of reciprocal irritability. Both know enough "psychology" to attack each other but not enough to understand themselves. The sketch is too accurate and painful to be very funny. Maureen Stapleton gives a ruthless picture of an aging woman, salvaging her dignity under a barrage of desperate jokes.

Walter Matthau, who performs with immense virtuosity in all three sequences, becomes in the second a Hollywood producer determined to seduce Barbara Harris as an old sweetheart from Tenafly, New Jersey. The third sequence is marriage at the Plaza

Hotel, with the bride beleaguered in the bathroom while her parents, Matthau and Lee Grant, rage outside the locked door. This erupts into slapstick and is great fun but is quite different, in tone and level of reality, from the opener. What unites the sketches and defines Neil Simon's world is a sense of the egomania bred by modern urban life. His characters are solipsists. They see no reality outside themselves. But they must live in crowds, entrapped by false relationships and compulsive rituals. Their form of communication is the wisecrack. It is a sterile world, enveloped in hostility, superficially hilarious but fundamentally bleak.

Naturally Simon's plays are an immense relief for people who are themselves involved in our contemporary urban hysteria. They can distance themselves from the reality of this world by recognizing their friends and enemies on the screen. Probably, however, they do not recognize themselves, and this may be the present failure of Simon's art. It is all a little too easy; caricature softens the blow of satire; in its slackest moments, it is too close to situation comedy on television.

The comedy of manners is the highest form of comedy, and Neil Simon is certainly today its most adept American practitioner. He has it in him to become another George Kelly or Philip Barry, but this would require an austerity and self-denial he has not yet achieved. They stripped their plays down and were ready to sacrifice their witticisms to their general ideas. Simon, one feels, still dislikes to disappoint his audience, so he will too often sacrifice his idea to his witticisms. The first sequence of *Plaza Suite* is far the least ingratiating. It is also far the most mordant and telling.

Penelope Gilliatt

Neil Simon's parish-pump Manhattan comedy, *Plaza Suite*, is the one thing connected with the island that *no one* seems to want ever to pull down. I daresay the new film of it will outlast us all. It is a minor agony: humorless, loveless, calorie-scared. It is also trivially malign, mostly because of Arthur Hiller's direction, slightly because of the casting of Walter Matthau, a good actor with a souring presence that has generally been better used. The witty hesitancy of Maureen Stapleton is here traduced into seeming a parody of our local comic acting, which is the acting of fluster, and the beauty and repose of Barbara Harris's performance can't quite salvage a part that is deliberately pitched in the writing to be silly.

HAPPY BIRTHDAY, WANDA JUNE

Vonnegut's Folly
HOLLIS ALPERT

Happy Birthday, Wanda June is actually the inscription on a cake purchased to celebrate, *in absentia,* the birthday of long-lost Harold Ryan, who disappeared while searching for diamonds in the dark reaches of some continent or other. Ryan, from the décor of the New York apartment he left behind (inhabited now by his wife and adolescent son), appears to be a compound of Hemingway and movie heroes played by John Wayne. Mementoes include a well-preserved Land Rover, a variety of animal tusks, and doorbells that, when rung, growl like tigers or roar like lions. As for that cake, we soon learn from a quick visit to Kurt Vonnegut's version of heaven that it was meant for a little girl who was killed by a truck just prior to her birthday celebration. Now she is very happy up there somewhere with such playmates as the Nazi colonel known as the Beast of Yugoslavia, sent there by the same Harold Ryan.

I'm sorry to have to report that I have just about exhausted the more amusing elements of Kurt Vonnegut's blend of black humor, savage satire, and all-around irreverence first encountered off-Broadway in his play and then adapted for the screen by the author himself. Things begin to go wrong very early on in the movie, for it is almost at once apparent that Vonnegut is imprisoned by his stage conception and hasn't the foggiest about how to open it up cinematically. Yes, here and there the action moves out of that fanciful Central Park West apartment—a couple of visits to "heaven," and a few brief scenes outside—but for the most part the entrances and exits of the principals are as contrived as anything in the "Tennis, Anyone?" school of playwriting of the Twenties.

Rod Steiger, for instance, as the monstrous symbol of violent American virility, conveniently arrives home a few seconds after his wife (Susannah York) has gone out for the evening. When she returns, the shock of reunion is further delayed by his need to visit the bathroom. When Ryan is moved to bash the violin of the effete doctor in the next apartment, the doctor has been sent off on an errand, only to appear in time for a confrontation with the beast of Central Park West. Naturally, every time someone arrives, the visit is heralded by the growl of a tiger or the roar of a lion—those doorbells. The device may have worked on the stage, but on the sound track the joke gets awfully thin, if loud. Aimed straight at the heartland of the college film audience, a film as stagy as this can only offend it.

Nor does the material translate well to film. Steiger's puffery is so ridiculous to begin with that one wonders why the bother to deflate it. And caricatured, too, are the others: the father-worshiping son, the wife torn between violent husband and non-violent, faggish doctor, the doltish pilot who dropped the bomb on Nagasaki (*should* he have followed orders?). These figures of fun are not so much tiresome as tired.

But how wrong can a movie get? The quite prestigious cast has long been accustomed to acting for the camera, and one's expectations are that Steiger, Miss York, Don Murray, and George Grizzard will create some sort of dazzle with the Vonnegut follies. Instead, under Mark Robson's direction, it's as though all are hyped up for facing Clive Barnes on opening night. The screen has a way of magnifying performances, and when the performances are already pumped up, the results are bound to be disastrous. In this regard, Miss York offends least, while Steiger offends most. He booms out four-letter expletives or rattles them like machine-gun fire at the hapless audience and, in general, puts on such a carpet-chewing display that, if there were actually carpets, they'd be the most expensive item in the budget.

In fact, maybe the blame should be put on the budget rather than on any of those involved. Getting a movie on these days, particularly for something as off-the-track as *Happy Birthday, Wanda June*, involves considerable sacrifice. And time, shooting time, is of the essence, because that's where the money goes. So, obviously, they had to settle for this spartan production, which meant few sets, sparse use of setups, and hopes that the actors would work themselves into their roles posthaste. Still and all, it's billed as "A Mark Robson Film." We can only assume that Mr. Robson deserted the filmic instincts that had previously brought him commercial success because here he was, finally, in the presence of art. His disappointment, I fear, will be general.

10

ADAPTATIONS

KING LEAR

Brook: Outplaying the Fool with Lear
Molly Haskell

Even those of us perverse purists who prefer Shakespeare on the page to Shakespeare on the stage accept the fact that every production sacrifices one thing to gain another and that a really original interpretation is worth a few trampled nuances and muffled meanings. Peter Brook's production of A *Midsummer Night's Dream* was just such a brilliant and bold conception, a whitewash of a play that stood in need of refurbishing anyway. But *King Lear* is something else again, and here the compromise entails more sacrifice than gain.

I didn't see the stage production, but in his film of *King Lear* Peter Brook has taken upon himself the function of the Shakespearean Fool: to expose the fundamental irrationality of the world and all human enterprise—and has come out a little bit of an ordinary fool in the process. Jack MacGowran's Fool is rendered superfluous by Brook's conception and direction, which consists of pulverizing the Shakespearean verbal universe. The Polish critic Jan Kott wrote a brilliant though by no means definitive essay ("*King Lear* or *Endgame*") situating *Lear* in the grotesque, absurdist school of Beckett and Ionesco rather than the tragic tradition founded on faith in Divine Justice and the premise of cosmic order. By limiting himself to this interpretation, Brook does not allow us to arrive at a vision of human absurdity, but immerses us in it from the beginning.

For his location, Brook has found a non-representational end-of-the-world landscape in the arctic region of Denmark. This unbroken grisaille of ice and snow and sea and Nothingness brings to mind previous attempts at apocalyptically abstract settings—the bleak but cluttered landscapes of *Shame*, Lester's *How I Won the War*, and *The Bed-Sitting Room*, and *Glen and Randa*, which failed more interestingly.

Over the immeasurable distances of this medieval limbo, Brook mobilizes his characters—by horse, carriage, and on foot. Dressed in heavy skins and thick furs, with an earthy, barroom-brawl atmosphere hovering around the edges, Lear & Co. move from one castle to another. Primitive lustiness, exciting as an idea, is a nuisance on the stage and a distraction on film, serving to further reduce an already drastically cut script. The action and outdoorsiness reminded one reviewer, somewhat comically, of John Ford. Actually Brook would do well to spend as much time studying Ford's compositions in time as he has Rembrandt's and Bruegel's in space. At this point in his career, after *Tell Me Lies* and the film of *Marat Sade*, Brook reveals no instinctive feeling for the medium, and it is difficult to tell in *King Lear* where the alienation effect leaves off and technical incompetence begins.

He divides the dialogue in the same way that he breaks up the narrative, cutting away from the speaker, filming him from the back of his head, slicing soliloquies into arbitrary components and cutting away the feeling as if it were fat instead of protein. This is Estrangement, ladies and gentlemen (may I show you to your seat?) and you are not allowed to respond. An audience longing to lose itself in the emotional power of the play got only one opportunity—the final scene between Paul Scofield's Lear and Alan Webb's Gloucester, a gentle, agonizing duet which somehow emerged, overpoweringly, intact. For the most part, Brook uses either static two-shots (two profiles at either end of the screen) or painterly close-ups which arrest the narrative rather than deepen it, and serve to separate the characters from each other rather than bring them closer to us.

In this way Brook shows us that he, like the Fool described by Kott, "knows that the only true madness is to regard this world as rational." But, to borrow Edmund's phrase, "the wheel is come full circle." The alienation which was the fool's exclusive province is become the territory of all mankind. We have caught up with the prophets of absurdity. The comfortable island at the edge of our consciousness is now the fluid that surrounds us, and we have to look for other truths and mysteries in his words.

The truth that remains, in Shakespeare and in Beckett, is not the absurdity of life but the absurdity of death, and, as a consequence, the awesome bond of individual suffering. And it is here, in tracing the pattern of Lear's suffering, that Brook's production like every production before it, falls short. And despite Scofield's brilliance, the exquisite delicacy and irony he can summon in the midst of the whirlwind, Brook's production falls even shorter than productions with less talent, because he has denied the play its emotional poetry and the main character the psychology whereby the story of his suffering becomes a progression, if not from sin to regeneration, at least to redemption, and from ignorance to enlightenment. Granted that *Lear* is the least psychological and most metaphysical of the tragedies, and that its alignment of good and evil, as Kott points out, is that of a morality play, at its center is still the fascinating study of a man who, spoiled and petted and protected by power, has acquired age without wisdom, and whose crisis could be that of any government leader or corporation executive about to retire. An energetic decision-maker, he became chairman of the board but now, after many years and with the ebbing of his authority, he is irritable, arbitrary, and willful. He wants simultaneously to get out from under his responsibilities and obligations, while still retaining his power, his entourage, his chauffeur and limousine. Halfway despising himself (his identity being defined entirely by his position), he suspects everyone who professes loyalty to him, makes unreasonable challenges, and surrounds himself with yes-men. He is a man with innate authority, a born leader who has never developed intellectual curiosity or spiritual awareness. Unbuttressed by self-knowledge, his natural virtues have become grim parodies of themselves, and the blindness which might have been acceptable, even charming, in a young man is grotesque in an older one. But Paul Scofield's Lear begins with sardonic control; he is willful but never unintelligent, and he has the elusiveness of a man with inner resources he is not revealing.

As Goneril, Irene Worth gives the single most exciting performance, standing out—perhaps too much—as the scheming, sexhungry queen. Susan Engel's Regan is vague; Annelise Gabol's Cordelia is simply a figurehead, never suggesting (though few Cordelias do) the underside of the compulsion to tell the truth at all cost, that manic honesty which inflicts the truth like a whiplash.

In turning Kott's insights into a directorial blueprint, Brook makes the same mistake as Olivier did in his Oedipal Hamlet based on the Ernest Jones interpretation. Both directors isolate drives and desires which in Shakespeare are half conscious, and whose power to disturb is precisely their subterranean pull and the fact that they merge paradoxically with other drives and turn them into skeleton keys which unlock every mystery.

"As flies to wanton boys are we to the gods," says Gloucester, one voice expressing one philosophy. But Peter Brook raises this to a guiding metaphor. Absurdity becomes a certainty and thus the very thing Brook's production is meant to deny—an absolute.

MACBETH

JOHN SIMON

Macbeth, the film Roman Polanski directed from his and Kenneth Tynan's adaptation of the play, is a much worthier experiment than Peter Brook's catastrophic *King Lear*; and though it still ends in failure, it at least holds our interest and juggles with Shakespeare rather than sabotaging him. Polanski, questionable as his taste may be, has a vivid film sense, and his *Macbeth* is eminently cinematic. In fact, it is so filmic that it fails to be poetic and tragic; because it is often, though not always, good cinema, it manages to be generally inferior Shakespeare. True, the Polanski–Tynan view of the world is as dark as the Bard's was in this play, perhaps even darker; but the film provides a horror that is mostly quantitative, fast-moving and lateral, whereas Shakespeare's horror is qualitative, gradual and vertical.

By making the thane and his lady attractive, sexy people in their twenties, in a world in which only Duncan is old and smarmy, while everyone else is young, tough and potentially treacherous, a curious shift occurs. The work no longer examines how evil enters the soul of a strong and upright man of maturity and stature—how both from without and within, by supernatural and natural agencies, his being is corroded into first causing and then suffering violence and death, until, with all hope gone, a certain nobility ironically reasserts itself at the end. With a young, lightweight, headlong Macbeth and his pretty, demurely sinning blond wife, we get a medieval Bonnie and Clyde, victims of a brutish society, out on a murderous lark. Duncan, after all, is a pompous old bore, whom his own scowling sons might easily have done in sooner or later. Indeed, as the film ends, a clubfooted, surly Donalbain is off to see the Weird Sisters and, presumably, start the wheel of fortune revolving again.

There are many generally demeaning touches in the screenplay. Reviewers have been particularly impressed by a Ross shown as the possibly unjust betrayer of Cawdor, then becoming Macbeth's stooge in the murders of Banquo and Macduff's family, then becoming a turncoat as Malcolm triumphs, and getting himself an earldom for being the first to snatch the crown off Macbeth's severed head and presenting it to the victor. But this "ingenious" notion is not new; it was first advanced by a certain Libby in *Some New Notes on Macbeth* in 1893. Tynan and Polanski have snatched up Libby's folly as eagerly as Ross the crown, thereby, of course, minimizing Macbeth's evil and dislocating the entire work.

Everywhere in the picture they have made brutality, violence, horror so universal as to suggest that Macbeth is a mere victim of social circumstances. Instead of three witches, there is a whole coven of ugly nude bodies decrepitly disporting themselves. The visions of the future conjured up for Macbeth are pure *Grand Guignol*. In the end, everyone deserts him, and he must defend his castle alone against Malcolm's army. This is a world in which a half-dead soldier, prone on the battlefield, is repeatedly clobbered by another's mace, until we can see the blood oozing out through the victim's coat of mail.

Uglinesses proliferate. Cawdor's execution is horrifying, Lady Macbeth's death, here a suicide, is mean, and her barely covered corpse is left lying about unattended. The dead Macbeth's head, crown and all, rolls ghoulishly across the courtyard. On the night of Duncan's murder, it rains heavily, and the Macbeths and their guests must run barefoot and in nightshirts all over the unpaved, muddy yard. A particularly doddering porter is shown urinating. Lady Macbeth, naked in her sleepwalking scene, is exposed to the eyes of a loathsome doctor. A dart from a crossbow hits Seyton smack in the face in close-up. And so on.

Along with excesses of such superficial, though often brilliantly directed and photographed, *verismo*, making for decreased tragedy, we get the filmic breaking up of long speeches with various business and movement and scene shifts, making for decreased poetry. There is continuous, highly cinematic action, but the pathos, penetrancy and depth of poetic words are scattered and largely forfeited.

If, for instance, Macbeth delivers his most famous soliloquy as he bounces down a set of stairs from the battlements of his castle, those repeated tomorrows no longer creep at a petty pace but jog along trippingly. If Macduff utters his piercing "He has no children!" against a background of swirling soldiery, armament and martial panoply, it loses most of its poignantly welling-up grief. If the lines about "our chief guest" at the fateful banquet are transferred from Banquo to a bear about to be baited, you get cinematic excitement and social commentary but lose the terrible irony of murderers fawning on their next victim.

What, then, is left? A marvelously paced action film that nevertheless preserves most of the original text; camera movements that are often breathtaking; poetic color photography by Gil Taylor, including a dawn view from the ramparts that is almost as beautiful as a Shakespearean metaphor; a convincingly reconstructed medieval world; some spectacular swordplay, though Macduff is made into an unduly dirty fighter. And there are fine performances within the limiting concept of the work: Jon Finch as Macbeth, Francesca Annis as the Lady, Martin Shaw as Banquo, and John Stride as Ross are particularly fetching both in acting and in looks.

THE TROJAN WOMEN

The Screen Bestrides the Stage
JOHN SIMON

Plays resist screen adaptation much more doggedly than novels. The former require additions, and these have a way of being easily deadlier than subtractions; the latter often lose much in their transfer to the screen, but the openness of the form—its ability to burrow into psyches and expand into landscapes—can be matched by the camera. A play, ensconced in limited stage space no matter what the stage directions call for and the set designer dreams up, contradicts the free-roaming tendencies of the camera. The lens magnifies everything, even a small room it may find itself locked into. That chamber promptly becomes a microcosm full of details: spots on the ceiling, irregularities in the wallpaper, shadows on the floor, not to mention a universe of furniture and bric-a-brac —and all of this constantly changing shape and size as the camera shifts its position.

Even if slide projections change the backdrop, pieces of scenery float or glide on and off, the lighting shifts drastically from *al giorno* to chiaroscuro, at a play we are still face to face with faces of relatively fixed size within the unelastic frame of the stage. The pores or blemishes of a countenance do not suddenly hit us, the intricate work of fingers is not spelled out for us, and we cannot take in exactly the sliding of a coffee cup from a table and its symbolic splintering into irredeemable fragments. We depend on large gestures, generous verbiage, carefully measured silences and, above all, on simultaneity: our ability to see protagonist and antagonist, or a whole group of interacting people, at once and without interruption—without the camera's selectivity and never quite impersonal mediation.

Consider Michael Cacoyannis' movie version of Euripides' *The Trojan Women*, an earnest effort by a man with ample theatrical and cinematic experience who has repeatedly returned to *The Trojan Women* in different places, languages, and now media. Granted, Euripides' work is not quite a play in the modern sense, rather a sort of tragic cantata. Troy has been conquered and its great women—the heroic Hecuba, the pathetic Cassandra, the profoundly human Andromache, the diabolic Helen—come on to speak their piece before they go off: the good to slavery and death, the evil to further life and lust. All this is framed by a chorus of ordinary women extending the drama downward, and prefaced by a colloquy between the gods Poseidon and Athena, stretching the tragedy upward into cosmic, metaphysical reaches.

What makes *The Trojan Women* a great play is that here in 415 B.C. someone managed to encapsulate in one short play every possible argument against war, which had previously been exalted, except in cases of civil war. The arguments are cogent, pregnant, po-

etic and complete, focusing on the defeated but showing, by implication, the toll on the victors as well. Given the originality, depth
of insight and poetic splendor, the essentially schematic, pat and
undramatic form of the presentation becomes relatively unimpor-
tant. But here, of course, the very unreality of theater proves
handy, indeed necessary: we are psychologically primed for stagi-
ness, unreality on the stage; whereas the camera, as every child
knows, does not, or is not presumed to, lie.

The problem for the film adapter and director then becomes
how to make this highly stylized play even moderately realistic for
his much more realistic medium; or, conversely, how to derealize
the film medium; or, perhaps, how to work out a fusion of both
modes. But Cacoyannis—no more than anyone else, possibly—is
unequal to the task. His setting (ably designed by Nicholas Geor-
giadis), for example, is real enough, though it shows a ravaged and
smoldering Troy from the beginning: To have built an undamaged
one and then destroyed it would have exceeded the budget. Yet
when at the end of the film the "city" goes up in colossal flames,
the sequence is a ludicrous anticlimax. Why would the Greeks
burn those burnt-out ruins, and how, for that matter, can those
remnants of stone walls catch fire?

But it is not just a matter of money; rather, of indecision and
wavering. When Astyanax is thrown off the battlements, the camera becomes, most naturalistically, the falling child, whirling and
crashing fearsomely. Yet when the corpse is carried on to become
the human pulpit from which Hecuba hurls her imprecations, the
boy is all in one piece and undented except for a modest bruise on
one cheek. Again, the recitations of the chorus are broken up in
various photographic as well as choreographic ways to make them
less formalized. But for all the distribution of choric speeches
among individuals, for all the close-ups of one face or part of it, we
never gain a sense of these being particular women with personal
tragedies, while we lose the massive sculptural and terpsichorean
image of stylized, ritual drama.

The toughest conundrum, of course, is what to do with the long
speeches, the solo arias in which these noble women lament their
falls. Cacoyannis lacks the nerve, the talent, or the actresses of an
Ingmar Bergman, who can keep his camera more or less immobile
on Ullmann, Thulin or Andersson against a blank background and
make a vast soliloquy incandesce.

For Geneviève Bujold's appealing but histrionically insufficient

Cassandra, Cacoyannis devises an elaborate balletic chase, with the Greek soldiers as supporting male dancers and the Trojan women as corps de ballet. Religious fervor and human pathos fizzle equally among studied compositions and calculated movements, combined with disconcerting jump cuts between medium shots and close-ups and extreme close-ups. For Vanessa Redgrave's intelligent and interesting Andromache—unfortunately lacking the ultimate warmth and depth—there is much soft-focus hovering over handsome blue-eyed blondness, and picturesque posing of the actress in front of her slain husband's mounted armor flapping abjectly in the wind like a martial scarecrow.

Only for Helen, shrewdly and forcefully if not very seductively incarnated by Irene Papas, has the director come up with some good business, and here his additions are effective: Helen's eyes, in extreme close-up peering out from between the logs of her private stockade; other Trojan women parched with thirst while Helen gets a basin of water for mere ablutions. But I am somewhat disturbed by Miss Papas' thick accent, Greek though it be, and her great confrontation scene is weakened by her antagonist being Katharine Hepburn. Hecuba is the most important character, the only one who remains present throughout, and she who plays the queen must dominate the action and hold its disparate set pieces together. But what is Hepburn to Hecuba? She offers no stronger stuff than brittle querulousness, head-waggling and lip-trembling, so that the Trojan indomitability shining through the uneasy Argive victory is as missing as Poseidon and Athena.

Cutting the gods' opening scene is understandable in 1971, but a strategic error all the same. For it is from the conversation of the deities that we learn of their weakness and fickleness, and of their intention to make the arrogant Greeks, on their journey home, pay dearly for their triumph. This rounds out the tragic image of war, in which even the victor falls victim to a fundamentally untrustworthy, unmanageable cosmos. Moreover, Helen's argument that Aphrodite is to blame for what happened, though meant to be in part sophistic, emerges, in the absence of visible gods, as sheer nonsense. Alfio Contini's color cinematography is appropriately muted and desolate, but black-and-white would have done the job better. The music of Mikis Theodorakis is disappointing when not embarrassing, and Edith Hamilton's translation should have been avoided by Cacoyannis, but then it was all English to him.

MEDEA

Tropism of a Transplanted Race
MOLLY HASKELL

Medea is Pasolini's interesting if not entirely successful attempt to get into the freer and more animalistic skin of prehistoric man. Roughly half of Pasolini's version, written by himself, takes place before Euripides' tragedy begins, elaborating on such formative influences as the young Jason's tutelage at the hands (or rather hoofs) of a centaur, and the bloody and barbaric civilization of Colchis in which the sorceress Medea was raised. Unlike Euripides, Pasolini is not concerned with the evolution of Medea's passion, or with seeing Athenian society through her eyes, but in a bold and characteristically Marxist interpretation, with Jason and Medea as products of their conflicting environments, engaged in the struggle between a rapacious, man-oriented civilization and a primitive, pantheistic one. Ironically, whereas Euripides was "modern" and psychological, Pasolini is atavistic in his insistence on the physical.

In reconstructing the world of Colchis, with its cave dwellings in tiers of stone, its ritual of human sacrifice, dismemberment, and "re-cycling of limbs and organs," its magic and incantations, Pasolini attempts to recapture a sense of the strangeness and wholeness of nature before it was called "natural." The world of Colchis is not so much prehistoric as preconceptual, its houses and vegetation and animals and human beings forming an unbroken chain of life and death.

A link in this chain and its crowning glory is Medea. To the role Maria Callas brings the magnificence not of an actress seeking modulation and motivation, but of an image, emblazoned across the film like a medallion. For Pasolini, Medea is not an individual woman with inner conflicts and complexes, but the quintessence of a primeval civilization which, even as she betrays and abandons it, hacking her own brother to pieces to delay the pursuers, she most clearly embodies, and which clings to her tragically in her new home.

Pasolini uses striking architectural and musical contrasts to set off the alienation of Medea, a story—to borrow a phrase of the centaur—"full of deeds and not of thoughts." Even her imaginings become concrete images, as, in the film's most exciting sequence, she plans the murder of her rival with the poisoned cloak and crown.

In her initial attraction to Jason, Medea is beguiled not, as Euripides suggested, by words, but by his flesh. In their final confrontation over the flames, he himself accuses her, in so many words, of treating him as a love object. I use the term advisedly because, although Pasolini means to make us feel something more than merely the desire of a woman for a man—something vaster and deeper, like the tropism of a transplanted race—when Maria Callas gazes at the Olympic limbs of Giuseppi Gentile, we see him, inevitably, as a love object. This arises partly because the image of sensuality on the screen obliterates subtler meanings. But it is a problem inherent in the kind of interpretation Pasolini attempts—i.e., the intellectual trying to inhabit the primitive sensibility. As he himself realizes, the very faculty that enables us to appreciate and long for early, undifferentiated experience is the distance that divides us from it, the river of no return.

There is a haunting moment when Medea arrives in Greece and searches desperately for a holy tree like some in Colchis. She must suddenly recognize, like a child discovering his separateness from people and objects, that the trees are not an extension of herself but have a place and time of their own. Just as with the loss of innocence we really discover it, with the loss of her tree Medea comes to know its beauty.

DEATH IN VENICE

Soul Destroyed

STEFAN KANFER

Vladimir Nabokov called it "*poshlost*," a Russian term he translates as "crude pseudo literature." Thomas Mann called it *Death in Venice*, perhaps the most celebrated novella of the twentieth century.

One can understand the great Russian's distaste for the work of the great German. In the story, the sun does not rise and set; instead "the naked god with cheeks aflame drove his four fire-breathing steeds through heaven's spaces." Venice is not a city, but "the fallen Queen of the Seas." The symbolism accompanying the dense, involuted prose is no less affected. But *Death in Venice* works, as a tale, a moral instruction and as art. Of all authors, Mann was the least ingenuous. He deliberately chose the Romantic mode to bid adieu to the romantic mood. Through the spacious andante of *Death in Venice*, one can hear the contrapuntal knell of the nineteenth century with all its values, poses and styles.

In his film adaptation, Luchino Visconti (*The Damned*) pays his utmost disrespect to the original by maintaining Mann's fustian and removing his intention. In the novella, the aging author-philosopher Gustave Aschenbach seeks renewal in Venice. But like the fugitive with an appointment in Samarra, he finds death awaiting him. An elusive and beautiful youth, Tadzio, attracts the writer. Though he never touches his beloved, never even speaks to him, Aschenbach is rendered immobile by his platonic affair. A plague of cholera racks the city. At any time the writer is free to leave, but he cannot. Eventually, rouged and dyed in imitation of youth, Aschenbach assumes the aspect of a broken clown. At beachside, he finally succumbs, still gazing at the elusive figure of Tadzio. "And before nightfall a shocked and respectful world received the news of his decease."

Those events would be difficult to render in the best of cinematic circumstances. Director Visconti provides the worst. Mann is supposed to have based his hero on Gustav Mahler. So Visconti, ruthlessly deleting Mann's imagination, makes the neoclassic author a Romantic musician—accompanied by plaintive strains of Mahler's *Fifth Symphony*, emphasized until it becomes as banal as the theme from *Love Story*. Mann's Aschenbach was a harrowed spent figure with a dead wife and a grown daughter. Visconti's is played by Dirk Bogarde, a man barely into middle age. Accordingly, he is equipped, like Mahler, with a young wife and a deceased child.

Most important, Mann's treatment of the unconsummated affair of man and boy was a metaphor for Europe's decaying society. But Visconti takes the veneer and calls it furniture. With infinite tedium, he pores over every facet of Tadzio's Botticelli visage; with stupid distortion, he makes the boy, played by Bjorn Andresen, a flirt whose eyes flash a come-on to his helpless elder, like some midnight cowboy off the Via Veneto. He even concocts an elaborate bordello scene in which Aschenbach is shown as a heterosexual failure—a moment that proves as barren of meaning as it is of style.

It must be acknowledged that even at his worst, Visconti remains a master of surfaces. The city's astonishing Adriatic streets, its gleaming planes and squares have never been so lovingly rendered. The epoch, with beautiful women haloed by immense hats and men elegantly attired merely for a saunter through the palm court, is flawlessly but tediously re-created. Still, there is no substance beneath the moving images. Adolescent Bjorn Andresen is properly androgynous but no more mysterious than a lump of sugar. Dirk Bogarde is miscast and misdirected—all hurt looks and empty cackle. The prize for most voluble player must, however, go to Mark Burns as the musician's friend. Invented for the film, he shrieks such Viscontian art-and-life lines as "Do you know what lies at the bottom of the mainstream? Mediocrity!"

This film is worse than mediocre; it is corrupt and distorted. It is one thing to change an author's lines or his characters. It is quite another to destroy his soul. Mann's *Death in Venice* is, in fact, no more about homosexuality than Kafka's *The Metamorphosis* is about entomology. Visconti's *poshlost* may aspire to tragedy, but it does not even achieve melancholia; it is irredeemably, unforgivably gay.

ONE DAY IN THE LIFE OF IVAN DENISOVICH

JOHN SIMON

Casper Wrede's movie version of Aleksandr Solzhenitsyn's *One Day in the Life of Ivan Denisovich* is a responsible, conscientious transposition of the short novel to the screen, yet, despite incidental felicities, it does not truly come off. Why?

The novella is told from Ivan's point of view: we get the bare, dismal facts of a day in a Siberian "special" camp of the Stalin (and, presumably, Brezhnev) era as filtered through the consciousness of a simple carpenter, a man of courage, cunning, pawky common sense, and also decency. He has been condemned to ten years' imprisonment merely because his speedy escape from Nazi captivity in 1941 looked suspicious to the Russians. He has outlasted eight years of subhuman forced labor in subzero colds and will maintain a sizable part of his dignity through the remaining years, thanks to resiliency, resourcefulness, and a sense of humor. But the way he looks at his life simply is not the way the camera sees it. Ivan, down-to-earth though he be, is reflective; and the camera does not reflect.

Take the incident involving another inmate, a former Navy captain who is led off to "the cells": for a petty protest, he is given ten days in a cell that is a barely heated icebox. There the cold penetrates deeper than the lashes of the knout, one sleeps on the wooden floor, rations are minimal. In the book, Ivan thinks: "Ten days! If you had ten days in the cells and sat them out to the end, it meant you'd be a wreck for the rest of your life. You got TB and you'd never be out of hospitals long as you lived. And the fellows who did fifteen days were dead and buried." The film briefly shows the captain hunched up helplessly in his cell. But it cannot give you the vital information of Ivan's interior monologue.

To be sure, the film uses voice-over narration where it considers it proper and necessary. This sparing use is absolutely judicious, but it manages to become obtrusive, even though the voice is, correctly and unmelodramatically, Ivan's own. The problem is that narration is the novel's medium; on film, it tends ever so slightly to clash with, or needlessly duplicate, the images we see. In the present case, because Ivan's reflection is a sort of parenthesis, the film had to omit it and we do not learn the full horror of the captain's ordeal. But something still more important gets lost: the offhand, almost humorous tone of Ivan's comments that, paradoxically, makes the dreadfulness even greater by showing how accepted, banal a part of existence it has become.

And something else. The brief comment, which in Solzhenitsyn often pierces the heart, cannot be rendered by any medium but print—especially if it is followed by some white space, inviting a pause for meditation. When the captain is led away, the others shout after him, "Keep your chin up!" and "Don't let 'em get you down!" This the film reproduces. But then the text reads. "What could you say?"—end of paragraph, blank space. What can the film do to equal these few plain, helpless, undramatic but shattering words? A great director, which Wrede is not, might have found a solution; but even the greatest could not find cinematic equivalents for every one of literature's major and minor triumphs.

The matter of parentheses is particularly important here: "and death i think is no parenthesis," ends one of E. E. Cummings' finest lyrics; but living death, life in a prison camp, is precisely a parenthesis. The body is confined in space and, even more, in a daily round of dreary and dehumanizing activities or brutish exhaustion. That leaves the mind free, indeed forces it, to roam obsessively in the backward, the forward, the sideways. What the body does is piddling and linear, although the line may be a frantic zigzag. But the mind, the mind creates desperate, speculative, life-giving parentheses of its own, where the abject prisoner lives superreally. And the camera is, for the most part, denied access to these.

Yet just as the camera underachieves in some areas, it accomplishes too much in others, with equally untoward results. The color photography here is by Sven Nykvist, Ingmar Bergman's superlative cinematographer. For the prison barracks scenes, Nykvist gives us exactly the right hues: soiled blues and lackluster browns, colors that do not improve on the situation. But when the prisoners are marched out to their terrible labor as the icy dawn is about to break, the screen becomes overwhelmingly beautiful. Strange, unsuspected colors appear in the Northern sky: nacreous, opalescent, boreally understated. As the camera comes in on or withdraws from the trudgers, we see less or more sky around them; and each time we see more, the color has subtly, insinuatingly modified.

No less lovely is the sky-show at evening, when the prisoners return. In both instances the snow on the ground provides an obbligato to the celestial color organ, a neutral, blue-white bass that modulates into white or black to stay in harmony. It is too beautiful, and it is no use saying that's how it is in Siberia or in northernmost Norway, where the film was shot. That is not the way Ivan Denisovich, or any of the other unfortunates, would have seen it. It is too ennobling.

Otherwise, the film has merits. It is faithful to the book; it is at least adequately directed; and it contains sober, apt performances. If *One Day* is sometimes hard to follow, that is in the nature of the material: the weird regulations and circuitous machinations of the camp. Regrettably, too, half the cast speaks with a Norwegian accent, and the other half with British ones, mostly Cockney or Yorkshire, to indicate humble origins. The result, to my ear, is less than convincing. But Tom Courtenay is a believable and likable protagonist who does not become overingratiating; and the various British and Norwegian character actors make much out of their generally small parts.

The centerpiece of the film is a lengthy chunk of toil, the building of a house with the most primitive means in far-below-zero weather. Both the biting cold and the hardbitten methods of scrounging for illegal heat are well conveyed. Moreover, film has seldom communicated so palpably the hardness, roughness, exhaustingness—the very feel—of labor; and also its minuscule, sneaky exultations when whatever shifty stratagem yields badly needed results.

Like the novel—and here it is a match—the film shows persuasively how even under the most bestial circumstances men can hold on to their humanity, can find crevices in the rock of inhuman discipline from which kindness sprouts. Now it is the saxifrage of a smile, now the hardy lichen of intellectual debate about the artistic merits of Eisenstein's films. In fact, such things as prisoners discussing *Potemkin* or avidly reading a newspaper account of Zavadsky's latest production are among the sunniest occurrences in this icy inferno.

It is to Solzhenitsyn's credit that he does not show extraordinary brutalities where the ordinary ones will do nicely. And, again like the book, the film records a *good* day in Ivan's life—which is the loveliest and saddest thing about it. There are some obviousnesses: I wish, for instance, that a debate about God did not take place between prisoners Karamazovishly named Ivan and Alyosha. Still, it is finally a life-enhancing movie, deserving a place somewhat higher than that of a mere respectable failure.

The film adaptation, however, cannot do for this book what Leoš Janáček's musical genius did for a very similar work, Dostoevski's *From the House of the Dead,* turned by Janáček into an opera as great as, if not greater than, the original. It is because music is farther than film from literature, because it does not invite close comparisons, that an autonomous success can result in it even from an adaptation.

II:

REFLECTIONS

THE RATINGS

Jacob Brackman

By tradition, we Americans abhor censorship, which is what the rating system of the Motion Picture Association of America is supposed to save us from. Censorship is where they make you change stuff or cut stuff out. The ratings, in theory, are no more than a labeling device—like those lists of ingredients which the law requires on food and drug packages—to give us some idea of what to expect inside. Ratings don't presume to "fix" movies, only to alert people—parents, specifically—when they contain potentially indigestible material.

Parents cannot screen all movies in advance; ratings offer them a handy guide. By warning parents away from unsuitable pictures, ratings free the film-maker, for the first time ever in this country, to treat any material he chooses. We want artists to be able to reflect the changes in society, pursue a vision wherever it leads. At the same time, we understand that not all children can handle everything they might come up with. The idea behind ratings is to reconcile this conflict.

If there were no ratings, the argument goes, all films would have to observe rigid proprieties; none could portray themes or incidents too strong for any member of the family. For decades, all American movies conformed to a Production Code with just such standards. Without the Code, and without ratings, state and local agencies—responding to pressure from their constituencies—would swoop down on "objectionable" films, banning them, or demanding cuts willy-nilly.

Indeed, since the inception of the rating system three years ago, domestic film-makers *have* realized unprecedented freedoms; their work *has* escaped meddling in all but a handful of cities and states. As they've evolved thus far, however, ratings remain troublesome.

The system currently has four categories. G (General admission) and GP (General admission: Parental guidance suggested) are the two unrestricted ones—anyone with the price of a ticket is admitted, regardless of age. R (no one under seventeen admitted unless accompanied by a parent or guardian) and X (no one under seventeen admitted period) are the two restricted categories. The significant line falls between GP and R—the line that is hardest to draw anyway. At issue here, essentially, is what teenagers should be allowed to see, since few children below the age of twelve *want* to attend the sorts of movies that get rated R and X.

One of the gravest inadequacies of the present restrictions is that they penalize sixteen-year-olds because of our fears for six-year-olds. An innovation—which likely will have gone into effect by the time you read this—proposes to split GP into two sub-categories, one warning parents more ominously than the other when a "film contains material which you may not consider suitable for pre-teen-age children." Nonetheless, the one and only restrictive line will still be drawn at seventeen years old. The further subdivision—in an already overcomplicated alphabet soup—seems a petty improvement.

Since few children over twelve go to movies with their parents, R is an unsatisfactory category. The R humiliates adolescents, and leads inevitably to a good deal of finagling. How excruciating to be turned away from any film one feels ready to handle—especially from *Woodstock*, *Alice's Restaurant*, *Taking Off* or others whose characters and themes are drawn from adolescence.

Teenagers on dates often choose unrestricted movies over preferred restricted ones rather than run the risk of an embarrassing hassle at the door. Many shy away from movies altogether—an avoidance which the faltering industry can ill afford. Our population has grown, but the weekly movie audience has shrunk to about one fifth of what it was twenty years ago—from nearly 100,000,000 to fewer than 20,000,000. Restrictive ratings don't help instill the moviegoing habit in tomorrow's adults.

Among those teenagers who decline to stay away, many find ways to cheat the system: lying to cashiers, procuring phony identification certificates, hitching up with a stranger on line who is agreeable to posing as one's guardian. These are trivial transgressions, to be sure, but the necessity of resorting to them must contribute, in its own small way, to youth's growing conviction that the Establishment is full of it. At lots of theaters, naturally, deceit is quite unnecessary. Nearly all theaters in the United States subscribe to the rating system, but who knows what percentage enforces restrictions rigorously. We do know that the theater manager more concerned with boosting his weekly receipts than with shielding the impressionable young is by no means uncommon.

Compared with official rationalizations of our pressing on in Southeast Asia, or of brutal penalties for drug possession, the prim hypocrisy of "protecting" adolescents from forbidden bodily zones —which they have likely viewed often in the flesh—or from words they hear every day scarcely seems to matter. But it does matter, especially when enforcement too is conducted inconsistently, hypocritically. Official hypocrisies, however differently they *ought* to be weighted, interweave, reinforce one another, become an agglomerate source of disaffection. They won't let you see a sexy movie until you're old enough to kill for them. You make Woodstock happen, then they don't let you into the movie of it. They insist pot is bad for you, the Stones are bad for you, the Vietcong is bad for you, *Medium Cool* or *Catch-22* is bad for you—and each of their prohibitions colors all the others.

Restrictive ratings are financially unfavorable. An R can easily cost a picture 20 or 25 percent of its potential gross. *Summer of '42*, for instance, doing an excellent trade, would be lots bigger still had it managed to squeak through for a GP. It is all about thirteen-to-sixteen-year-olds, and thirteen-to-sixteen-year-olds would enjoy it and flock to it if they were permitted to flock without their parents. (It's the last thing you'd want to see with your parents! Particularly since you might run into some classmate who'd faked it in on his own.) *Summer of '42* concerns itself with the first fevers of sexual awakening, but its comedy is so homey and the actual scenes of initiation so discreet that most adolescents would take it in stride.

Here is another point of view. A psychologist on the rating board, Dr. Jacqueline Bouhoutsos, has repeatedly stated that sex concerns her far less when viewed by children than by teenagers who are not yet in full command of their sexual responses. Presumably, Dr. Bouhoutsos fears such viewing might arouse teenagers, though to what perils their arousal might lead remains unclear. Even the government's Commission on Obscenity and Pornography concluded that ". . . empirical research . . . has found no evidence to date that exposure to explicit sexual materials plays a significant role in the causation of delinquent or criminal behavior in youth or adults."

If an R can cost a film a fifth or a quarter of its potential gross, an X can literally cut its revenues in half. Many newspapers refuse advertising, no matter how sedate, for X-rated films. (Much of the public believes X simply means Porno Trash.) Many theaters refuse to book them; in many cities and towns they are never shown at all.

This is not to say that X pictures can't make money—a handful, such as *Midnight Cowboy*, have made it big. But X is a grievous handicap, one under which increasing numbers of serious films will likely have to labor. For ratings will now become tougher than at any time since they went into effect three years ago. This is a short-run prediction—the stringency or leniency with which they get applied fluctuates oddly, almost from month to month. If *Midnight Cowboy*, for instance, had been released a bit later, it would most probably have garnered an R, and still heftier receipts. But if it came out today, with decisions tightening way up again, another X would likely be its fate.

Similarly, *Summer of '42* might well have received a GP (and another $5,000,000 or so in revenues) had it come up a month or two *earlier*. The film-makers were understandably resentful. *Ryan's Daughter* featured an adultery with more passion and more skin, yet its rating had recently been changed from R to GP. Moreover, Ryan's daughter had left her husband's bed to deceive him, whereas the married lady who copped the moony adolescent's cherry that summer of '42 was in fact no married woman at all, but a widow —she'd just received word of her husband's death overseas. Some rater therefore might have argued that, strictly speaking, no adultery occurred; borderline cases are often resolved on the basis of just such silly distinctions.

In truth, the appeals board gave in on *Ryan's Daughter* precisely because it knew restrictions would cost the picture heavily and might even sink MGM, whose fortunes were riding on it at the time. (MGM's president had threatened to withdraw his studio from the Motion Picture Association if that R were upheld.) Warner Brothers, who released *Summer of '42*, was not in comparable trouble and did not press for a change. But either company might have compiled a long list of GP-rated films—all those gory Italian Westerns, for instance—which any sensible parents would consider "worse." The board has been too squeamish about language, nudity and love play right along, and insensitive to "harmfulness" in even the most wholesale slaughter.

The renewed strictness today is different from the strictness of a couple of years ago. Then, judgments tended to be routinized, simple-minded. Board members would consign a film to this or that category on the basis of unmistakable cues. A glimpse of pubic hair or a four-letter word automatically demanded restriction. The raters were disinclined to worry over thematic implications, over disturbingness cast deep in a picture's warp and woof. It followed, therefore, that they could often be assuaged by small excisions: a few frames, a word or two looped out of the sound track. Producers willing to bowdlerize their own films a bit could usually escape threatened restrictions.

In an as yet unpublished book about his internship on the rating board, Stephen Farber, a young West Coast film critic, cites instance after instance in which the board agreed to loosen ratings in exchange for cuts amounting to no more than ten or fifteen seconds. As if such token expurgation could make the difference! Farber reports that almost all complaints of excessive leniency arose, significantly, over films whose ratings had been softened on the basis of these trivial concessions. As many as one third of all American movies make such "voluntary" cuts to accommodate the board's objections.

But if a movie is fundamentally okay for kids, a flash of snatch or a few naughty words won't transform it into a traumatic experience. Conversely, if it's suffused throughout with sadistic sexuality, say, or cruelty to children, snipping its one or two worst minutes cannot turn the remaining ninety-nine minutes innocuous.

The raters appear to be moving toward a more thoughtful evaluation of a film's *gestalt*. The industry, however, responds with wounded cries: "Thought-control!"

Dr. Aaron Stern, a psychiatrist who previously served as consultant to the board, has become chief rater. His guidelines seem to have grown increasingly diffuse and subjective. He can decide, for example, that although *Summer of '42* lacks serious nudity or profanity, it subtly excites infantile oedipal fantasies; that the boy's getting to sleep with the older married woman embodies a wish-fulfillment so subliminally potent that it's irrelevant how lyrically, how tenderly his defloration is carried out. In this way, psychological jargon can replace the language of sin and corruption.

The moguls most outraged by Dr. Stern's new "dictatorial" powers had grown accustomed to squeaking questionable pictures past the board with last-minute surgery. Indignation from industry stalwarts like Samuel Arkoff, whose American International Pictures foists dozens of horror flicks (saturated with blood and bizarre erotic innuendos) onto the GP market, underscores the moral ambiguities of the rating game. If A.I.P. needs unrestricted ratings in order to release its creepy-cheapies to drive-in-theater chains, it will tend "willingly" to make cuts the raters ask for. Typically, a kind of bargaining ensues and is resolved in compromise.

Exploitative film-makers are more prone to compromise, or knuckle under, than film-makers with serious commitment to their own rhythms and intentions. The result, of course, is that exploitation films become available to young audiences far more readily than quality films do—even when they fall within the same broad spectrum of "maturity." The unrestricted categories fill up with flaccid family musicals and violent genre pieces, while teenagers are denied easy access to nearly all the most humane and stimulating films.

Dr. Stern is now *the* crucial arbiter of what a sixteen-year-old American is psychologically equipped for. As he is obviously steering by more sophisticated machinery, we might expect more enlightened judgments. But so far he looks like an out-of-the-frying-pan-into-the-fire.

While he was still an adviser to the board, Dr. Stern recommended that any film treating rebellion against the Establishment —even one lacking in sex or violence—should be restricted. In the G category, he stipulated, "the broadly practiced social mores are not challenged." In the GP, "the broadly practiced social mores are not significantly challenged." He further proposed that in unrestricted films violence should always be "represented as a force in the service of law and order," and sex should be portrayed "within the context of a loving relationship." It is possible Dr. Stern's sophistication will make us long for a return to nipple-counting.

As I write this, news arrives of Dr. Stern's intention to bestow the dreaded X upon *The Last Picture Show*, a disciplined, truthful portrait of a small Texas town folding up in the early 1950's. That parents should ever be deprived of their right to expose their own children to whatever art they see fit seems a proposition of dubious wisdom and constitutionalty—cases like *Medium Cool* and *The Last Picture Show* illustrate just how dubious.

More and more studio representatives, producers, even directors are eager to confer with Dr. Stern—not merely after their films are done (over what sequences best be eliminated to secure more favorable ratings) but before they even go into production. Some companies have committed themselves never to make an X film. Although they are not required to do so, most companies submit prospective scripts to raters—a practice the board encourages—to pinpoint "troublesome elements" in advance and avoid restrictions later. They then receive "script letters," itemizing the "corrections" needed to win an "improved" rating or even (as in the case of MGM's *Pretty Maids All in a Row*) going so far as to recommend junking a project altogether. These policies are not so different from censorship.

A rating system is a good idea. That the present system seems moving toward renewed repressiveness strikes me as unfortunate. But it is happening because the burden of pressure on the M.P.A.A. has come from the right—from church groups and parents' associations, whose loudest complaint is that ratings are too lenient; that it's still impossible to determine what's safe.

The Catholic and Protestant film councils recently withdrew their support from the ratings altogether. And they have their side. Not because even unrestricted movies, such as *Love Story*, employ language still forbidden to writers in adult magazines, such as this one. But because movies are powerful image-makers to the mind—I keep realizing, "I had no idea *how* powerful"—and the minds of children should sometimes be shielded from that much power.

It will take some good heads to straighten out the mess, but I guess our immediate goal should be to allow teenagers easy access to movies like *Walkabout, Adalen '31, Stolen Kisses, Catch-22, Five Easy Pieces,* and *The Last Picture Show.*

HORROR '71

BRUCE WILLIAMSON

The cinematic blood bath has been shaping up as a national sport since *Bonnie and Clyde* set the tone of American-style violence by pumping slugs into people's faces—but the current vogue for sanguinary shockers dates back to 1957 or thereabouts, when England's Hammer Films launched its gory *The Curse of Frankenstein*, paving the way for an even gorier *The Horror of Dracula*, a spin-off *Count Yorga*, a flood of brutal Italian Westerns and such pretentious excuses for mayhem as *Soldier Blue, The Sporting Club* and *The Hunting Party*.

In the American hinterland, drive-in theaters mop up with double- and triple-bill scream shows at a dollar per carload. A typical duo might be *I Drink Your Blood* and *I Eat Your Skin*, billed AS 2 GREAT BLOOD-HORRORS TO RIP OUT YOUR GUTS. In Manhattan's Greenwich Village, one neighborhood theater launched a summer festival of fear with midnight showings of *The Night of the Living Dead*, a crude but spine-tingling sci-fi thriller that was slapped together in 1968 in Pittsburgh for $150,000 and has become a campy semiclassic. Graphic dismemberment, cannibalism and uninhibited bloodletting make *Living Dead* a must for viewers who come to shiver, and remain to squirm, at scenes in which a demon-possessed child carves up her mama with a trowel, then gobbles most of her papa's right arm.

While violence may well be the true-blue pornography of our time, the shock merchants have gradually been adding sex to their line as well. The distressed damsels of yesteryear, who retired to their chambers clutching a crucifix or a sprig of wolfsbane to ward off evil, have been replaced by a bevy of bosomy wenches right out of *Tom Jones*. Before they catch Frankenstein's eye, these lusty ghoul diggers go tumbling into bed with any lout who might be sufficiently grateful to lead a rescue party in the last reel. Comely Ingrid Pitt, German-born star of *The House That Dripped Blood* and *The Vampire Lovers* ("an erotic nightmare of tormented lusts . . . where even the lifeless can love . . . even the dead can desire"), introduced a new kink to the latter by sapping the lifeblood from her acquiescent female victims while pretending to kiss their breasts just above the nipple, a brand-new place for those telltale puncture marks.

Blood money turns out to be a sound investment for film companies such as American International Pictures, a firm that seldom spends more than $500,000 to turn out a handsomely horrific feature that stands to earn up to several million, with reissues ad infinitum. A few are first-rate, despite the gratuitous gouts of gore, and serve as showcases for horror stars such as Christopher Lee, Peter Cushing and the ubiquitous Vincent Price, as well as for ambitious young directors. Roger Corman (*The Masque of the Red Death*) inspired a cult while directing classic tales of terror for A.I.P. and went on to bigger if not better things.

Now, as more and more "straight" films become glutted with sex and violence, the makers of horror flicks are under pressure to find something new. So far, they appear to be settling for relatively costly remakes of the classics and pale imitations of past successes, all garnished with livid flesh and blood. The only faintly visible shadow of a trend is a tendency to play foul deeds for outright laughs, cluing the addicted audience not to take sadism and mass murder too seriously.

If common sense prevails, the spate of such nightmarish entertainments that are rated G or GP may finally lead some sane tastemaker to suggest applying letter labels to films in a choice of colors —with bright red, perhaps, for family shows that eschew explicit lovemaking but offer a full quota of gouged eyes, torn limbs and stakes through the heart.

Director Daniel Mann, whose past efforts include *Butterfield 8* and *Come Back, Little Sheba*, scores a freakish near hit with *Willard*, a shocker starring Bruce Davison, Ernest Borgnine and approximately 500 rats. While young Davison (an alumnus of *Last Summer*) performs capably in the title role as a maltreated orphan lad who avenges injustices by turning rodents loose on his enemies, *Willard*'s effectiveness is due mostly to the efforts of Hollywood animal trainer Moe Di Sesso, the man responsible for the rats. A cunning wretch named Ben steals the show—and wraps it up by making a banquet of the hero. Even dependable Elsa Lanchester, whose mother role is canceled out by a heart attack before the patter of little feet begins to swell like thunder, can do little to top *that* brand of showmanship.

She's nutty as a fruitcake, that's *What's the Matter with Helen?*, a chintzy period piece concocted by screenwriter Henry Farrell, remembered for *What Ever Happened to Baby Jane?* and *Hush . . . Hush, Sweet Charlotte*. It's more of the same pseudogothic claptrap, with Shelley Winters (as Helen) and Debbie Reynolds (as Adelle) playing two dragon-ladies who operated a Hollywood dancing school for professional kids back in the days when every self-respecting American mom wanted her daughter to challenge Shirley Temple. According to the plot, Adelle and Helen are the mothers of two convicted thrill killers and they've come to Tinseltown to re-establish their peace of mind and anonymity after all those ugly headlines. Believe that and you can believe everything: Shelley going stark mad with plenty of help from an off-screen orchestra and Debbie—bleached and painted in reasonable facsimile of a girl who yearns to be like Jean Harlow—nipping through her tap routine, her tango and a bad case of the shudders. In a cast of seasoned troupers, Dennis Weaver, Agnes Moorehead and the Irish theater's Michael Mac Liammoir cannot quite alter the impression that they're all working to revive a stiff.

Made in Belgium with an English-speaking cast, *Daughters of Darkness* is a sickly-elegant vampire tale based on the legendary exploits of a sixteenth-century countess who was said to preserve her beauty by bathing in the blood of slain virgins. *Daughters* is updated to the present and stars exquisite Delphine Seyrig (of *Last Year at Marienbad*), wearing some dazzling *couturier* threads that are fashion throwbacks to the Thirties and courting a couple of tasty young things (Danièle Ouimet and Andrea Rau) at a splendid seaside hotel during the off-season. Among the registered guests there's also a young man (John Karlen, from American TV's *Dark Shadows*) who seems equally naïve about lesbians and werewolves and believes the countess wants him for himself, until she starts describing the dissection of virgins she's known while she's fondling him. Tearing off their nipples is one of her beauty secrets. Belgian director Harry Kümel spares his audience that particular atrocity, but he does appear partial to red and uses it like catsup to smarten up what he calls "a Gothic fairy tale for full-grown adults."

American International's remake of the Edgar Allan Poe classic

Murders in the Rue Morgue borrows nothing from Poe save his tingling title. With a slew of celebrated actors, such as Jason Robards, Christine Kaufmann, Michael Dunn, Herbert Lom and Lilli Palmer, director Gordon Hessler went to Spain and obviously lavished a lot of money on sets and costumes to dress up the tale of a crazed killer's bloody revenge on the members of a *Grand Guignol*–style theatrical troupe. As the company's actor-manager and husband of the leading lady (Miss Kaufmann, whose eyes fill with fear quite fetchingly—and frequently), Robards handles himself as if he enjoyed his work but seems much too crisply contemporary for this turn-of-the-century thriller. Rated, GP, *Rue Morgue* offers a heady measure of bestiality, ax murder, torture, decapitation, acid in the face (also poured down the throat) and other GP-rated diversions. Just the ticket for the pure in mind who would forbid youngsters to watch beautiful men and women lolling around with their clothes off.

Proof that the purveyors of routine horror can scarcely keep pace with so-called serious film-makers may be found in *The Devils*, Ken Russell's adaptation of a mediocre play based on Aldous Huxley's book *The Devils of Loudun*. It's witch-burning time in seventeenth-century France, the era of Richelieu and rising Protestantism. But Russell seldom pauses to keep the historical record straight or even coherent; he's too busy dreaming up sick, sicker, sickest shock tactics to illustrate Huxley's account of how a swarm of sexually possessed nuns was manipulated by the authorities of church and state to bring a licentious priest, Father Grandier (Oliver Reed, defending freedom of conscience between orgies), to his death at the stake. Admirers of *Women in Love* must be perplexed at the directions Russell's career has since taken—first his lurid Tchaikovsky biography, *The Music Lovers,* and now this. Playing hostess to the ersatz-Fellini decadence in a white-on-white city that looks oddly Techbuilt, Vanessa Redgrave assumes a witch's cackle and a hunchback in her role as Sister Jeanne, the overheated mother superior whose sexual fantasies include a wingding in which Father Grandier, as Jesus, climbs down from his cross to molest her on the floor of the chapel (she frenziedly licking the blood off his hands). The grisly scenes of torture show bones being broken, tongues being pierced by needles and nuns being purged of evil with jumbo enemas and douches. One of the most vulgar movies ever made.

ABEL GANCE'S *BONAPARTE AND THE REVOLUTION*

VINCENT CANBY

If the ninth New York Film Festival had shown nothing else of value during its recent run at the Vivian Beaumont Theater, it still would have justified itself by its presentation of Abel Gance's 4½-hour *Bonaparte and the Revolution*, a movie that makes me more than a little penitent for all of the times I've called something an epic—most recently Pier Paolo Pasolini's adaptation of *The Decameron*.

The Pasolini film has a grand, painterly sweep and vision to it, but it simply shouldn't be compared to—or described in the same language as—the remarkable Gance production, which is a history of the achievements of not only Napoleon and the French Revolution but also (more interestingly, to me) of movies and of Gance himself. At eighty-two, Gance is approximately the same age as the medium he continues to inhabit with such amazing vigor.

This is not to slight *The Decameron* or the two other important films that the festival premiered—Bogdanovich's *The Last Picture Show* and Bresson's *Four Nights of a Dreamer,* a film that I can admire without really liking a great deal. (All of Bresson's films since *Au Hasard Balthazar* have been, for me, like preliminary exercises in a foreign language whose words remained undifferentiated.) Nor is it to slight some festival films that—due to conflicting commitments and human endurance—I had to miss (Zanussi's *Family Life,* Kurosawa's *Dodes'ka-den* and Ophuls's *The Sorrow and the Shame*).

All of this is beside the point, however, because *Bonaparte and the Revolution* is unique in contemporary film annals, as the original film was when it had its premiere at the Paris Opera in the spring of 1927 under the title of *Napoléon Vu Par Abel Gance.* The story of Napoleon, as seen by the comparatively young Abel

Gance, was unlike any film ever seen before, a gigantic, patriotic spectacle that utilized just about every screen technique then known, plus a few that weren't, including Polyvision, the three-screen system that was later refined by Cinerama. (In 1962, when Cinerama opened its own theater in Paris—the remodeled Empire Theater—it was named the Empire-Abel Gance.)

Gance originally planned to make the life of Napoleon as six separate features, the first three of which made up *Napoléon Vu Par*. . . . Although the film caused a sensation in Paris, the grand design eventually fell apart. According to Kevin Brownlow's account in *The Parade's Gone By*, the film played in its massive, three-screen form in only eight cities in Europe. MGM bought the rights to the film for $450,000, showed it intact only in London, and then in a cut-down form in the United States, apparently because the company did not want to further confuse motion-picture exhibition, which was then wondering whether or not sound was really there to stay.

According to Henri Langlois, Gance's problems were also aggravated by the death of Hugo Stinnes, the wealthy German industrialist who had initiated the financing of *Napoléon Vu Par* . . . and had agreed to finance the others. The remaining films were never made, at least, not by Gance. The director eventually sold the screenplay for what was to be the last feature of the series, *Napoleon at St. Helena*, to a German director named Lupu Pick, who shot it in 1929. As far as I can find out, the film has never been seen in the United States.

Because *Napoléon Vu Par* . . . was so unwieldy, it quickly suffered the fate of Von Stroheim's *Greed*, being cut up and edited by just about everyone who could lay hands on it. In the early 1930's, Gance himself put together a 1½-hour sound version, which seems to have impressed no one very much, after which there came to be almost as many different versions of the film as there were prints. In 1967, the New York Film Festival showed a four-hour silent version that had been pieced together by Langlois and the Cinémathèque Française.

Bonaparte and the Revolution, I'm told, uses much of this version, as well as much of the early sound version (which, among other fascinations, features the voice of Antonin Artaud, who plays Marat), but it is, obviously, a different movie. Not only has Gance redesigned the film to emphasize Napoleon's relation to the revolution (the early film was a straight chronological history), but he has shot new scenes, dubbed those sections (with extraordinary success) that weren't used in the abbreviated sound version, and created new montages and superimpositions of almost reckless passion and splendor. What one sees when watching *Bonaparte and the Revolution* is not a jazzed-up modernization of some ancient classic, but a movie that has literally been over forty years in the making.

The emotional effect is both immensely moving and more than a little spooky, as only movies—because they freeze action within time—can be. Watching it is like looking through an enchanted telescope that allows us to observe, simultaneously, several different ages of one man, which is actually what we are doing in the case of Gance. We see not only the shifting interests and sensibilities of the director, but also Gance himself, who, at the age of thirty-six, played the revolutionary immoralist, Saint-Just. He speaks, however, with the voice of Gance in his forties, and then, quite late in the film, we see the silhouette of Saint-Just-Gance, in a scene shot last year, as Saint-Just stands in a shadowy alcove listening to charges being brought against him on the Convention floor. There's no mistaking the silhouette as that of anyone but an indomitable old man. Yet the scene works beautifully within the context of the drama. Saint-Just is the one leader of The Terror who is firmly convinced that history will acknowledge his brilliance, if not justify his actions, and seeing the almost ghostly silhouette of an old Saint-Just, who was actually guillotined at the age of twenty-seven, amounts to another one of Gance's more nervy poetic projections, with which the film is positively dense.

Some people, I suspect, will object to anyone's daring to tamper with a classic in such a high-handed way, even if it's the original director himself. This is nonsense, however, not only because the silent version continues to exist but because such an objection would deny us the unique privilege of seeing, in one film, an effective anthology of the best that a certain kind of popular, commercial cinema has offered us since movies began, conceived by a man who has survived all the ages.

Bonaparte and the Revolution is, in the politics of art, nothing if not conservative (the original *Napoléon Vu Par . . .* was reportedly DeGaulle's favorite film), an epic poem dedicated to an historical ideal; yet it is so full of willful, personal energy as to seem, in this day and age, revolutionary. It has the headlong pace and the piety of Cecil B. De Mille, the taste and technical mastery of

D. W. Griffith, and an audacity that is Gance's alone. With the exception of *Intolerance*, the first *King of Kings* and *Ivan the Terrible*, it is the most stunning film about Great Events and/or Great Personages I've ever seen.

Given a certain amount of cash, or the manpower and resources of the Soviet Army, spectacle scenes aren't all that difficult to do. Gance's real triumph is in editing and montage, in his unabashed romanticism that permits him to equate the storm-tossed Napoleon, escaping from Corsica in a tiny sailboat that has a tricolor as its sail, with the tempest taking place on the floor of the Convention in revolutionary Paris. He also manages to shift from the epic to the individual view without losing his focus, from, say, an amazingly precise summation of the infighting among the various revolutionary leaders—Danton, Robespierre, Marat, Couthon and Saint-Just—to a lovely, comic sequence of Napoleon's courtship of Josephine.

There seems to be no technique that Gance does not use, including the 1927 equivalent of the hand-held camera. He also straps the camera to the back of a horse, suspends it from overhead wires, and ties it to a pendulum. There are magnificent long-shots of real-life vistas, still pictures studied by a moving camera, scenes staged before blow-ups of contemporary prints, plus a few tableaux vivants (David's "Assassination of Marat") that, in Gance's view, I'm sure, are simply another way of saying that the glory that is France is also France's art treasures.

There are anachronisms, but even these are in the spirit of the popular historical film. *Le Bal des Victimes* sequence, the party at which Bonaparte literally wins Josephine at a chess game, looks like pure 1927 revelry in the dresses and hairdos, and even in the Charlestonlike steps being danced by the pleasure-mad celebrants. In a few years, we will be equally amused—and with as little real justification—by Faye Dunaway's 1967 hair styles in *Bonnie and Clyde*.

Few of Gance's good films (he apparently made a number that weren't very good) have been seen in this country in anything approximating their original versions. His pacifistic *J'Accuse*, which he shot during World War I, had been so re-edited when it was shown in this country in 1921 that it received the endorsement of the American Legion's state executive committee. According to the man who reviewed it for *The New York Times*, the film had ceased to be an indictment of war and was, instead, "inferentially an indictment of Germany and, directly, a sentimental appeal to patriotism."

I assume that Gance's monumental, new-old film, which is as much an international treasure as a French one, will be luckier.

THE FILM CRITICISM OF OTIS FERGUSON

ANDREW SARRIS

The long-overdue republication of Otis Ferguson's movie reviews within a single binding, *The Film Criticism of Otis Ferguson* (edited and with a preface by Robert Wilson, Temple University Press, Philadelphia, 475 pp., $12.50), should help correct much of the nonsense written elsewhere about the period from 1934 through 1941. There is no better film chronicle of this era anywhere, but try selling this proposition to most publishers. *We* don't want merely another collection of faded clippings, they cry in unison. What *we* want is an authoritative history written especially for us by a recognized film scholar, and we have just the man for the job: Wolfgang Krockhaus of the Altamira Academy of Cinematic Art. As it happens, Herr Krockhaus has seen only nineteen movies in his life, but he has accumulated secondary reference material on 19,000 more. At the drop of a footnote, he can quote you what Vachel Lindsay wrote about Mae Marsh in 1916, but he himself has not had an original insight into acting since *Birth of a Nation*. What makes Krockhaus such a renowned authority is his sociological certitude even in the face of contrary aesthetic evidence. As Eric Sevareid has said of the persuasive man in the Pentagon with the blackboard and pointer, Krockhaus may be in error, but he is never in doubt. Nor is he ever afflicted with the specialist's ambivalence toward his subject. Official film historians cannot afford to be either specialists or particularists, but must pose instead as generalists par excellence so as to present publishers with the illusion of unity in a field in which unity is impossible. However, when the need arises for even random specificity, Krockhaus is clever enough to have access to every word Otis Ferguson ever wrote, and thus is free to render clumsy paraphrases of Ferguson's opinions as his very own.

If I seem to have spent an inordinate amount of space exposing poor old Krockhaus, it is simply to prepare the reader for the possibility of encountering echoes from forgotten readings and conversations in Otis Ferguson's critical prose, a bit like the old lady in Henry Fielding's *Tom Jones* with her complaint about Shakespeare's being made up of old quotations. I had that same sensation reading Ferguson on *Modern Times* to the effect that Chaplin had borrowed the assembly line from René Clair's *A Nous la Liberté*, released four years earlier. A very knowledgeable and knowing young lady dispensed that little tidbit back in my high-school days in the Forties, and I was very impressed, but, looking back, I think she must have gotten her scholarly insight (and many more like it) from Ferguson, perhaps subliminally from the pulpy but otherwise politically fashionable pages of *The New Republic*.

To my knowledge, reprints of Ferguson's movie pieces have popped up only in Alistair Cooke's *Garbo and the Night Watchmen*, along with criticism by Cecelia Ager, Cooke himself, Robert Forsythe, Graham Greene, Don Herold, Robert Herring, Meyer Levin, and John Marks, all very good critics indeed. And I would add to their number the eminently seminal Gilbert Seldes, far ahead of his time as the high priest of pop culture. Still, taking into account Ferguson's distinguished contemporaries mentioned above, and such distinguished predecessors as Vachel Lindsay, Hugo Munsterberg, and Robert E. Sherwood, and such distinguished successors as James Agee, Manny Farber, and Robert Warshow, I think a strong claim can be made for Ferguson as the writer of the best and most subtly influential film criticism ever turned out in America.

If Agee's criticism reflects a passion for poetry, and Farber's a passion for painting, Ferguson's reflects a passion for music. No other film critic has come as close as Ferguson to X-raying the connective tissue—physical, visual, soniferous, psychological—that binds isolated images into an organic narrative on the screen. He managed on more than one occasion the difficult stylistic feat of describing the tedium of movie-making without being tedious himself. His hilarious blast at the boredom of Dziga Vertov's *Three*

Songs about Lenin in 1934 consisted mostly of an improvised mock montage à la Ferguson, and like all first-rate parodies it really isn't too far from the real thing.

Ferguson was very much in tune with the technocratic spirit of the Thirties, and very much in sympathy with the working stiffs who were both the subjects and the labor force of so many movies. His instinctive populism, however, never degenerated into crudity, vulgarity or philistinism. And he was deadly serious about the craft of film criticism even when he was poking fun at its pedantic excesses. In fact, Ferguson was one of the few professional reviewers of his time with more than a rudimentary interest in the history of the medium, and film research in those days was a far more strenuous proposition than it is today.

Why then has Ferguson not been more widely recognized as the trail-blazing beacon of film criticism that he was? The most obvious reason is that no critic can address any meaningful portion of posterity except between the covers of a book. As it happened, James Agee not only followed Ferguson; he completely supplanted him on the cultural scene. Agee was blessed with the kind of bookish credentials that enabled the trolls and Trillings of the literary establishment to hail him as the one and only compleat film critick. Ferguson's enormous influence on Agee (and Farber) was never mentioned even by people who had been reading *The New Republic* since the year one, and the new breed of American Bazinians and Cahierists (to which this reviewer belongs) never paused to consider the possibility that Ferguson might have anticipated many of Bazin's ideas on film history from an entirely different vantage point. Indeed I can think of no higher tribute to pay Ferguson than to say that he is the one American movie critic who most closely resembles Bazin even to the point of anticipating Bazin's very dubious overestimation of Wyler at the expense of Welles and Ford.

Even today, however, an appreciation of Ferguson depends largely upon an appreciation of movies. Ferguson reads even better when you know what he's writing about than when you don't. His style is often more ritualistically judgmental than novelistically descriptive, and he never got around to editing out flabby adjectives like "swell" and "terrific." But then, unlike Agee, he was more often pointing than preening. Ferguson understood movies too well to attempt to duplicate the sensuous sweep of their detail, and he was observant enough to stand relatively mute before their ultimate magic and mystery.

Ferguson had no idea at the time that he was witnessing the final flowering of the classical tradition of movie-making. Like any reviewer worth his salt, he took each movie as it came along, shook out its inevitable puerilities and pretensions, measured whatever conscience and craftsmanship were left, and seldom missed the slightest semblance of style, whether of a Humphrey Bogart in his early gangster period or of a Fritz Lang in his back-to-the-wall exile. He could appreciate the finer points of W. C. Fields, Charles Laughton, and the Marx Brothers without overlooking how sloppy and undisciplined they could be without half trying. Actually, his outstanding surgical specialty was the funnybone, and no one else of his time or since has so perceptively appreciated the comic genius of the early sound film, that most mindlessly abused of all periods of production. There was in Ferguson none of the numbing nostalgia for the "Golden Age of Comedy" celebrated in Agee's elegant essay. Agee was of course emotionally driven by memories of laughing uproariously with his father at Chaplin's antics in the midst of a softly focused childhood in Arcadia. Ferguson's childhood seemed to have been somewhat harsher and less protected than Agee's, and his view of childhood was therefore more Dead End Kids and less sweetness and light than Agee's. Similarly, Ferguson's theory of comedy was more devil-may-care and less angelic than Agee's. Thus, it follows that Ferguson barely noticed the loss of the stylized clown personae of Chaplin, Keaton, Lloyd, Langdon, *et al.* in the rush of a mob of bit players full of roaring realism and bustling individuality. And it is at this point that Ferguson and Bazin intersect most strikingly, Ferguson more through intuition perhaps and Bazin more through theory, but both arriving at the unfashionable conclusion that the coming of sound had not only been commercially inevitable but also aesthetically desirable as an extension of realism. Actually, the breadth of Ferguson's sympathies provided him with a European sensibility tempered with American skepticism, a tough mixture that was never soured by either European knowingness or American know-nothingness. Hence, his critical vision could expand through the evidence of his senses, and not congeal in the molds of preconception.

I cannot pretend or presume to measure the full meaning of

Ferguson's life as a man on this planet, especially a life of thirty-six years snuffed out prematurely in 1943 on a cargo ship in the Bay of Salerno. Alfred Kazin has written eloquently of Ferguson's tough-minded iconoclasm in the days when everyone seemed to be Waiting for Lefty. Kazin knew where Ferguson lived and worked, but surprisingly little of what he was about as a film critic. To read Kazin one would think that Ferguson wrote about films merely to spite the literary aristocracy. Nothing could be further from the truth. Ferguson may have started movie reviewing as a lark, but once he plunged in he dedicated himself with a fervor that is still exciting to read thirty years later. His Hollywood articles alone are worth the price of admission to this testament of intellectual faith in a mass medium, and his pieces on *Citizen Kane*, the first Louis-Schmeling fight, *It Happened One Night*, and a couple of hundred other film-related subjects rank so close to the top of American journalism that it isn't worth measuring the difference. The important thing to remember is that Ferguson, like Agee after him, was not merely a disconnected stylist writing about nothing in particular. He was writing about something very important, something that went beyond the screen to the furthest reaches of art and life, but without ever completely bypassing the screen. Ferguson plus Film equals the best of autobiography and the best of aesthetics.

ABOUT THE CONTRIBUTORS

HOLLIS ALPERT was a film critic for *Saturday Review* from 1950 until early 1972 and is now critic of *World Review*. He is working on his sixth novel and is also the author of a collection of essays, *The Dreams and the Dreamer*, and a biography, *The Barrymores*. He has taught at New York University, the Pratt Institute, and Yale.

GARY ARNOLD is film critic of the Washington *Post*.

JACOB BRACKMAN was film critic of *Esquire* from 1969 until 1972. He has contributed stories and articles to *Playboy*, *Ramparts*, *The New York Times*, and *The New Yorker* and has written songs for Carly Simon and the original screenplay of Bob Rafelson's most recent movie.

VINCENT CANBY is film critic of *The New York Times*; he was a critic and reporter for *Variety* from 1960 until 1965. He is an associate fellow of Pierson College, Yale.

HAROLD CLURMAN is theater and film critic for *The Nation*. An active stage director, he was one of the co-founders of the Group Theatre and has been a film producer and director. He received the George Jean Nathan Prize for dramatic criticism in 1958 and another from Knox College in 1968. His published works include *The Fervent Years*, *Lies Like Truth*, and *The Naked Image*. He has written articles for *The New York Times*, the London *Observer*, *Harper's Bazaar*, *Partisan Review*, *Harper's*, and others. A book on stage direction will be published in October 1972.

JAY COCKS is a film critic for *Time* magazine.

DAVID DENBY is film critic of *The Atlantic*. He has written articles for *New York* magazine and *The New York Times* and taught at Stanford and UC Santa Cruz. He was editor of the previous volume in this series.

PENELOPE GILLIATT is a film critic for *The New Yorker* and was formerly film critic of the London *Observer*. Her latest books are *Nobody's Business*, a collection of short fiction and a short play, and *Unholy Fools*, a collection of writing on film and theater. She has also written two novels, *One by One* and *A State of Change*, and two collections of stories entitled *Come Back If It Doesn't Get Better* and *Penguin Modern Stories No. 5*. Her original screenplay for *Sunday, Bloody Sunday* is available in hardcover and paper.

PHILIP T. HARTUNG, film critic of *Commonweal,* has contributed articles on film for the Encyclopedia Americana Annuals and The Book of Knowledge Annuals. He has also reviewed movies for *Woman's Home Companion, Charm, Scholastic Magazines,* and *Esquire.*

MOLLY HASKELL is a film critic for *The Village Voice* and a free-lance writer on film and theater. Her pieces have appeared in *Vogue, Saturday Review, Intellectual Digest, Show, USA, Film Comment, Film Heritage, Inter/VIEW,* and *Cahiers du Cinéma in English.*

ROBERT HATCH is film critic and executive editor of *The Nation.*

PAULINE KAEL is a movie critic for *The New Yorker* and was formerly the movie critic of *McCall's* and *The New Republic.* She has written for *Partisan Review, Sight and Sound, Film Quarterly, The Atlantic,* and *Harper's.* Her criticism has been collected in *I Lost It at the Movies, Kiss Kiss Bang Bang, Going Steady,* and a new volume to appear early in 1973. Her long essay "Raising Kane" appears in *The Citizen Kane Book.*

STEFAN KANFER is film critic of *Time* magazine. He has contributed articles to *Life, Harper's, Esquire, The Atlantic,* and *Playbill.*

STANLEY KAUFFMANN is the film and theater critic of *The New Republic* and a visiting professor of drama at Yale University. A former drama critic of *The New York Times,* he is the author of seven novels and two collections of film criticism, *A World on Film* and *Figures of Light.*

ARTHUR KNIGHT is film critic of *Saturday Review,* writes a weekly column for *The Hollywood Reporter,* and is a professor in the Cinema Department of the University of Southern California. He is the author of *The Liveliest Art* and *The Hollywood Style* and co-author with Hollis Alpert of *The History of Sex in the Cinema* and has contributed to the Encyclopaedia Britannica and Collier's Encyclopedia.

ANDREW SARRIS is film critic of *The Village Voice* and Associate Professor of Cinema at Columbia University. His books are *The Films of Josef von Sternberg* (1966), *Interviews with Film Directors* (1967), *The Film* (1968), *The American Cinema: Directors and Directions 1929–1968* (1968), *Film 68/69,* co-edited with Hollis Alpert (1969), and *Confessions of a Cultist: On the Cinema 1955–1969* (1970). A new collection of criticism, *The Primal Screen,* will be out shortly.

RICHARD SCHICKEL is film critic of *Life* magazine. His books include *The Disney Version, The Stars, The Movies: The History of an Art and Institution, The World of Goya,* and a collection of film criticism, *Second Sight*. He co-edited *Film 67/68* with John Simon and is now completing a biography of D. W. Griffith.

ARTHUR SCHLESINGER, JR., formerly film reviewer for *Show* magazine, is now a reviewer for *Vogue*. He is also a historian and writer.

JOHN SIMON is film critic of *The New Leader* and drama critic of *New York* magazine and the *Hudson Review*. He has taught at Harvard, the University of Washington, M.I.T., and Bard, and is the author of three books of criticism, *Acid Test, Private Screenings,* and *Movies into Film,* which was nominated for a National Book Award. He is the winner of a Polk Award in film criticism and the George Jean Nathan Award for dramatic criticism.

BRUCE WILLIAMSON is film critic and Contributing Editor of *Playboy* magazine and teaches at St. John's University, Long Island; he was a film critic at *Time* magazine from 1963 to 1967 and has written for *Life*. His humor and travel articles and stories have appeared in numerous magazines and newspapers, and he has written songs and sketches for satirical revues in New York and London.

PAUL D. ZIMMERMAN is film critic of *Newsweek* and the author with graphic designer Burt Goldblatt of *The Marx Brothers at the Movies*. He teaches at the Columbia School of Journalism.

INDEX

289